COMMUNITY COHESION IN CRISIS?

New dimensions of diversity and difference

Edited by John Flint and David Robinson

This edition published in Great Britain in 2008 by

The Policy Press
University of Bristol
Fourth Floor
Beacon House
Queen's Road
Bristol BS8 1QU
UK

Tel +44 (0)117 331 4054
Fax +44 (0)117 331 4093
e-mail tpp-info@bristol.ac.uk
www.policypress.org.uk

British Library Cataloguing in Publication Data
A catalogue record for this book is available from the British Library.

Library of Congress Cataloging-in-Publication Data
A catalog record for this book has been requested.

ISBN 978 184742 023 7 paperback
ISBN 978 184742 024 4 hardcover

Cover design by Qube Design Associates, Bristol.
Front cover: image kindly supplied by www.istockphoto.com
Printed and bound in Great Britain by MPG Books, Bodmin.

Contents

List of tables and figures

Tables

Figures

Acknowledgements

John Flint and David Robinson wish to thank Emily Watt, Jessica Hughes and Philip de Bary of The Policy Press for their help in producing the typescript. The editors are also grateful for the insightful comments provided by the anonymous referees at The Policy Press and for the contribution of our colleagues who attended a symposium event at Sheffield Hallam University on 6 June 2007.

Census output in Chapter Three is Crown copyright and is reproduced with the permission of the Controller of HMSO and the Queen's Printer for Scotland.

Notes on contributors

Sameera Ahmed is a Research Fellow in the Cathie Marsh Centre for Census and Survey Research at the University of Manchester, UK.

Sarah Blandy is a Senior Lecturer in Property Law in the School of Law at the University of Leeds, UK (www.law.leeds.ac.uk/lawstaff).

Jon Burnett is an information and communications officer for the Positive Action for Refugees and Asylum Seekers project in Leeds. He has recently completed a PhD on community cohesion at the Centre for Criminal Justice Studies, University of Leeds, UK. The views expressed in Burnett's chapter are those of the author and not necessarily representative of the organisation he works for.

Roger Burrows is a Professor in the Department of Sociology at the University of York, UK, and Co-Director of the Social Informatics Research Unit (SIRU) (www.york.ac.uk/depts/soci/about/s_burr. htm).

Ian Cole is Professor of Housing Studies and Director of the Centre for Regional Economic and Social Research at Sheffield Hallam University, UK (www.shu.ac.uk/cresr/sp_ian_cole.html).

Ed Ferrari is a Research Fellow in the Department of Town and Regional Planning at the University of Sheffield, UK (www.shef. ac.uk/trp/staff/ed_ferrari).

Del Roy Fletcher is a Reader in the Centre for Regional Economic and Social Research at Sheffield Hallam University, UK (www.shu. ac.uk/cresr/sp_del_roy_fletcher.html).

John Flint is Professor of Housing and Urban Governance in the Centre for Regional Economic and Social Research at Sheffield Hallam University, UK (www.shu.ac.uk/cresr/sp_john_flint.html).

Robert Furbey is Principal Lecturer in Urban Sociology at Sheffield Hallam University, UK (www.shu.ac.uk/geography/furbey.html).

Keith Kintrea is a Senior Lecturer in the Department of Urban Studies at the University of Glasgow, UK (www.gla.ac.uk/departments/urbanstudies/staff/keithkintrea).

Deborah Phillips is a Reader in Ethnic and Racial Studies in the School of Geography at the University of Leeds, UK (www.geog.leeds.ac.uk/people/d.phillips/).

Kesia Reeve is a Senior Research Fellow in the Centre for Regional Economic and Social Research at Sheffield Hallam University, UK (www.shu.ac.uk/cresr/sp_kesia_reeve.html).

David Robinson is Professor of Housing and Public Policy in the Centre for Regional Economic and Social Research at Sheffield Hallam University, UK (www.shu.ac.uk/cresr/sp_david_robinson.html).

Ludi Simpson is Professor of Population Studies in the Cathie Marsh Centre for Census and Survey Research at the University of Manchester, UK (www.ccsr.ac.uk/staff/ss.htm).

Naofumi Suzuki is Assistant Professor in the Department of Civil Engineeriing at the University of Tokyo, Japan (www-e.civil.t.u-tokyo.ac.jp/lab/staff-index.html).

Peter Wells is Professor of Public Policy Analysis and Evaluation in the Centre for Regional Economic and Social Research at Sheffield Hallam University, UK (www.shu.ac.uk/cresr/sp_peter_wells.html).

Introduction

John Flint and David Robinson

Britain is more and more often portrayed as a broken society. Politicians, religious leaders, media commentators and academics appear increasingly convinced that the social cement that binds local and national social systems together is crumbling and the established standards and values essential for maintaining civic order are collapsing around us. The demise of 'community' is presumed, by Left and Right alike, to be the key driver of this breakdown in society. Problems as diverse as Islamic terrorism, educational underachievement, gang violence, teenage pregnancy, worklessness, drug crime and anti-social behaviour are all explained through reference to the erosion of the informal ties and reciprocal arrangements that bind communities together.

This reasoning, evident in the pronouncements of the Prime Minister (see for example, Brown, 2006) and the Leader of the Opposition (see for example, Cameron, 2007a, 2007b), was first applied to the problems of urban society in the aftermath of the street disturbances in various Pennine mill towns in the summer of 2001. The political response to the disturbances centred on the perceived crisis of cohesion in the social fabric of the affected towns. Various reports were commissioned and charged with explaining this situation (Community Cohesion Independent Review Team, 2001; Home Office, 2001; Oldham Independent Panel Review, 2001; Ouseley, 2001; Burnley Task Force, 2002). In response to the reports, the paradigm of 'parallel lives' was forged, whereby particular ethnic and religious groups are presumed to be self-segregating into ethnic enclaves, limiting contact between themselves and wider society, undermining a common sense of belonging and purpose and allowing misunderstanding and suspicion to flourish. In response, the challenge was identified as being the promotion of cohesive communities.

The presumption at the heart of the community cohesion agenda – that towns and cities increasingly consist of socially cohesive but divided neighbourhoods – has become the starting point for public policy efforts to understand and respond to a wide range of contemporary problems in urban society. This is not to suggest that all residentially segregated and socially isolated communities are considered problematic. Problems are only perceived to arise when either internally cohesive, segregated communities nurture a culture that asserts values and allegiances at odds with the dominant moral order (for example, in ethnic or religious enclaves) or where the mainstays of community governance collapse and the void is filled by values and practices at odds with accepted norms of behaviour (for example, in residualised housing estates). Whether the consequence is persistently high levels of worklessness, anti-social behaviour and crime, social disorder or community conflict, policy is presented with the short-term challenge of establishing order and the longer-term objective of creating communities that nurture a sense of belonging and citizenship.

Through the application of this logic, peoples labelled as 'different' and 'distinct' are problematised, along with the neighbourhoods in which they reside, while attention is deflected away from the increasing spatial polarisation of society on the basis of income and class (Dorling and Thomas, 2004). While the media report from the front line of the broken society – typically portrayed as inner-city neighbourhoods and peripheral estates – the retreat of the wealthy into gated communities and the self-segregation of the middle class into zones of sameness continues unquestioned.

Of course, concerns about the cohesiveness of society are nothing new. Perceived crises in the bonds between citizens and between citizens and the state were a common feature of the classical world, as were concerns about national identity and allegiance (Fox, 2006). During the 20th century, urban studies was dominated by analyses of the residential clustering of particular groups of the population and the social tensions arising from cultural diversity (eg Park et al, 1925; Zorbaugh, 1929; Cohen, 1980). It is important to remember this history when considering the current 'moral panic' over a crisis of cohesion in British society. Current debates are distinctive, however, for their foregrounding of community as both the problem and solution to so many of the ailments affecting urban society (see Giddens, 1998; Bauman, 2001).

Community cohesion and the new politics of community

The community cohesion agenda that emerged in the immediate aftermath of the street disturbances in Bradford, Burnley and Oldham in 2001 represents the most unequivocal application of the new policy agenda that seeks to address social problems through the reinvigoration of the idea of community. It also provides the most explicit rationalisation of the logics underlying this new politics of community. Yet, community cohesion was not present in the lexicon of either urban theory or public policy before the disturbances of 2001 (Robinson, 2005). As with other contemporary UK policy concepts, such as 'respect', community cohesion represented an empty vessel into which a variety of public policy concerns (social exclusion, race relations, national identity, immigration, law and order) were poured and re-articulated (Robinson, 2005). The first 'official' policy definition of community cohesion appeared in a guidance document for local authorities in 2002 (LGA et al, 2002). This defined a cohesive community as one where:

- there is a common vision and a sense of belonging for all communities;
- the diversity of people's backgrounds and circumstances is appreciated and positively valued;
- those from different backgrounds have similar life opportunities; and
- strong and positive relationships are being developed between people from different backgrounds in the workplace, in schools and within neighbourhoods.

The community cohesion agenda has subsequently been shaped by events, including the war in Iraq, the London bombings of 2005, disturbances in the Lozells district of Birmingham in November 2005, new immigration from the European Union accession states and attempted terrorist attacks in London and Glasgow in 2007. The result has been an increasing focus on, and problematisation of, Muslim communities. There has also been a broadening of the localities considered to be experiencing cohesion problems, most notably rural areas where migrant workers have increasingly settled following the expansion of the European Union.

In a bid to respond to these events, the government sponsored a Commission on Integration and Cohesion, which reported in 2007, and launched a new £50 million fund to support the implementation of some of the Commission's recommendations. The Commission (2007, para 3.15) also generated a new and expanded definition of an 'integrated and cohesive community' as one where:

- there is a clearly defined and widely shared sense of the contribution of different individuals and different communities to a future vision for a neighbourhood, city, region or country;

- there is a strong sense of an individual's rights and responsibilities when living in a particular place – people know what everyone expects of them, and what they can expect in turn;
- those from different backgrounds have similar life opportunities, access to services and treatment;
- there is a strong sense of trust in institutions locally to act fairly in arbitrating between different interests and for their role and justifications to be subject to public scrutiny;
- there is a strong recognition of the contribution of both those who have newly arrived and those who already have deep attachments to a particular place, with a focus on what they have in common;
- there are strong and positive relationships between people from different backgrounds in the workplace, in schools and other institutions within neighbourhoods.

Although community cohesion is largely a political concept, it has its corollary in academic attempts to define social cohesiveness. There are, however, important distinctions to be drawn between political definitions of cohesion and the ruminations of academics regarding the essential elements of a cohesive society. Take, for example, the work of Kearns and Forrest (2000). In an attempt to break down a cohesive society into its constituent parts and provide a basis for empirical investigation, Kearns and Forrest identify five elements of *social* cohesion:

- common values and civic culture
- social order and social control
- social solidarity and reductions in wealth disparities
- social networks and social capital
- place attachment and identity.

This schema is directly referenced in the Cantle Report, although relabelled as a definition of *community* cohesion, and these five dimensions of cohesion underpin the broad working definition of community cohesion presented in official guidance (LGA et al, 2002; Commission on Integration and Cohesion, 2007). However, there are important differences between the two official definitions and the conceptualisation presented by Kearns and Forrest. Note, in particular, the emphasis within the two 'official' definitions on equality of opportunity rather than on Kearns and Forrest's assertion regarding the importance of reducing wealth disparities, a subtle variation indicative of the reticence of the community cohesion agenda to acknowledge and address structural inequalities rooted in economic processes. These definitions are also incredibly broad and abstract and this has had two consequences. First, it has enabled political discourse to prioritise certain forms of cohesion (in particular, racial and religious) over others (such as gender and class) and to problematise particular groups (for example, Muslim or white working-class communities). Second, local areas have been given considerable autonomy to define their own 'community cohesion' problems (or lack of them) and implement local solutions, creating ambiguity about what constitutes a 'community cohesion' problem or intervention and how these are distinctive from, for example, equal opportunities, race relations or social exclusion policies.

The rudiments of the new politics of community are clear to see within the scope and focus of the community cohesion agenda. The spotlight is very much on local communities. Social responsibility is promoted as the natural corollary of individual rights; the importance of generating a shared sense of belonging and purpose is emphasised; there is a recognised need to engender trust in local institutions; and social interaction between people from different backgrounds is considered an essential to cohesion. The attention of policy is therefore inevitably directed towards communities perceived as internally cohesive but socially isolated and asserting values and forms of behaviour at odds with presumed norms or standards. The essentials of this perspective are shared with contemporary policy responses to a range of challenges in urban society, ranging from religious extremism through to concentrated worklessness, and reflect the rooting of this new politics of community in the principles of political communitarianism that emerged in the 1990s in response to the perceived failings of both Left and Right.

The proponents of political communitarianism, most notably Etzioni (1995), asserted that the welfare policies of the Left had undermined key institutions of civil society and had centralised decision making, thereby disempowering local communities. The Right, meanwhile, was criticised for supporting the rights of the individual at the expense of social responsibility and the well-being of society. Charting a path between the perceived failings of these two positions, political communitarianism championed community as the vehicle through which people could be reintroduced to the fundamentals of civil society; cooperation and reciprocity. In doing so, allegiances and affiliations to society could be forged and democracy could be reinvigorated. The central tenets of this ideology are clearly evident in the New Labour rationales that view membership of, and participation within, a community as the principal mechanism for forging shared values and regulating the conduct of individuals.

The emphasis on the curative powers of community also reflects the centrality of social capital theory to contemporary British governance, in which collective and cultural dynamics are given prominence in the explanation of social outcomes (Putnam, 2000). In particular, 'bonding' social capital, inferring strengthening ties within groups, is regarded as potentially problematic for community cohesion, while 'bridging' social capital is viewed as a mechanism for facilitating interaction and solidarity across groups, and therefore for establishing a national community of communities. A number of theories more specific to debates about cohesion have also informed the spotlighting of community, including underclass theory, with its focus on cultural explanations for socio-spatial segregation (Murray, 1990), and contact theory, which posits that physical proximity and interaction will foster local inter-group solidarities (Community Cohesion Independent Review Team, 2001). All of these theories will be examined in the chapters within this book.

The aims of this book

This book aims to explore the policy agenda that seeks to address social problems through the reinvigoration of the idea of 'community'. This approach cuts across conventional analytical frameworks based on national policy change, legislative developments or institutional transformation, by exploring the neighbourhood-level manifestations and responses (by individuals, communities and policy) to this perceived crisis in cohesion. The logic behind this approach is to reflect the increasing concern within public policy on increasing differentiation and fragmentation at the neighbourhood level and the recognised possibilities for promoting social change through the reconstitution of local communities.

Unpacking this statement of purpose a little further, the first aim of the book is to connect the rationales and policy developments within the community cohesion agenda to the changing dynamics of neighbourhood diversity and cohesion. In other words, it seeks both to explain how some forms of cohesion are changing at the neighbourhood level and to assess critically whether the political and policy programme badged as the 'community cohesion agenda' is responsive to the lived realities of community dynamics and social interaction. In order to do so, the book critically engages with some of the key conceptual frameworks supporting the community cohesion agenda, including communitarianism, social capital, contact theory, cultural explanations of social exclusion and 'parallel lives'.

The book's second aim is to provide an explicit neighbourhood dimension within the new politics of community. The community cohesion agenda initially emerged as a response to disorders in particular neighbourhoods in 2001, and was largely viewed at that time as being a problem specific to these localities. However, subsequent events, including the Iraq war, the terrorist attacks of 2005 and 2007, political devolution and the migration resulting from EU expansion have seen the policy discourse around community cohesion, and academic critiques of this discourse, increasingly focused at the national level and debating issues of citizenship and British identity. However, as Amin (2002) and many of the contributors to this book argue, there is a need to recognise that dynamics of diversity and manifestations of cohesion or disconnection are dependent on very localised circumstances and play out at the neighbourhood level. We suggest therefore that both policy and further research should emphasise the centrality of the neighbourhood to social cohesion.

The book's third aim is to counter the lack of evidence upon which debates about cohesion are often based. In doing so, it presents a range of recent empirical research evidence about the changing dynamics of difference and diversity in a variety of locations in Britain. This evidence illustrates the complexities of diversity and difference and the dynamism of neighbourhood trajectories and social relations, which is at odds with the assumptions and generalisations often evident in community cohesion discourse about the motivations, opportunities and behaviour of particular groups and the interactions between them. Related to this point, the book's fourth aim is to identify further areas of research that are urgently required if policymakers are to construct appropriate and effective mechanisms for addressing the negative outcomes of neighbourhood dynamism and diversity, and – equally importantly – to begin to tackle the wider structural causal factors underpinning social disconnection and tensions.

Finally, the book aims to identify important dimensions of neighbourhood disconnections that are either new, or have not been given sufficient attention to date by either policymakers or academics within the community cohesion agenda. These include, for example, new immigration, advances in information technology and new forms of residential development and spatial differentiation. This also involves a broadening of the community cohesion agenda that recognises historical and traditional forms of social division, including conflict within ethnic groups and the socio-spatial segregation of British society on the lines of class and income.

In order to deliver on this ambitious manifesto, a range of academic perspectives on debates about various aspects of community cohesion in the UK have been drawn together from disciplines including geography, housing studies, legal studies, political economy, political science, sociology, social policy, public theology and urban studies.

The structure of the book

The opening two chapters provide a critical assessment of the rationales underpinning the community cohesion agenda. In Chapter One, David Robinson explores the disputed territory of community cohesion. Reflecting on the lack of evidence upon which the community cohesion agenda is based, Robinson challenges some of its underlying themes, concepts and assumptions and describes the dynamism and diversity within local neighbourhoods that is not captured in policy discourse or interventions. Robinson illustrates how community cohesion is constructed by government in a process that excludes some important dimensions of cohesion from official scrutiny and debate. In Chapter Two, Jon Burnett argues that the community cohesion agenda represents a neoliberal governance programme of integrationism, through which particular norms and values are prioritised. Using a case study of Bradford, one of the sites of the 2001 urban disorder that acted as a catalyst for the community cohesion agenda, Burnett shows how community cohesion has become entwined with the quest for urban renaissance, regeneration and a modernity believed necessary to ensure the economic prosperity of cities and neighbourhoods. Burnett argues that such processes result in the exclusion of particular groups and populations who are subject to an increasingly coercive strategy of integrationism that neglects the structural factors of deprivation, racism and cultural inequality.

The following three chapters explore how the dynamics of housing and labour markets affect diversity and cohesion at the neighbourhood level. Ian Cole and Ed Ferrari, in Chapter Three, highlight the need to explore the connectivity of neighbourhoods within housing market systems. Based on evidence from a study of two local housing markets in Birmingham, Cole and Ferrari show how varying structural constraints in local housing markets, including geography, population characteristics, stock and price, affect residential outcomes for particular ethnic groups. Arguing for the importance of micro-level analysis of housing processes and not just outcomes in community cohesion

—

debates, they analyse 'context-free' theories that link the trajectories and demographic profiles of neighbourhoods to cultural preferences.

Similarly, in Chapter Four, Deborah Phillips, Ludi Simpson and Sameera Ahmed reveal the nuanced and complex factors shaping the residential decisions and aspirations of different ethnic groups. Based on qualitative work with British Asian and white individuals in Oldham and Rochdale, the chapter explores how understandings of community have an impact on perceptions of neighbourhood. Although Phillips and her colleagues identify barriers to achieving greater social mix at the neighbourhood level, including housing affordability, racial harassment and anti-social behaviour, they also find a commonality in housing aspirations between ethnic groups and a considerable desire for multi-ethnic neighbourhoods that is at odds with the 'self-segregation' and 'parallel lives' paradigms underpinning the community cohesion agenda.

In Chapter Five, Del Roy Fletcher uses a historical study of the Manor Estate in Sheffield to critique policy rationales linking labour market behaviour to the 'disconnection' of deprived communities. Like the preceding two chapters, Fletcher's study shows the inadequacy of cultural theories in explaining the physical and/or social isolation of particular populations. He evidences the strong work ethic on the estate, but reveals how both individual and community identities were strongly related to manual employment, and highlights the importance of rooting community tensions and divisions within economic restructuring and housing allocation policies. Fletcher also reveals how contemporary concerns about a crisis in community cohesion ignore similar concerns about neighbourhoods like the Manor in earlier historical periods.

The next three chapters focus on the role of particular types of organisations and institutions within the community cohesion agenda. In Chapter Six, Rob Furbey discusses the impact of faith and faith organisations on social cohesion. While acknowledging the potential divisiveness within certain religious interpretations and practices, Furbey provides evidence that faith, expressed both individually and collectively, is positively related to civic and community participation that has enhanced bridging, as well as bonding, social capital in many local neighbourhoods. However, Furbey also comments on the instrumental role ascribed for faith communities in the community cohesion agenda, and argues that the complexity and independence of faith groups should not be misrepresented as a non-allegiance to the secular state within overly simplistic functional and consensual definitions of community cohesion.

Peter Wells, in Chapter Seven, assesses the roles that third-sector organisations operating in deprived neighbourhoods have been ascribed in the community cohesion agenda. Like Furbey, Wells highlights the need to understand the complexity of the third sector and uses data from the New Deal for Communities evaluation to challenge some of the assumptions about both the nature of diversity and attachment in deprived communities and the contribution of third-sector organisations to fostering cohesion. Wells uses the example of debates over single group funding to illustrate the complex relationship between policy frameworks and consequences for community cohesion. He argues for the need to locate the third sector within wider concepts of civic participation and associative democracy, and concludes that there is a need for a broadening of the conceptualisation of community cohesion interventions to encompass all of the contributions that third-sector organisations make within local neighbourhoods.

In Chapter Eight, John Flint examines how particular forms of welfare state institutions are conceptualised within the community cohesion agenda. Flint uses the examples of state-funded faith schools and social housing allocation policies and black and minority ethnic (BME) housing associations to show how the welfare state is a particularly controversial site of contestation over the relationships between different religious and ethnic groups and the compact between citizen and state. Flint provides evidence that neither faith schools nor BME housing associations are inherently divisive institutions within local neighbourhoods. Rather, he argues that there is a need to address the challenges in governing institutionalised diversity within the welfare state, and to locate developments in the public sector within wider processes of community and neighbourhood secession.

The final four chapters examine either new dimensions of disconnection that are emerging at the neighbourhood level, or provide evidence on longstanding sources of tensions in neighbourhoods that have, to date, been ignored in the community cohesion agenda. In Chapter Nine, Kesia Reeve discusses the neighbourhood impacts of new immigration to the UK. She shows that new immigrants are both arriving from a very diverse range of countries and settling in neighbourhoods, including those in rural areas, that have not previously experienced significant immigration. Patterns of new immigration interact in complex ways with policy developments, economic restructuring, local housing markets and changing settlement patterns of established ethnic minority populations. Reeve shows the dramatic scale and pace of change that is occurring and the considerable challenges that this raises for community cohesion. She argues that the knowledge base on the housing needs of new immigrants, and their impacts upon local neighbourhoods, needs to be substantially improved.

Keith Kintrea and Naofumi Suzuki, in Chapter Ten, explore territoriality among young people in Edinburgh and Glasgow. Their chapter highlights how socio-spatial manifestations of division are neither new, nor limited to inter-ethnic or religious rivalries, as the community cohesion agenda often suggests. Kintrea and Suzuki show how territoriality plays out in different ways, depending on local neighbourhood histories and dynamics and the age and gender of the groups affected by it. They illustrate some of the negative consequences of territoriality for young people, including constraints on mobility and social interaction and limited access to neighbourhood facilities and educational institutions. However, they also reflect on their findings that territoriality represents a type of belonging and attachment to a neighbourhood that denotes a form of cohesion that, while problematic, may potentially be reshaped towards more positive outcomes.

In Chapter Eleven, Roger Burrows explores an issue that has been completely absent from the community cohesion agenda to date: the role of new technologies in the representation and construction of neighbourhoods. Burrows uses case studies of the Mosaic software system and the cities of Sheffield and York to examine the relationship between digital representation and social geography. He highlights how new technologies enable ever more fine-grained classifications and sorting of populations and neighbourhoods and how this has an impact on both governmental and commercial processes. Burrows points out that geodemographic technologies may be increasingly influencing the residential decision making of particular groups, with as yet unknown consequences for neighbourhood formation, trajectories and social cohesion.

Sarah Blandy, in Chapter Twelve, examines the consequences for social cohesion of the growing number of gated communities in England. Blandy assesses the evidence about levels of community cohesion within such developments, and explores the wider social cohesion outcomes of locating gated communities in their wider neighbourhood contexts. Blandy develops a five-part typology of 'host' neighbourhoods within which gated communities may be situated, and argues that the siting of affluent gated communities adjacent to deprived neighbourhoods may have the most detrimental impact on community dynamics and social cohesion. She concludes that the processes of social secession evident in the emergence of gated communities requires a national government response that places these forms of residential developments within a community cohesion, as well as a planning, framework.

References

Amin, A. (2002) 'Ethnicity and the multicultural city: Living with diversity', *Environment and Planning A*, vol 34, no 6, pp 959–80.

Bauman, Z. (2001) *Community: Seeking safety in an insecure world*, Cambridge: Polity Press.

Brown, G. (2006) 'The future of Britishness', Speech to the Fabian Society, 14 January 2006.

Burnley Task Force (2002) *Report of the Burnley Task Force, chaired by Lord Clarke*, Burnley: Burnley Task Force.

Cameron, D. (2007a) Interview with Andrew Marr on *BBC Sunday AM*, 7 July, http://news.bbc.co.uk/1/hi/programmes/sunday_am/6281810.stm (accessed January 2008).

Cameron, D. (2007b) 'No one left behind in a Tory Britain', *Observer*, 28 January 2007.

Cohen, S. (1980) *Folk devils and moral panics: The creation of the Mods and Rockers*, New York: St Martin's Press.

Commission on Integration and Cohesion (2007) *Our shared future*, London: Commission on Integration and Cohesion.

Community Cohesion Independent Review Team (2001) (Cantle Report) *Community cohesion: A report of the Independent Review Team, chaired by Ted Cantle*, London: Home Office.

Dorling, D. and Thomas, B. (2004) *People and places: A 2001 census atlas of the UK*, Bristol: The Policy Press.

Etzioni, A. (1995) *The spirit of community: Rights, responsibilities and the communitarian agenda*, London: Fontana.

Fox, R.L. (2006) *The Classical world: An epic history of Greece and Rome*, New York: Basic Books.

Giddens, A. (1998) *The third way: The renewal of social democracy*, Cambridge: Polity Press.

Home Office (2001) (Denham Report) *Building cohesive communities: A report of the Ministerial Group on Public Order and Community Cohesion*, London: Home Office.

Kearns, A. and Forrest, R. (2000) 'Social cohesion and multilevel urban governance', *Urban Studies*, vol 37, no 5/6, pp 995–1017.

Local Government Association (LGA), Office of the Deputy Prime Minister, Home Office and Commission for Racial Equality (2002) *Guidance on community cohesion*, London: Local Government Association.

Murray, C.A. (ed) (1990) *The emerging British underclass*, London: Institute of Economic Affairs.

Oldham Independent Panel Review (2001) *One Oldham, one future. Panel report, chaired by David Ritchie*, Oldham: Oldham Metropolitan Council.

Ouseley, H. (2001) *Community pride not prejudice: Making diversity work in Bradford*, Bradford: Bradford Vision.

Park, R., Burgess, E.W. and McKenzie, R.D. (1925) *The city*, Chicago: University of Chicago Press.

Putnam, R. (2000) *Bowling alone: The collapse and revival of American community*, New York: Simon & Schuster.

Robinson, D. (2005) 'The search for community cohesion: Key themes and dominant concepts of the public policy agenda', *Urban Studies*, vol 42, no 8, pp 1411–28.

Zorbaugh, H.W. (1929) *The Gold Coast and the slum: A sociological study of Chicago's Near North Side*, Chicago: University of Chicago Press.

ONE

Community cohesion and the politics of communitarianism

David Robinson

Introduction

It is difficult to find any reference to community cohesion in the statements of public policy or the work of urban theorists prior to the street disturbances that rocked a number of northern UK towns and cities in the summer of 2001. Yet, community cohesion quickly emerged as the favoured reference point of politicians and policymakers seeking to explain and articulate a response to the violence and disorder. A flurry of policy statements and guidance documents on community cohesion followed, ranging from advice about promoting community cohesion during the delivery of Area Based Initiatives (ABIs), to advice to schools about how to contribute to community cohesion. Local authorities were charged with taking the lead in promoting community cohesion and the agenda was mainstreamed into national policy through its integration with race equality issues (see Home Office, 2005). Community cohesion was born and raised to maturity as a policy concern in just a few short years. The significance of the agenda appears questionable, however. Centred on an ill-defined concept that can be interpreted and understood in very different ways, it is a policy agenda with no statutory framework to underpin its delivery and no dedicated funding stream. This chapter asserts, however, that the importance of the community cohesion agenda lies beyond such formal manifestations of policy and in the pioneering role that the agenda has played in the practical application of the new politics of community that is the focus of this book.

In the weeks and months that followed the disturbances in the summer of 2001 – and the subsequent events of 11 September 2001 in New York City – the empty concept that was community cohesion was imbued with meaning. The various reports into the disturbances commissioned or sanctioned by the government were published in

December 2001. They presented a shared vision of the root causes and required response to the disturbances. This storyline focused on the perceived residential segregation of the South Asian population in Bradford, Burnley and Oldham – the towns and cities where the troubles had erupted in 2001 – and the limited interaction that resulted, which was undercutting shared values and allowing social disharmony and unrest to flourish. The settlement patterns of South Asian populations were problematised for allowing values and forms of behaviour that were at odds with the dominant social order to flourish. The proposed response, captured in the working definition of community guidance (LGA et al, 2002), was to promote shared values and a common sense of belonging through the development of positive relationships between people from different backgrounds at the neighbourhood level. This diagnosis and proposed remedy represent one of the most explicit and committed applications of the communitarian logic that has increasingly informed public policy making since the mid-1990s. Particular places were problematised as areas of conflict where social norms, values and practices are undermining essential aspects of civil society. The recognised challenge was to support the development of new and more valued forms of community in these areas in order to protect and promote civic society.

As subsequent chapters will reveal, the ideological footprint of this new politics of community is now evident across a wide policy spectrum. Efforts to tackle worklessness, for example, are more focused on reshaping particular places thought to reproduce cultures resistant to work; the response to anti-social behaviour has included a concentration on challenging values and practices that have emerged in neighbourhoods where community governance is perceived as weak or to have collapsed completely; and immigration policy is increasingly aimed at civil integration and nurturing of a sense of belonging and citizenship. Community cohesion, however, remains the most vivid representation of this new politics and provides the clearest illustration yet of the process through which particular places and the people who reside therein are being problematised within public policy discourses for asserting values, principles and modes of behaviour at odds with the dominant moral order. This chapter sets out to explore this disputed territory of the community cohesion policy agenda.

Discussion begins with a review of the storyline that emerged to explain the 2001 disturbances and how this perspective has subsequently been reiterated and reinforced through policy statements and guidance documents. Analysis traces the fundamentals of this narrative back to the central tenets of communitarianism and spotlights the kinds of places that are being problematised through the application of this political ideology for breeding social disharmony and civil unrest. Attention then turns to the evidence base, in an attempt to substantiate the validity of the claims made about these problematised places of community cohesion. Discussion reveals that the political commitment to communitarianism is overriding attention to empirical evidence, despite claims of evidence-based policy making (Wells, 2007). Finally, some overarching lessons regarding the character of this new politics of community are drawn out from this exploration of community cohesion.

The community cohesion agenda: offering change through communitarianism

Community cohesion might have had no place in the vocabulary of public policy prior to the street confrontations of 2001, but the Home Secretary's immediate response to the disturbances was to establish an interdepartmental Ministerial Group on Public Order and Community Cohesion (Home Office, 2001). Chaired by John Denham, the group was charged with reporting on what the government should do to minimise the risk of further disorder and to build more cohesive communities. With the concept still undefined, the Home Secretary also established a Community Cohesion Independent Review Team (chaired by Ted Cantle), charged with reviewing the views and opinions of different interests in the affected towns and beyond. Focusing attention on the vague, undefined issue of community cohesion served an obvious political purpose. Attention was steered away from more intractable problems, such as the high levels of deprivation and social marginalisation in the effected locations, and directed towards virgin political territory that the government could colonise with its own priorities and preoccupations. This mission was accomplished with the publication of the Denham and Cantle reports in December 2001.

The reports of the Ministerial Group (Home Office, 2001, Denham Report) and the Community Cohesion Independent Review Team (2001, Cantle Report) focused their analysis on the related issues of segregation and values. The Denham Report drew heavily on the findings of local reviews commissioned in the immediate aftermath of the disturbances in Oldham (Oldham Independent Panel Review, 2001) and Burnley (Burnley Task Force, 2001) and a report into 'community fragmentation' in Bradford (Ouseley, 2001) that had been commissioned before the disturbances but was published shortly afterwards. Striking in their similarity, these local reports pointed to three key concerns that were regarded as underpinning the unrest – ethnic segregation, limited cross-cultural interaction and the absence of a shared identity and values.

The Ouseley Report set the tone for what followed in the other reports with its focus on 'the very worrying drift towards self-segregation' and 'the necessity of arresting and reversing this process' (Ouseley, 2001, Foreword). The corrosive effect of social deprivation and disadvantage on life in the city was acknowledged, but the key concern for the district was identified as being the fact 'that relationships between different cultural communities should be improving, but instead they are deteriorating' and that 'there are signs that communities are fragmenting along racial, cultural and faith lines' (Ouseley, 2001, p 6). This issue of fragmentation – in the form of ethnic residential segregation – was the central theme of the report of the Oldham Review Team. Various drivers of residential segregation were acknowledged, including the operation of the housing market and the practices of housing institutions, as well as the inclinations and preferences of different population groups that were identified as being rooted in fears, preferences and prejudices. The result, it was argued, was 'a substantial degree of educational segregation, and in turn … a very low level of contact between most white people and most Pakistanis and Bangladeshis within the town' (Oldham Independent Panel Review, 2001, p 10). Similarly, the Burnley Task Force concluded that 'the Asian and White communities live separate and parallel lives and have very few ways of learning from and understanding each others' cultures and beliefs' (2001, p 7). Ouseley went on to portray civil society within the city as breaking down, as 'different communities seek to protect their identities and cultures, discouraging and avoiding contact with other cultures and institutions' (2001, p 10). In response, he concluded that there is an urgent need, within the Bradford context, for the promotion of a 'single common identity to a diverse population' (Ouseley, 2001, p 1).

The Cantle Report captured the essential essence of this causal story with its reference to 'parallel lives'. Although much-quoted, this section of the report is worth revisiting:

> Whilst the physical segregation of housing estates and inner city areas came as no surprise, the team was particularly struck by the depth of polarisation of our towns and cities. The extent to which these physical divisions were compounded by so many other aspects of our daily lives, was very evident. Separate educational arrangements, community and voluntary bodies, employment, places

of worship, language, social and cultural networks, means that many communities operate on the basis of a series of parallel lives. These lives often do not seem to touch at any point, let alone overlap and promote any meaningful interchanges. (Community Cohesion Independent Review Team, 2001, p 9)

This short section of the Cantle Report provides a précis of the official storyline that emerged to explain the 2001 disturbances: residential segregation leads to social isolation and limited cross-cultural contact, which allows misunderstanding and suspicion to flourish and can lead to inter-community tensions and violence and disorder. If we invert this storyline, we can see a route map out of this dystopian world of community conflict. What we need to do is challenge the 'them and us' attitude apparent in such situations and develop common goals and a shared vision. To this end, greater contact should be promoted between different communities by tackling the residential segregation that promotes separation in schooling, employment, service use and social life.

The development of the community cohesion agenda is clearly rooted in the politics of communitarianism that emerged in the 1990s and was a key influence on the New Labour administration that took office in 1997. This new wave of communitarian thinking bought into the pessimism being expressed by various urban theorists about the dissolution of the 'social glue' that had bound society together, in the context of social and economic change (see, for example, Castells, 1997; Fukuyama, 1999; Forrest and Kearns, 2001). To communitarians, both Right and Left were to blame for this social malaise. The libertarian solutions of the Right had eroded social responsibility and valued aspects of community life and reciprocity. The Left was blamed for its centralising tendency, involving the shift of powers away from local communities and towards centralised bureaucracies, and for promoting welfare policies that undermined key institutions and social ties in civil society, including the family (Bell, 2005). In response, the new politics of communitarianism sought to rebalance the emphasis in contemporary politics, away from the individual – who needed to recognise a responsibility for promoting the well-being of friends, relatives and others within the various communities to which they belonged – and thereby towards the interests of society (Etzioni, 1995). Community emerged as central to the pursuit of this political project.

Dixon et al (2005) point to two presumptions, central to the political ideology of communitarianism, that help explain why community reigns supreme within communitarian political thinking. First, communitarianism understands normal human relations as requiring cooperation. The liberal self, bereft of shared values and attitudes is considered an unnatural state. Community relations are presumed to be an essential component of identity and a vehicle through which individuals can reach improved levels of personal well-being. Second, communitarianism asserts that it is only through cooperative participation in community discourses that the social cohesion required to constrain authoritarianism can be secured. Through 'community', members 'can create a democracy that is united around shared core values ... thereby constraining authoritarianism, nurturing mutuality and promoting a more egalitarian society' (Dixon et al, 2005, p 14).

This emphasis on community raises the inevitable question of definition. Bell (2005) suggests that communitarianism recognises communities as taking three essential forms. Communities of place are linked to a particular fixed locality and involve association with familiar surroundings and a sense of 'home'. Communities of memory have a shared history, ideals and aspirations, with members seeing their efforts as contributing, in part, to a common good. Examples might include the nation and ethno-cultural and faith groups. Communities of interaction are governed by sentiments of trust and cooperation, the family being the most obvious example. Life is bound up in these different community forms, and identity is constituted through their membership. Communities therefore hold the potential to serve society, by expressing commitments to which community members align themselves. The corollary of this, however, is that communities can challenge the dominant moral order by promoting values, modes of behaviour and allegiances at odds with a particular model of citizenship. The communitarian political project therefore centres on identifying valued forms of community and devising policies designed to promote and protect such communities where they already exist and to reconfigure community forms that stray from this ideal.

This new politics of community is plain to see in the Cantle and Denham reports. Central to the analysis presented therein is the assumption that towns and cities increasingly consist of internally cohesive but socially isolated neighbourhoods. Following the communitarian logic, none of this is necessarily problematic; problems arise when segregated communities nurture a culture that asserts values and allegiances at odds with the dominant moral order. The retreat of middle-class households into white British zones of sameness, discussed in Chapters Eleven and Twelve, can therefore be tolerated because such communities of place are presumed to reinforce dominant values and standards. In contrast, the perceived retreat of particular minority ethnic populations into ethnic enclaves to protect diaspora traditions and Muslim values is problematised because it is seen as generating communities of place, memory and interaction that assert identities and values at odds with the dominant notions of British standards and principles that politicians have been so eager to discuss and define in recent years (Burnett, 2007). Seeking academic legitimisation for this conclusion, the Cantle Report refers to the work of Kearns and Forrest (2000) and their observations regarding the contradictory connectiveness of neighbourhoods, whereby tensions can exist between internally cohesive neighbourhoods. In such situations, the stronger the ties that bind such communities, the greater may be the conflict between them. The challenge, therefore, according to the Cantle Report, is to help such micro-communities gel or mesh into an integrated whole (Community Cohesion Independent Review Team, 2001, p 70).

The dominant discursive themes of the community cohesion agenda – the assertion of shared values and the problematising of places where difference is allowed to flourish – were updated and reinforced in the report of the Commission on Integration and Cohesion (2007). The Commission was established by the government in the aftermath of the bombings in London on 7 July 2005 and was charged with examining the issues raising tensions and leading to segregation and conflict, including large-scale immigration into the UK, driven by the twin engines of asylum and labour migration.

The report of the Commission is laced with references to two issues – immigration and fundamentalism – which were largely absent from the 2001 reports and subsequent guidance documents. A number of familiar themes, however, frame the Commission's recommendations. The problematising of difference, associated with the retreat from multiculturalism discussed by Burnett in Chapter Two, is asserted in the opening lines of the report, which sketch out a vision of a society 'where people are committed to what we have in common rather than obsessing with those things that makes us different' (Commission on Integration and Cohesion, 2007, p 3). Reference is frequently made to 'shared futures' and an emphasis put on 'what binds communities together rather than what differences divide them' (Commission on Integration and Cohesion, 2007, p 43). The central tenets of communitarianism are, meanwhile, reinforced through repeated references to mutuality and respect and the need to promote 'a new model of responsibilities and rights ... that make clear both a sense of citizenship at national and local level and the obligations that go along with membership of a community, both for individuals or groups' (Commission on Integration and Cohesion, 2007, p 43).

The Commission report also shares with the Denham and Cantle reports a concern about segregation, separation and isolationism. A fundamental problem is recognised as being alienation within particular communities and the 'parallel lives' perceived to be lived in some places. Segregation therefore remains central to the cohesion agenda, although it is suggested that the national debate on integration and cohesion should not be boiled down to this one specific issue. Rather, invoking communitarian fundamentals, the report argues that at the national level, government should assert a shared national vision of integration and cohesion and lead a national shared futures campaign. At local level, it is suggested that the focus will depend upon the particular challenges evident within a location. Residential segregation will be the issue to focus on in some areas, where efforts to bring people together and counter the divisive effect of segregation will need to be championed, but not in others. However, no attempt is made to chart this uneven geography of community cohesion and, ultimately, the centrality of segregation to the cohesion agenda is reinforced through the focus on the two 'interlocking concepts' of integration and cohesion, which are both considered as being related to the challenges of persistent separation in some communities (Commission on Integration and Cohesion, 2007, p 38).

So, to summarise, community cohesion was an empty concept that the government filled with meaning in an attempt to manage the response to the disturbances in northern towns and cities in 2001. It involved tapping into emergent notions of what constitutes an ideal society and, in particular, the celebration of shared values and common bonds, promoted through social contact. Communitarian ideology ran thick in the veins of this new policy creation, reflecting the growing influence of this political ideology on public policy making since the mid-1990s, and legitimised the focus on shared values and the problematising of the segregation and separation perceived to allow attitudes and standards at odds with these values to emerge in certain locations. The agenda has been reinforced and subtly updated in response to events, including the London bombings of 2005 and the large-scale immigration of migrant workers from Eastern Europe, but the fundamentals have remained the same. Through all of this, however, some critical questions of definition have been left unanswered. Where are the segregated and separated communities that urgently need to be meshed into wider society? Would we recognise these communities if we stumbled across them? These questions raise two challenges, one philosophical and one empirical. The former relates to the definition of community, which is a far more ambiguous concept than is allowed for in communitarian thinking (Brent, 2004). The second challenge relates to the identification of evidence that substantiates the assumptions regarding segregation and separation and associated parallel lives that are central to the community cohesion agenda. Leaving political philosophers to ruminate about the former, the following section of this chapter moves on to explore the evidence base that might be called upon to support the thrust of the community cohesion agenda.

Segregation, separation and parallel lives: in search of an evidence base

There is no disputing that the events of summer 2001 in Bradford, Burnley and Oldham and subsequent disturbances in other towns and cities (for example, the Lozells area of Birmingham in 2005) raise very real questions about the exclusion of certain population groups in particular locations from the opportunities and choices available within contemporary society. Nor is there any denying that the experience of exclusion can prove highly divisive and can undermine relations between different population groups, who often perceive themselves to be in direct competition for scarce resources. Neither is there any question that the events of 11 September 2001 in New York City and 7 July 2005 in London have redefined public attitudes towards Islam in the UK. Islamophobia is increasing, as are attacks on Muslims. Meanwhile, what Modood (2003) refers to as Muslim assertiveness has emerged as a new voice in majority–minority relations, challenging policy to extend protection from discrimination to the UK's Muslim population. There is also little doubting that new immigration, whether driven by asylum or labour migration, has the potential to promote change at the neighbourhood level and raise challenges for community relations and service provision (Robinson and Reeve, 2006). What is in doubt is the assumed cultural separatism and self-segregation of particular communities, which is taken as indicative of the failure of the multicultural project and its celebration of difference over shared futures, which has promoted fragmentation instead of integration. Where is the evidence to substantiate this storyline?

The various reports into the 2001 disturbances and subsequent reports and guidance notes on community cohesion provide little or no evidence to support the picture they paint. This lack of evidence is openly acknowledged in the Denham Report:

> It is difficult to identify what is cause and what is effect
> in the development of segregated communities. It is

> equally difficult to be certain whether the geographical
> concentration of different communities in different areas
> always give rise to problems of community cohesion or
> whether other factors have to be present for difficulties to
> arise. (Home Office, 2001, p 13)

This would appear a rather startling admission, given the assertions
that are made within the Denham Report about the problems of
segregation. However, an apparent lack of data does not appear to
be a concern when it comes to asserting the storyline of community
cohesion. The final report of the Community Cohesion Panel (2004),
for example, which had been set up to work with and advise ministers,
reported that, despite its best efforts, including requests to government
departments and agencies, it had not been able to acquire information
that allowed it to 'take a really informed view about patterns of
segregation and integration' (2004, p 17). The panel was therefore
forced to 'rely on anecdotal and limited information' (Community
Cohesion Panel, 2004, p 17). However, this did not stop it going on
to recommend that a 'suite of policies be developed in response to
segregated neighbourhoods' (Community Cohesion Panel, 2004,
p 17). Yet, there is a wealth of data that can be drawn on to explore the
changes in residential settlement and the preferences and actions that lie
behind these patterns. The problem for policy is that this evidence base
challenges rather than substantiates the causal story of the community
cohesion agenda.

An ethnic identity question first appeared in the 1991 Census of
Population. Analysis of the Census revealed there to be no ghettos in
England, that is, no polarised enclaves where a large proportion of an
ethnic group's population reside (Phillips, 1998). Analysis also suggested
that assimilation best describes the shifting pattern of minority ethnic
residential settlement in England, with the clustering of certain
groups reflecting the early stages of concentration, which in all cases
has been followed by dispersal, although this process has taken place
at different rates for different groups in different locations (Johnston
et al, 2002). Analysis of the 2001 Census of Population has revealed
this process of residential dispersal from established areas of settlement
to have continued during the 1990s. Indeed, at a time when spatial
polarisation is becoming a more pronounced feature of British society
– most notably along lines of income and class – analysis of the 2001
Census has revealed that this is generally not the case for ethnicity
(Dorling and Thomas, 2004). Minority ethnic groups, including the
Indian, Chinese and Black Caribbean populations, are moving out of

cities to more distant suburbs and small towns, a shifting pattern of settlement consistent with processes hinted at in analysis of the 1991 Census of Population. Dorling and Thomas (2004) also reveal that the Pakistani and Bangladeshi populations were actively dispersing out of established areas of settlement during the 1990s, a finding clearly at odds with the assumption made by the community cohesion agenda that these populations are resistant to moving beyond established areas of settlement and have more recently been retreating back into these 'comfort zones'. Added to this, the geography of new immigration has been revealed to be distinct and different to what has gone before, with new immigrants often settling beyond the metropolitan centres that have traditionally been the first port of call for new immigrants to the UK and moving into small towns and rural areas (Audit Commission, 2007; Bauere et al, 2007).

There are clearly dangers in relying on anecdote and perception when it comes to demographic trends and the shifts in residential settlement, which the various reports promoting the community cohesion agenda have failed to heed. This is most starkly exposed by Simpson's (2004) analysis of demographic change and settlement patterns in Bradford. Analysing time series data with a racial dimension, Simpson reveals that, rather than the South Asian population self-segregating into ethnic enclaves, as suggested by Ouseley (2001), overall segregation between South Asian and 'other' populations remained unchanged in the city during the 1990s. This general picture, however, masks two significant trends. First, the city experienced an increase in the number of areas that could be described as majority South Asian. However, rather than driven by the self-segregation of the city's South Asian population into 'comfort zones', this growth was the result of the arrival of new Pakistani immigrants into areas of established settlement, as well as the relatively high reproduction rates associated with the population's young age profile. As the population grew, so new households were formed and moved into housing vacated by people leaving the area. The second significant trend, however was that the people leaving the area were both white and South Asian, dispelling simplistic notions of 'white flight'. Indeed, the net migrationary trend for both white and South Asian groups was out of the city. Consequently, there were far fewer mono-racial areas of the city at the end of the 20th century than there had been 10 years earlier.

The motivations and actions that lie behind these changing patterns of minority ethnic residential settlement in towns and cities across the UK have been revealed by numerous qualitative studies of the residential preferences and drivers of mobility among different minority ethnic groups. Such studies have reported a common aspiration among – particularly younger – minority ethnic households to move beyond established areas of settlement (Harrison with Phillips, 2003). Preferences often focus on neighbourhoods adjacent to or within easy reach of established areas of settlement, although the preference for such areas is often explained with reference to their essential qualities (quality of housing, living environment, facilities, services and perceptions relating to issues of safety) rather than their location (see, for example, Ratcliffe et al, 2001). It is true to say that for some groups in certain locations, the realisation of these aspirations is proving problematic and dispersal is proceeding at a relatively slow rate. However, the factors putting a brake on the process of dispersal have been found to centre on restricted opportunities and choice in the context of poverty and racism, rather than the self-segregating tendencies of any particular group.

Three broad reasons can be called on to explain the slow pace of dispersal for certain groups in particular locations. First, problems are often perceived and can be experienced by households living beyond established areas of minority ethnic settlement. The result can be the heavily racialised notions of space discussed in Chapter Four, which serve to restrict residential choices to particular neighbourhoods seen as being safer and more welcoming. In certain situations such notions can effectively foreclose residential choice. In some towns and cities, for example, the minority ethnic population might be too small to secure and maintain a recognisable presence beyond the established area of settlement. In contrast to the situation described in Chapter Four, where young Pakistani men described different parts of Oldham and Rochdale as 'white' or 'Asian', minority ethnic households might therefore perceive there to be no other neighbourhoods in the town or city where they live that they would consider safe and welcoming places that are able and willing to accommodate ethnic and cultural diversity. This was certainly the case among respondents to a recent study of minority ethnic housing preferences and neighbourhood attitudes in Newcastle and Gateshead (Robinson et al, 2007b). Similarly, a study in the rural district of North Lincolnshire (Reeve and Robinson, 2007) revealed a shared aspiration across the minority ethnic population to move beyond the neighbourhood in Scunthorpe where the minority ethnic population of the district has historically been clustered. However, few households appeared able to realise this aspiration, and the minority ethnic cluster was proving a persistent feature of the residential landscape. Exploring this issue further, racialised notions of space, associated with the fear or experience of racism, emerged as a critical factor in explaining the relatively slow process of dispersal and the virtual exclusion of the population from the small towns, villages and hamlets within the district.

A second brake on the process of dispersal is the fact that for many minority ethnic households residential mobility remains closely associated with the ability to buy into the opportunities provided by the owner-occupied sector in locations beyond traditional areas of settlement. This is particularly true for the Pakistani population (Ratcliffe et al, 2001; Bowes et al, 2002; Robinson et al, 2005; Robinson et al, 2007a). The supply, allocation and management of social housing has largely failed to recognise that the needs, requirements and preferences of minority ethnic populations, including the Pakistani population, differ from those of the majority ethnic, white British, population. This has served to render the sector an unpopular or unsuitable housing option for some groups.

The policies and practices of social landlords also continue to have discriminatory consequences, despite the outlawing of more overt forms of racism. The failure of landlords to deal effectively with racist harassment and persecution, for example, serves to restrict the location choices of minority ethnic applicants. The Pakistani population is therefore largely reliant on the private sector to satisfy its housing needs and residential aspirations. However, financial resources, rather than housing need, are the principal determinant of a household's position in the market place. Pakistani people are more likely to live in low-income households and experience unemployment; their housing options are therefore severely curtailed. Hence the reported comments of the South Asian people surveyed by Ratcliffe et al (2001) in Bradford that the only people likely to move out of the inner city were 'middle class professionals', 'business people' and 'those who can afford it'. Added to these financial constraints, all minority ethnic groups have been persistently disadvantaged by the discriminatory actions of private institutions (landlords, letting agents, estate agents and mortgage finance companies) in the housing system (Harrison with Phillips, 2003).

A third restraint on the dispersal of some minority ethnic populations from established areas of settlement is the fact that, although such locations do have their problems, including poverty and social exclusion, they can also provide substantial benefits (Robinson, 2007). Clustering can provide the critical mass required to sustain community-led shops and services, which offer an alternative for people unable to access formal provision, as well as often providing a bridge into statutory services. In addition, these community-led agencies can provide job opportunities for local people, while clustering can give a particular group the visible presence required to prompt statutory service providers to recognise and respond to their needs, often through targeted initiatives. A sense of safety and security can also stem from living in a neighbourhood where one does not stand out merely by virtue of not being white. Such neighbourhoods can also provide a territorial focus for a sense of identity and belonging, which serves to foster security in the face of persecution and oppression. Population clustering, meanwhile, can also allow a group to exert greater power through the structures of representative and participative governance. These last two points are of particular importance, as they point to the possibility that the problematised spaces of community cohesion might actually provide the security, stability and confidence that marginalised and disadvantaged groups require in order to engage with wider society and to begin to overcome their exclusion from social and economic opportunities. In the parlance of social capital, these problematised ethnic clusters represent a source of both bonding and bridging capital.

This brief review of the evidence base has focused on the process of self-segregation through which the problematised community archetype of the isolated minority ethnic enclave is presumed to be (re)produced. The existence of these problematised places, as well as the process of their production, has been thrown into doubt. Even if one was happy to ignore such evidence, as the community cohesion agenda chooses to do, various unanswered questions surround the proposed responses to the problem of community cohesion. How is the greater residential integration deemed necessary to be promoted? Does the commitment exist to release the brakes on the residential dispersal discussed above? Even assuming that residential integration proceeds apace, will the fruits of social interaction inevitably follow? Will multicultural social ties emerge and bind people together around a common interest? Will cooperation be promoted, reciprocity norms be generated and all forms of segregation reduced? Certainly, lessons from an analysis of interaction within socially mixed neighbourhoods question whether residential integration inevitably results in social interaction between different groups (Robinson, 2005). Evidence also suggests that habitual contact is no guarantor of cultural exchange and can even reinforce animosities (Amin, 2002).

However, such questions are ultimately academic. Sustaining the narrative of community cohesion demands an indifferent attitude towards evidence and elucidation. Evidence that complicates or refutes the fundamental principles of the agenda has to be ignored. The challenge facing the government after the 2001 disturbances and subsequent events in New York City and London was the generation of what Stone (1989) refers to as a causal story that 'sounded right' and identified the cause of harm. In doing so, this story invested policymakers with the right to invoke power to stop further harm. How this power has been applied has been revealed to be determined more by ideological priorities, rooted in the logics of political communitarianism, than a considered review of empirical evidence.

Conclusion

This chapter has explored one of the most distinct expressions of the new politics of community; the community cohesion agenda. This case study has argued that the roots of this new politics can be traced back to the political communitarianism that emerged in the 1990s, which seeks to address the perceived erosion of community life and the increasing fragmentation of society by tackling the imbalance between rights and responsibilities. The vehicle to carry us forward towards this goal is 'community'. The challenge for policy is to identify valued forms of community and to devise policies designed to protect and promote them. The corollary of this is that policy is also required to counter community forms that are regarded as undermining the promotion of some assumed notion of social responsibility.

Through the focus on community cohesion, insights have also been provided into the change offered to society through the application of this ideology. In conclusion, the first point to make is that this agenda for change is not based on rigorous analysis of the evidence. At best, the new politics of community appears to have an indifferent attitude to evidence and, like all political ideologies, it seeks to avoid questions that call into doubt its 'comprehensive vision'. Instead, it tries to assert an explanation that generates demands for reform that invoke and represent a legitimate basis for the particular policy solution that it prefers. Through this particular ideological lens, the 2001 disturbances and the subsequent disorders in other towns and cities, as well as the London bombings, are interpreted as an 'Asian problem'. Triggers of unrest and disturbance – which in Bradford, Burnley and Oldham were reported to include deprivation and social marginalisation, the vilification of young Pakistani and Bangladeshi men in the local media, the local activities of the Far Right and the insensitivity of local policing – are denied and the dominant themes of media representations – that the young men involved were criminals, ungrateful immigrants, disloyal subjects, cultural separatists and Islamic militants – go unchecked (Amin, 2002).

Another point of note is that, despite the importance of this ideology to contemporary politics and its ongoing application in response to various policy challenges, this new politics of community is sustained by only a vague and ambiguous system of abstract thought. In particular, for a political ideology focused on community, surprisingly little effort is put into defining this core concept. Group belonging and identity is central to the concept of community promoted by the community cohesion agenda, but no effort has been made to clarify, confirm or define any clear sense of either problematised or preferred identities. Of course, glossing over contradictions and uncertainties can prove a useful approach to managing inherent weakness within an ideological position. It also allows concepts to be adapted to political objectives. This would certainly appear to be the case with the political rhetoric on identity associated with the community cohesion agenda. This agenda has involved, on the one hand, an attempt to assert some notion of the shared values and principles of Britishness. On the other hand, rhetoric has sought to harden up the differences associated with particular groups, in order that they can be problematised for being different. In particular, attention has focused on a South Asian/Muslim identity category, which is assumed to be bounded, homogeneous and distinct. However, no reference is made to the connections that define this group, or to the multiple and hierarchical identifications that might exist among group members. The group is presumed to exist and to be reproduced in segregated ethnic enclaves and this identity is assumed to be an important driver of behaviour that can sometimes challenge accepted norms and standards.

The impression that we are left with is that, rather than buying into the communitarian belief that there are many valued forms of communal life in the modern world, the new politics of community prefers to assert a hierarchy of communities and group identities. This assessment is reinforced by the way in which the new politics of community has quietly disregarded another inconvenient aspect of political communitarianism: the concern of communitarian thinkers regarding the erosion of valued forms of communal life and social responsibility at the hand of unregulated free market capitalism. An obvious example is the reluctance to problematise middle-class segregation and isolationism, most vividly represented in the growth of the gated communities discussed in Chapter Twelve. The exclusion of such forms of segregation from discussion and debate is justified by reference to the supposed cultural neutrality of these communities and their role in affirming, rather than challenging, 'normal' and 'accepted' values and standards of behaviour. Communitarian critics, however, condemn such developments on the grounds that they undermine connectivity to neighbouring communities and the local and national polity, and erode the trust and common understanding required to sustain social justice and the democratic process (Bell, 1995).

There is no doubting that the street disturbances of 2001 and the subsequent disorder in other towns and cities, together with the London bombings of July 2005 and the failed bomb attempts in London and Glasgow in 2007, present very real challenges for society that policy must address. What is in doubt is that the diagnosis and policy response, rooted in political communitarianism and encapsulated in the community cohesion agenda, represents a valid or effective response. Not only has any commitment to evidence-based policy making been overrun by ideology. The new politics of community appears to be slipping into the worst excesses of political communitarianism, observed by Fraser (1999), whereby a notion of community is applied that justifies hierarchical arrangements and delegitimises areas of conflict and contest in modern society. There would, therefore, appear to be good reason to view this new politics of community with a good dose of scepticism and no small amount of concern.

References

Amin, A. (2002) 'Ethnicity and the multicultural city: Living with diversity', *Environment and Planning A*, vol 34, no 6, pp 959–80.

Audit Commission (2007) *Crossing borders: Responding to the local challenges of migrant workers*, London: Audit Commission.

Bauere, V., Densham, P., Millar, J. and Salt, J. (2007) 'Migrants from Central and Eastern Europe: Local geographies', *Population Trends*, vol 129, pp 7–19.

Bell, D. (1995) 'Residential community associations: Community or disunity', *The Responsive Community*, fall, pp 25–36.

Bell, D. (2005) 'Communitarianism', in Edward N. Zalta (ed) *The Stanford Encyclopedia of Philosophy*, Spring 2005 edn, http://plato.stanford.edu/archives/spr2005/entries/communitarianism (accessed February 2008).

Bowes, A., Dar, N. and Sim, D. (2002) 'Differentiation in housing careers: The case of Pakistanis in the UK', *Housing Studies*, vol 17, no 3, pp 381–400.

Brent, J. (2004) 'The desire for community: Illusion, confusion and paradox', *Community Development Journal*, vol 39, no 3, pp 213–23.

Burnett, J. (2007) 'Britain's "civilising project": Community cohesion and core values', *Policy & Politics*, vol 35, no 2, pp 353–7.

Burnley Task Force (2001) *Report of the Burnley Task Force, chaired by Lord Clarke*, Burnley: Burnley Task Force.

Castells, M. (1997) *The Power of Identity*, Oxford: Blackwell.

Commission on Integration and Cohesion (2007) *Our shared future*, London: Commission on Integration and Cohesion.

Community Cohesion Independent Review Team (2001) (Cantle Report) *Community cohesion: A report of the Independent Review Team, chaired by Ted Cantle*, London: Home Office.

Community Cohesion Panel (2004) 'The end of parallel lives? The report of the Community Cohesion Panel' (www.communities.gov. uk/publications/communities/endparallellives, accessed February 2008).

Dixon, J., Dogan, R. and Sanderson, A. (2005) 'Community and communitarianism: A philosophical investigation', *Community Development Journal*, vol 40, no 1, pp 4–16.

Dorling, D. and Thomas, B. (2004) *People and places: A 2001 census atlas of the UK*, Bristol: The Policy Press.

Etzioni, A. (1995) *The spirit of community. Rights, responsibilities and the communitarian agenda*, London: Fontana.

Forrest, R. and Kearns, A. (2001) 'Social cohesion, social capital and the neighbourhood', *Urban Studies*, vol 38, no 12, pp 2125–43.

Fraser, E. (1999) *The problems of communitarian politics*, Oxford: Oxford University Press.

Fukuyama, F. (1999) *The great disruption: Human nature and the reconstitution of social order*, London: Profile Books.

Harrison, M. with Phillips, D. (2003) *Housing and Black and Minority Ethnic Communities: Review of the evidence base*, London: Office of the Deputy Prime Minister.

Home Office (2001) (Denham Report) *Building cohesive communities: A report of the Ministerial Group on Public Order and Community Cohesion*, London: Home Office.

Home Office (2005) *Improving opportunity, strengthening society. The government's strategy for race equality and community cohesion*. London: Home Office.

Johnston, R., Forrest, J. and Poulsen, M. (2002) 'Are there ethnic enclaves/ghettoes in English cities?', *Urban Studies*, vol 39, no 4, pp 591–618.

Kearns, A. and Forrest, R. (2000) 'Social cohesion and multilevel urban governance', *Urban Studies*, vol 37, no 5–6, pp 995–1017.

Local Government Association (LGA), Office of the Deputy Prime Minister, Home Office and Commission for Racial Equality (2002) *Guidance on community cohesion*, London: LGA.

Modood, T. (2003) 'Muslims and the politics of difference', *Political Quarterly*, vol 74, no 1, pp 100–15.

Oldham Independent Panel Review (2001) *One Oldham, one future. Panel report, chaired by David Ritchie*, Oldham: Oldham Metropolitan Borough Council.

Ouseley, H. (2001) *Community pride not prejudice: Making diversity work in Bradford*, Bradford: Bradford Vision.

Phillips, D. (1998) 'Black minority ethnic concentration, segregation and dispersal in Britain', *Urban Studies*, vol 35, no 10, pp 1681–702.

Ratcliffe, P., with Harrison, M., Hogg, R., Line, B., Phillips, D. and Tomlins, R. (and with Action Plan by Power, A.) (2001) *Breaking down the barriers: Improving Asian access to social rented housing*, Coventry: CIH, on behalf of Bradford MDC, Bradford Housing Forum, Housing Corporation and FBHO.

Reeve, K. and Robinson, D. (2007) 'Beyond the multi-ethnic metropolis: Minority ethnic housing experience in small town England', *Housing Studies*, vol 22, no 4, pp 547–71.

Robinson, D. (2005) 'The search for community cohesion: Key themes and dominant concepts of the public policy agenda', *Urban Studies*, vol 42, no 8, pp 1411–28.

Robinson, D. (2007) 'Living parallel lives? Residential segregation, community cohesion and housing', in H. Beider (ed) *Residence, renewal and community empowerment: Comparing approaches in the US and UK*, London: Macmillan.

Robinson, D. and Reeve, K. (2006) *Neighbourhood experiences of new immigration. Reflections on the evidence base*, York: Joseph Rowntree Foundation.

Robinson, D., Reeve, K and Casey, R. (2007a) *The housing pathways of new immigrants*, York: Joseph Rowntree Foundation.

Robinson, D., Reeve, K., Casey, R. and Goudie, R. (2007b) *Minority ethnic residential experiences and requirements in the Bridging NewcastleGateshead area*, Newcastle: Bridging NewcastleGateshead.

Simpson, L. (2004) 'Statistics of racial segregation: Measures, evidence and policy', *Urban Studies*, vol 41, no 3, pp 661–81.

Stone, D.A. (1989) 'Causal stories and the formation of policy agendas', *Political Science Quarterly*, vol 104, no 2, pp 281–301.

Wells, P. (2007) 'New Labour and evidence based policy making: 1997–2007', *People, Place and Policy Online*, vol 1, no 1, pp 22–9.

TWO

Community cohesion in Bradford: neoliberal integrationism

Jon Burnett[1]

Introduction

Following a series of urban disorders in northern towns and cities in England in 2001, the New Labour government embarked upon a community cohesion agenda that has significantly shifted the terrain of race relations policy and thought.[2] While gaining popular cross-party political support (see for example Oaten, 2005; BBC, 2007a; Cameron, 2007, p 31; Johnston, 2007, p 2), the aims and rationales of this agenda have been subjected to considerable criticism from anti-racist campaigners (see in particular Campaign Against Racism and Fascism, 2002; Fekete, 2004; Sivanandan, 2006; Kundnani, 2007a).

As Sivanandan (2007, pp 48–9) has argued, the community cohesion agenda – consolidated through a concerted attack on the (assumed) values of multiculturalism – has marked a shift towards an assimilatory framework of race relations policy making. This, in turn, has embedded what Kundnani (2007b, pp 26–31) calls a 'rise of integrationism' whereby a set of British core values are in the process of being both defined and rewritten. In this context, a climate of hostility towards Muslims, in particular, but diversity in general has been fostered through a perception that certain people are potentially threatening to national security, stability and identity. Consequently, the integrationism that Kundnani (2007b) speaks of sets out to garner a form of national homogenisation through which an emerging set of boundaries mark out acceptable and unacceptable forms of difference.

This chapter seeks to follow this analysis of the community cohesion agenda as a concrete framework of integrationism. In doing so, it will explore the manner in which the core values that are said to be necessary for cohesion to exist portend a shifting relationship between the citizen and the state. A redefining and championing of 'Britishness' serves to act as a banner around which citizens – and indeed would-be citizens – are expected to adhere and, as such, provides an indication of the form of community cohesion that is desired by those who champion the ongoing attack on multiculturalism. However, by analysing this form of community cohesion that is being consolidated, this chapter will further consider the way in which a neoliberal conception of citizenship is being crafted through the community cohesion agenda.

In grounding its analysis in the discussion of integrationism earlier, this chapter will explore the implementation of community cohesion policies in the Metropolitan District of Bradford in West Yorkshire. As one of the locations of the 2001 urban disorders, Bradford has received considerable attention, funding and investment in order to consolidate community cohesion. Consequently, it represents a specific location from which the idea of community cohesion has both emerged and been implemented. In particular, a significant programme of urban regeneration put in place after the 2001 disorders has prompted ideals of an urban renaissance through which Bradford is envisioned to emerge as a competitive, global district. This renaissance, it will be argued, affords a particular set of neoliberal structural changes into which integrationist policies are channelled. Further, it consolidates an emerging provision of coercive measures reinforcing the changing basis of citizenship and belonging that is being constructed.

From multiculturalism to community cohesion

Following the 2001 urban disorders, the principal thrust of New Labour's response was the creation of a Community Cohesion Review Team (CCRT) – led by Ted Cantle – whose findings (the Cantle Report) went on to form the basis of community cohesion as a 'new framework for race and diversity' (Cantle, 2005).[3]

Central to the ethos of community cohesion was the much-quoted evocative phrase of the Cantle Report that 'many communities operate on the basis of a series of parallel lives' (Community Cohesion Independent Review Team, 2001, para 2.1).[4] The theory of parallel lives insinuated that communities were divided along a number of lines – primarily by ethnicity – and in turn segregated from each other both geographically and culturally. Thus, according to Cantle, Britain *was* (and indeed in his analysis *is*) seeing 'the development of separate identities, often reinforced by segregated or "parallel lives" and by transnational and diasporic identities' (Cantle, 2006, p 85). In this context, Cantle evoked a picture of a country that was ghettoised in all but name.

As Kundnani (2001) has explained, this image of segregation presented through the community cohesion agenda relies fundamentally upon a historical reading that is, at its core, decontextualised. The analysis offered fails to address the structural basis of 'forced segregation', the fear of racial attacks, the decline of particular industries, and discriminatory council housing frameworks, but instead shows: 'The segregation of communities, the roots of which lay in institutional racism, came to be perceived as "self segregation" – the attempt by Asians to create their own exclusive areas or "no go areas" because they did not want to mix with whites' (Kundnani, 2002, p 107).

Consequently, what the community cohesion agenda evoked was an understanding of segregation based upon a (racialised) emphasis on culture and identity. However, in order to explore this further it is necessary to discuss how the emergence of the community cohesion agenda has occurred alongside a concerted criticism of multiculturalism. For it is through this attack on multiculturalism that community cohesion has been consolidated as a marked shift in understandings of contemporary race relations.

Attacking multiculturalism

In September 2006 the Institute of Race Relations (IRR) held a one-day conference titled 'Racism, liberty and the war on terror'. As a collective of campaigners, the IRR has been at the forefront of analyses of an emerging offensive on multiculturalism and a panel discussion was held called, quite aptly, 'The attack on multiculturalism: A discussion'. This attack on multiculturalism has been consolidated through an ongoing – and, as the director of Statewatch (Bunyan, 2005, p 15) has suggested, evidently now permanent – 'war on terrorism' following the terrorist attacks on 11 September 2001. Through this framework, the spectre of an alien enemy within is now invoked as a lasting feature of the national landscape.

In this context Muslims, cast as this new 'enemy within', are the principal (although not only) subjects of an ever-increasing series of anti-terrorism and criminal justice legislative advances.[5] These reforms are, in turn, tied directly to a set of ideological assumptions that identity politics is more important than political context (see Burnett, 2005). Multiculturalism, in this analysis, has been recast as a set of relations that contribute to internal divisions and ultimately violence. Indeed, as Bourne (2007, p 2) has argued, 'Multiculturalism, a term generally accepted across the political spectrum for some three decades, has suddenly become a term to be scoffed at, rather like "Political Correctness".' This has fed into a shifting contour of racism that has gained currency from a range of perspectives:

> What is unusual and worrying about the new anti-Muslim racism is that erstwhile liberal-thinking people who would normally eschew any form of personal racism, now find it possible to join in the clamour against Islam and Muslims. And they do so because the idea of a fundamental clash of civilisations – between enlightened, western Christendom on the one hand and benighted, barbaric Islam on the other – has become commonplace and accepted. (Bourne, 2007, p 6)

As Bourne makes clear, one of the hallmarks of this attack on multiculturalism is a perception of divergent and incongruent values between groups of people. Consequently, community cohesion policies appeared to provide an answer to these misguided assumptions. Where multiculturalism is now seen by many as being a source of division, the community cohesion agenda promises a solution through fostering core values, shared mores and national allegiance.

Fostering core values

> The gradual integration and the improvements in cohesion of societies, which were expected to develop over time, have not yet been achieved and there are renewed doubts about the value of diversity, particularly in terms of civic and social solidarity. (Cantle, 2006, p 85)

According to Ted Cantle, unmanaged diversity represents a fundamental problem for a given understanding of cohesion. Solidarity is undermined and stability threatened. Where evidence is needed in order to support this claim, a misreading account of violence is put forward in relation to urban disorders in 2001 and terrorist attacks in 2005.[6] Community cohesion offered a depoliticised account of the causes and responses. Accordingly, the community cohesion agenda proposed to articulate a set of core values that would bind the nation together through a common vision and sense of belonging.

The most recognisable aspect of this attempt to cohere core values upon the populace has been through the instigation of a drive to promote, in some senses to rewrite, and to foster a sense of 'Britishness' in citizens and would-be citizens. While an enthusiasm for setting out the meaning of national identity pre-dates the advent of a community cohesion agenda,[7] it was this agenda that helped open up a political space in which such manoeuvrings could garner considerable support (for discussion see Burnett, 2007).

Upon its publication, the Cantle Report set out that the core values desired to maintain community cohesion should be amalgamated with a sense of nationality and allegiance to the state. Indeed, the community cohesion agenda, from its outset, had set out a desire to prioritise and rework a sense of national identity. In 2004 John Denham maintained that a 'common national identity' was necessary to foster cohesion where there was a 'real clash of cultures', and continued to state: 'Until now, the political leadership in this country has avoided articulating a 21st-centruy Britishness ... We've now got to grasp that challenge, which was set out cogently in Ted Cantle's report on the northern riots' (2004, p 1).

This discourse assumed that a sense of shared values could be achieved through a reworking of national identity to which all citizens were aligned. It was envisioned that this 'modern British identity' would 'draw heavily on the history of the white majority' (Denham, 2004, p 1) and, according to the then Home Secretary, David Blunkett (2004, p 7), inform an 'inclusive notion of active British citizenship ... articulating a sense of pride in being British and the rights and responsibilities we share'. The then head of the Commission for Racial Equality (CRE) – and later chair of the Commission for Equality and Human Rights (CEHR) – made it explicit that this evocation of national allegiance was understood as an antithesis to the perceived pitfalls of multiculturalism, maintaining that multiculturalism encouraged 'separateness' between communities and that there was an urgent need to 'assert a core of Britishness' across society (Baldwin and Rozenburg, 2004, p 1; see also BBC, 2004).

Consequently, through invoking Britishness as a cornerstone of the core values that are said to be necessary in order to build community cohesion, what has been consolidated is a policy context in which those who are deemed 'threatening' to national unity are expected to display their national allegiance openly. Compulsory citizenship ceremonies ensure that those who obtain citizenship must swear loyalty to the state;[8] Britishness is now intended to be taught to children through the national curriculum (BBC, 2007b)[9] and Muslims are told through a variety of means that they are required to articulate their national credentials (see Burnett, 2005). A framework of race relations has been constructed where attacking multiculturalism underpins an agenda of 'enforced assimilation' (Sivanandan, 2006).

Core values and 'integrationism'

Exploring the marked shifts in race relations policies as a rise of integrationism, Kundnani (2007a) sets out a lucid account of not only the basis of national belonging, but also a set of shifting state contours in contemporary Britain. As he has explained, the concerted focus on establishing a national story and British identity has fostered the enthusiasm for core values whereby: 'These core values would also be the mechanism by which limits could be set on multiculturalism, while allegiance to these values would be a factor in assessing the merits of different categories of migration as well as a necessary condition for the settlement of immigrants' (Kundnani, 2007a, p 122).

Within this evocation of asserting core values as necessary for a given understanding of community cohesion, integrationist theories ensure that structural understandings of exclusion and segregation are downplayed in favour of those that focus on culture and identity. In short, where the basis of social policy becomes integration and cohesion, inequality, discrimination and ultimately institutional racism are downplayed. Further, institutional racism can remain a feature of the national politic while particular groups of people are encouraged (and coerced) to integrate into this same structural landscape.

Kundnani's analysis provides a means to explore the interests and power relations that cohesion and integrationism serve. It is here that the introduction of a policy of managed migration coincided with the community cohesion agenda in order to articulate a specific way of managing diversity. In particular, Kundnani discusses the importance of the 2002 White Paper 'Secure borders, safe haven: Integration with diversity in modern Britain' that sought to establish how immigration could be aligned to market dictates, while a definable national identity was to be set out in order to stem the perceived divisive nature of multiculturalism. Consequently, 'Thereafter, immigrants were themselves to be divided into categories of wanted and unwanted according to market needs (managed migration) while "ethnic minorities" were to be ranked – and expelled – according to their perceived assimilation to British values (community cohesion)' (Kundnani, 2007a, p 129).

What is emphasised here is the way in which managed migration policies – themselves directly tied to a given understanding of community cohesion – originated irrevocably with a desire to maintain certain economic interests and to construct an economic framework within which people are expected to integrate. The fact that this framework is inherently power laden – propping up a series of global relationships between countries that by their nature are unequal (Fekete,

2001) – is downplayed. The community cohesion agenda articulates that cohesion serves only certain interests, and it is the duty of citizens, and would-be citizens, to uphold them. Viewed from this perspective, the active citizenship that the New Labour government so champions (see Blunkett, 2003), and the rights and responsibilities that are being (re)defined in contemporary Britain (see Blair, 1998; Giddens, 1998; Blunkett, 2003), require analysis in terms of the *form* of community cohesion that they are expected to underpin, which is now illustrated in a case study of Bradford.

The District of Bradford – a brief demographic overview

As one of the scenes of the 2001 urban disorders, Bradford occupies a unique place in the community cohesion agenda as an archetype of the 'parallel lives' theory. Bradford District, in the county of West Yorkshire, is the fourth-largest metropolitan borough in England with an estimated population of 480,000, predicted to rise to half a million by the year 2020 (Bradford Vision, 2000). By the mid-19th century, Bradford had become recognised as the textile capital of the world (James, 1990, p 11; see also Jowitt, 1991) but, following the 'wholesale demise' of such UK industries in the 1980s, Bradford came 'to recognise ... the hardships involved in industrial restructuring' (Jowitt, 1991, p 5; see also Bühler et al, 2002, p 6; Colborn, 2003). According to Jowitt (1991, p 5), 'That process has brought about in its wake unemployment, poverty and deprivation ...'

Currently, Bradford is marked by severe deprivation spread unevenly throughout the District.[10] Of the 30 wards in Bradford, in 2004 nine were ranked within the most deprived 10% in the country; the majority of these were based within the city rather than the surrounding areas (Greenhalf, 2004). Thus it is suggested that, 'Bradford, it seems, has its own North–South divide' (Greenhalf, 2004; see also Bradford Vision, 2005, p 12). This stark geographical variation emphasises the impact of the demise of Bradford's textile industries, with high levels of deprivation linked integrally to the location of former textile industries. However, the contrasts of 'deprivation' within the District also emphasise patterns of both inward and outward migration and settlement. Bradford's comparatively large 'Asian' population[11] has felt the demise of the textile industries keenly, and in 2001 concerns were noted that 'middle-class' movement away from the city centre area was consolidating the stagnation of an 'underclass of relatively poor white people and visible minority ethnic communities' (Ouseley, 2001, para 2.5.1).

Consolidating community cohesion in Bradford

Following the 2001 urban disorders in Bradford, significant funding was provided in the District in order to embed policies of community cohesion. In 2002 Bradford Vision,[12] working with the Home Office Community Cohesion Unit and Local Government Association, and supported by approximately £3 million of Neighbourhood Renewal Fund (NRF) and Home Office funding, produced a *District outline community cohesion plan* that focused upon specific concerns regarding the 2001 urban disorders. These concerns were based upon perceptions that within Bradford there had been some kind of collapse of 'social order, and control' and 'social solidarity' (Bradford Vision, 2002, p 14). A localised community cohesion agenda was informed by the 'Ouseley Report',[13] the Bradford 2020 Vision[14] and the framework set through central government for fostering community cohesion.

Central to both the Ouseley Report and the 2020 Vision was an ideal of Bradford as an economically competitive District around which a new identity would be rebranded. Responding to the publication of the Ouseley Report, Bradford Vision stated that 'The District has struggled to make a new image for itself as a modern, 21st century, competitive, multi-cultural and desirable place to live, learn, work, and play' (Bradford Vision, 2001, p 1). Consequently, the community cohesion agenda was amalgamated explicitly with a vision to change the District. Where Bradford was taken in popular discourse as a signifier of a crisis of multicultural policies and, as such, a prime symbol for the critique of multiculturalism discussed earlier; multiculturalism was in turn articulated as related to a vision of Bradford that needed to be modernised. Setting out a 'new' way in which to manage multiculturalism tied in with an attempt to establish Bradford as a '21st-century District':

> Now Bradford has a chance to change. To reverse the sense of fear and to promote a sense of pride in our District. To be renowned for industry and innovation, culture and cutting edge commerce, not to be notorious for disorder and tension, crime and poverty. To be somewhere we can all be proud of. (Bradford Vision, 2001, p 1)

The post-2001 economic restructuring envisioned in this modernisation project was consolidated in plans to regenerate the city centre. A £2 billion initiative was instigated 'spearheading the renaissance of the city centre' through the creation of a banquet hall, the construction of new housing and leisure facilities in the centre and schemes that claimed to be 'paving the way to make Bradford a great place to work, live and learn' (Bradford Centre Regeneration, 2006a). In 2003 architect Will Alsop launched a 15-year 'Masterplan' of the city centre. Led by Bradford Centre Regeneration – an urban regeneration company – elements of this process included the ongoing development of a £300 million retail centre and a £350 million 'canal-side urban village' (BBC, 2005). That the regeneration of the city centre was explicitly tied to visions of establishing Bradford as an attractive proposition for future investment was made clear by the then chief executive of Bradford Centre Regeneration: 'We believe it [the Masterplan] will help to regenerate Bradford's core, bringing more wealth and jobs to the city. This, in turn, will lead to knock-on benefits for the rest of the district' (Marshall, 2003, p 1).

This unambiguous invocation of neoliberal visions of regeneration – relying on a perception of 'knock-on benefits for the rest of the district' – was further reinforced through a significant marketing campaign in 2005 entitled 'The Birth of a New City', aiming to further encourage inward investment (see BBC, 2005; Bradford Centre Regeneration, 2005b). This consolidated a perception of the city centre as a source of trickle-down benefits: not just economically, but culturally, socially and environmentally (see Goudie and Ladd, 1999 for critical discussion). In this context, the Masterplan and 'renaissance' of the city centre was articulated as central to ideas of community cohesion in the District: 'It is hoped that social exclusion can be reduced by attracting new wealth creation opportunities to the city. We also hope that greater cohesion will result from increased civic pride as regeneration gathers pace' (Bradford Centre Regeneration, 2006c).[15] This framework established a particular vision of community cohesion within Bradford that engendered attempts to 'repackage' multiculturalism within the city.

Redefining multiculturalism – 'culture', capital and cohesion

A regeneration programme tied directly to setting out a 'new' vision of Bradford aimed unambiguously at drawing in investment, particular kinds of people and establishing a landscape in which to 'live, learn, work and play'. It was envisioned that a particular form of cohesion would underpin such structural change and, consequently, inform Bradford's neoliberal (re)imagining.

In this context, a set of institutional alignments were put in place where particular interests and sectors were consolidated as viable definers of a localised community cohesion agenda. This in turn underpinned a series of alliances between state and private interests that shifted the local contours of statecraft. Through the community cohesion agenda, funding for a series of institutional realignments was channelled in particular ways that ultimately reduced the scope for projects to raise questions about power and inequality. This point was articulated most clearly in a critique of the community cohesion agenda by the author of the Bradford Race Review, Herman Ouseley:

> to attract funding in modern Britain today, you must not talk about racism; you must not talk about challenging inequalities. Not criticising the government enables you to attract funds. But then, when you do attract funds, that so called 'social inclusion' doesn't happen – because what you are actually engaged in is a kind of 'beauty contest' where you all compete for funds but only the ugliest wins! (Ouseley, 2007, pp 80–1)

What was being consolidated through the amalgamation of community cohesion within a neoliberal restructuring process was an embedding of power relations that, in turn, bolstered certain interests. According to Jones and Ward (2002, p 485), shifts in British urban policy have consolidated 'the incorporation into the state apparatus of members of local business communities in the regulation of regeneration projects'. Within Bradford a variety of schemes were put in place to ensure that businesses and business interests were high on the agenda for setting out how ideas of communities and 'cohesion' could assist in the regeneration of the District. For example, when in 2005 the council entered a £10 million bid of funding for 'deprived areas' in the District it first commissioned a survey of businesses to ensure that the bid reflected 'accurately what local businesses think would work' (Bradford District Economic Partnership, 2005, p 8). The rhetoric of a new vision for Bradford as a place to 'live, learn, work and play' was subtly altered: '[How] the renaissance of the heart of the city can be taken forward … was through establishing a great opportunity for the people who live, work, learn and invest …' (Bradford Centre Regeneration, 2006b). From the very outset, the community cohesion agenda in Bradford actively sought to consolidate a form of cohesion that was conducive to neoliberal economic interests.

A new set of institutional structures was put in place, along with a policy framework that ensured that it was particular communities and groups of people that would be inaugurated within this agenda. However, amidst the (re)imagining of Bradford, the intense restructuring in order to draw in capital, and among the visions of an urban renaissance, one problem remained. Bradford was still viewed as a signifier of a crisis of multicultural reality and this had to be managed in ways that could benefit the new vision of the District. Consequently, through a localised community cohesion agenda a surface-level programme of championing diversity was instigated. A myriad of initiatives were put in place attempting to articulate a specific vision of multiculturalism that fitted with a new vision of Bradford. This was a vision where communities met each other in shared cultural events; where multiculturalism could be packaged in such a way as to appear attractive to capital; and, crucially, where multiculturalism was managed in a framework that underpinned dominant understandings of community cohesion. In one example, a Bradford 'Spice' initiative focused on promoting the Asian population within the city as a facet that would encourage outside interest and utilise particular ideas of 'community' as an incentive for investment. Further, such approaches were subject to criticism about cultivating particular cultural stereotyping and pastiches of 'communities':

> 'Spice, we gave that £20,000. This woman came up with the idea of this big multicultural series of promotions and events about spice. The idea was that spices have been used in all cultures, in all countries, and the idea was that it would be like the Eden Project; but about spices. It wasn't fantastic. It was a bit patronising. It cost a lot of money.' (Representative, Bradford Local Authority)[16]

However, one of the key impacts of these initiatives was to consolidate a form of integrationism that sought to limit diversity in a set of particular and recognisable ways.

Neoliberal integrationism – community cohesion in Bradford

At the same time as multiculturalism was redefined through a localised agenda of community cohesion, a policy framework was enacted that sought to promote a set of core values necessary for Bradford's urban renaissance. This integrationism aimed to ensure that particular communities and individuals – and specifically those who were defined as potentially detrimental to a given definition of community cohesion – were encouraged to engender necessary values and mores. Consequently, notions of a 'can-do' culture – adapted significantly from their incorporation into the Bradford Race Review (Ouseley, 2001, p 3) – were utilised to foster the 'correct' values among particular groups within Bradford, and the core values necessary for community cohesion were evidenced through engaging quite literally within the ongoing urban renaissance:

> 'There was [a] programme which looked at the construction industry and young people with no qualifications. One of the barriers is that often ethnic minorities see working in the building trade as a dirty job. They want their children to be doctors, lawyers, barristers, respectable professions. They don't recognise construction, but there is a lot of money made out of building, particularly at the moment with what is going on in Bradford. So what they did was get young people involved and gave them an intense training course and got the construction industry to set up placements. They got the youngsters to lay foundations, put windows in and so on, and the courses were properly accredited – NVQ, I think – and they got the whole training. A number of people came out with jobs and it broke down barriers as well.' (Representative, Bradford Local Authority)

What lay at the heart of such integrationist strategies, then, was an attempt to harness multiculturalism within the District. In doing so, a form of multicultural managerialism simultaneously put limits on acceptable levels of diversity and, as such, sought to stem core values that were not seen as conducive. The reframing of the values, mores and behaviour of residents is central to the community cohesion agenda (Burnett, 2004; see Chan, 2006 for similar findings from Birmingham), and was articulated within Bradford through a form of neoliberal integrationism. A framework of 'active and participative citizenship' put in place by Bradford Vision made this explicit through defining a spectrum of 'good behaviour', which both defined and legitimised acceptable forms of participation, at the same time as discouraging others. Drawing from the New Labour mantra of rights and responsibilities, this framework aimed to encourage active citizens 'who take responsibility and contribute to the common good'

(Bradford Vision Active Citizenship Working Group, 2004a, p 3). In doing so, a continuum of active citizenship was drawn up – starting from 'voter' at the bottom and 'public office holder' at the top – that identified each 'step' of active citizenship.[17] This 'climbing frame', or 'continuum', worked along the construction of a relationship between 'opportunities' and 'responsibilities'. The further 'up' an active citizen progressed, the more opportunities they would be presented with. As such, certain communities – particularly those who were perceived as leading parallel lives – were made the target of active citizenship strategies and encouraged to engage in legitimised ways within the District. Predominantly, this was attempted through a programme of formal accreditation (Bradford Active Citizenship Working Group, 2004b, p 1) on individuals' CVs when applying for work or work-related promotions.

Yet, while certain forms of participation were accredited and encouraged, the Bradford Active Citizenship Working Group was clear that certain activities were not recognised as valid. Consequently religious activities, caring within a family unit and 'social activities' were excluded (Bradford Active Citizenship Working Group, 2004a, p 6).[18] Core values underpinning forms of active citizenship that were not seen as conducive to community cohesion were defined out of the community cohesion agenda. Herein lay the rub. The integrationism on offer was based largely on market dictates that primarily saw ideas of entrepreneurialism and self-advancement within a framework of redefining a new, neoliberal Bradford as valuable for community cohesion. Those values that did not fit within this framework were disregarded. Thus at the same time as a 'modern' – limited and restricted – view of multiculturalism was championed through a vernacular of community cohesion, community cohesion acted as a rationale for proactive policing of multi-ethnic areas described as 'sink estates' (Home Office, 2003, p 47). Similarly, while Asian residents were encouraged to show their commitment to a cohesive Bradford by 'integrating' within its urban renaissance, unwillingness to engage within such strategies was taken to denote a reluctance to contribute to community cohesion. In this context, community cohesion became coercive, rather than cohesive.

Conclusion

One of the most significant contributions of the community cohesion agenda has been to legitimise and give voice to an ongoing and wide-reaching attack on multiculturalism. This portends significant changes in the way race relations are perceived, and responded to, in the UK. At the heart of community cohesion policies is an attempt to limit and repackage notions of multiculturalism in ways that serve particular interests.

Within Bradford, the attack on multiculturalism and enthusiasm for community cohesion has been consolidated through its location as one of the scenes of the 2001 urban disorders. In this context, a localised framework of community cohesion has sought to foster a set of core values that explicitly tie in with an ongoing strategy of urban renaissance and political reconfiguration of the city. Attempts to redefine multiculturalism within this neoliberal vision have on the one hand articulated particular ideas of diversity as a magnet for capital, while, on the other hand, strategies of integrationism have sought to ensure that 'problematised' communities work within this script. In short, a 'cohesive' District is regarded as a better target for investment.

There may be some truth behind this claim that an area that displays polarised levels of inequality may be unattractive for investment. Yet, this conceptualisation of a cohesive District does not appear to require interventions to address glaring inequalities. Rather, an understanding of community cohesion that is at its heart assimilatory seeks to blame levels of inequality on understandings of culture and values, rather than the contours of statecraft.

Within Bradford a series of initiatives seeking to highlight and capitalise upon visions of culture are presented as beneficial for a given understanding of community cohesion. However, as Kundnani (2007a, p 52) has discussed, dressing up images of multiculturalism that play upon ideas of 'excitement' does little for the lived reality of multiculturalism for many communities and does not address racism. Nor is it meant to: the community cohesion agenda rests upon an assumption that racism stems from different cultures underpinning parallel lives. In this analysis, limiting (or repackaging) diversity will consequently lead to a common culture that somehow dissipates racism, an analysis that ignores the roles of the state and the structures that legitimise and embed racist practices.

What is put in place of such analysis is a championing of core values that, in Bradford at least, increasingly point to a neoliberal idea of citizenship. By considering the interests that frame such strategies, it is possible to consider the implications of this reassessment of the relationship between the citizen and state. We already know that neoliberal citizenship is insecure (Odekon, 2006), that capital ultimately homogenises (Simms, 2007), that inequalities are compounded (Stiglitz, 2003) and that polarisation among and between communities is embedded (Brenner and Theodore, 2002). Yet we do not know enough about the relationship between a community cohesion agenda and a neoliberal conception of citizenship and participation. Kundnani's concept of integrationism enables us to begin to consider the interests that community cohesion underpins and the contours of the core values that are being articulated. Through understanding the integrationism at the heart of the community cohesion agenda, strategies of community cohesion that appear on the surface to suggest a benign, benevolent state on the contrary legitimise localised forms of coercion. We are witnessing a fundamental shift in the basis of race relations in the UK. In this context, the use of community cohesion policies to legitimise an unfettered market populism, and the means by which to coerce this, portend a form of creeping authoritarianism.

Notes

[1] The author would like to thank Abdul Karim Aldohni, John Flint and David Robinson for comments on this chapter.

[2] The disorders were set against a context in which activity by the Far Right was either real or threatened, and predominantly involved Asian (mainly Pakistani or Bangladeshi) youths fighting pitched battles with white people or the police.

[3] For critical discussion see Burnett (2004, 2007)

[4] The Cantle Report was published in December 2001 to considerable media attention. See, for example Grice, 2001, p 1; Pascoe-Watson, 2001, p 1; Walker, 2001, p 2; and Williams, 2001, p 8.

[5] Here, the work of the Campaign Against Criminalising Communities has been particularly important. See, for example, Campaign Against Criminalising Communities (2003); and Campaign Against Criminalising Communities, in association with Index on Censorship (2003).

[6] As one example, following terrorist attacks in London in July 2005 *The Observer* launched a 'debate' that was, rather provocatively, focused upon the question 'How can we celebrate our national diversity, while harbouring communities who would seek to murder us?' (*The Observer*, 2005, p 18).

[7] See, for example, *The future of multi-ethnic Britain* (The Parekh Report) by the Runnymede Trust (Runnymede Trust, 2000).

[8] The first citizenship ceremony was held on 26 February 2004 (see Home Office, 2004). The pledge reads 'I, (name), (swear by almighty God)/(do solemnly and sincerely affirm) that, on becoming a British citizen, I will be faithful and bear true allegiance to Her Majesty Queen Elizabeth II, her heirs and successors according to law. I will give my loyalty to the United Kingdom and respect its rights and freedoms. I will observe its laws faithfully and fulfil my duties and obligations as a British citizen' (see Travis, 2003, p 7).

[9] Of particular note, after the terrorist attacks in London on 7 July 2005 a former headteacher, Sir Keith Ajegbo, was commissioned to write a 'Diversity and Citizenship Curriculum Review' that focused on whether 'modern British social and cultural history should be a fourth pillar of the citizenship curriculum' (Ajegbo, 2007, p 14). The report recommended that understanding core British values should be central to the school syllabus.

[10] In 2004, the Bradford local authority was ranked the 30th most deprived of 354 local authorities in the newly created Indices of Deprivation, covering 22 separate social and economic variables (Office for National Statistics, 2004). For details of this deprivation see Office for National Statistics, 2001; Bradford Metropolitan District Council, 2002, p 10; West Yorkshire Economic Partnership, 2004, p 18; Bradford Vision, 2005, pp 11–12; Bradford Metropolitan District Council, 2006, p 1.

[11] According to the 2001 Census, 19% of the population in Bradford described themselves as 'Asian or Asian British' compared with 5% in England overall; 78% of the population described themselves as 'White', compared with 91% in England (Darlow et al, 2005, p 20). For discussion see Singh, 1997; Office for National Statistics, 2001; Phillips, 2001; Bradford Metropolitan District Council, 2002, p 10; Singh, 2002; Simpson, 2004.

[12] Formerly the Bradford Congress, Bradford Vision is a strategic partnership made up of public, private and voluntary sector organisations.

[13] After the 2001 disorders, independent reports were commissioned in Oldham (Ritchie, 2001), and Burnley (Clarke, 2001). In Bradford Sir Herman Ouseley had already presented a report to Bradford Vision, written before the disorders in July 2001, focusing on 'race and community relations'. It was decided that this report would act in place of a further review, avoiding the duplication of Ouseley's findings (Ouseley, 2001).

[14] Bradford Vision was articulated as the primary body overseeing 'the Bradford 2020 Vision'; launched in 2000 following the largest public consultation exercise in the history of the District (Eaton, 2002, p 3).

[15] It is worth noting that attempts to tie ideas of cohesion to regeneration are by no means exclusive to Bradford, and indeed underpin strategies of urban policy under New Labour (see Atkinson, 2003).

[16] This, and the following quotes are taken from fieldwork conducted as part of a PhD study.

[17] From the 'bottom', the typology was set out in the following order: voter, participant, activist, campaigner, organiser, informal volunteer, (unregistered) formal volunteer, (registered) formal volunteer, group member, group leader, management committee member, (locally based) community representative, (sector-based) community representative, (district-based) community representative, parish councillor, ward councillor and public office holder (Bradford Vision Active Citizenship Working Group, 2004a, pp 5–6).

[18] There is a wealth of discussion regarding the impacts and significance of 'active citizenry' linked to notions of 'community' that has been discouraged and even criminalised. Ramamurthy (2006), for example, develops a detailed account on the impact of grassroots Asian Youth Movements in Britain that are examples of 'active citizenship', yet not recognised as such 'formally'. In another context Miraftab and Wills (2005) discuss what they term 'insurgent' active citizenship effecting progressive political change while challenging dominant (in their example, explicitly neoliberal) ideas and policies.

References

Ajegbo, K. (2007) *Curriculum review: Diversity and citizenship*, Nottingham: Department for Education and Skills.

Atkinson, R. (2003) 'Addressing urban social exclusion through community involvement in regeneration', in R. Imrie and M. Raco (eds) *Urban renaissance? New Labour, community and urban policy*, Bristol: The Policy Press, pp 101–20.

Baldwin, T. and Rozenburg, G. (2004) 'Britain "must scrap multiculturalism"', *The Times*, 3 April.

BBC (2004) 'Race chief wants integration push', *BBC News Online*, 3 April (http://news.bbc.co.uk/go/pr/fr/-/2/hi/uk_news/3596047.stm).

BBC (2005) 'A "brighter future" for Bradford', *BBC News Online*, 23 December (http://www.bbc.co.uk/print/bradford/content/articles/2005/12/23).

BBC (2007a) 'Britain "must resist extremists"', *BBC News Online*, 29 January (http://news.bbc.co.uk/go/pr/fr/-/1/hi/uk_politics/6309427.stm).

BBC (2007b) 'Schools "must teach Britishness"', *BBC News Online*, 25 January (http://news.bbc.co.uk/1/hi/education/6294643.stm).

Blair, A. (1998) *The third way: New politics for the new century*, London: Fabian Society.

Blunkett, D. (2003) *Active citizens, strong communities: Progressing civil renewal*, London: Home Office.

Blunkett, D. (2004) *New challenges for race equality and community cohesion in the 21st century*, Speech to the Institute of Public Policy Research, 7 July, London: Home Office.

Bradford Centre Regeneration (2006a) '£90million student village planned for Bradford City Centre', 24 July (www.bradfordurc.co.uk).

Bradford Centre Regeneration (2006b) 'City park and mirror pool star in final neighbourhood', 14 November (www.bradfordurc.co.uk).

Bradford Centre Regeneration (2006c) 'Why does Bradford need a masterplan?', (www.bradfordurc.co.uk).

Bradford District Economic Partnership (2005) *Bradford District Economic Bulletin*, vol 2, Winter, Bradford: Bradford District Economic Partnership.

Bradford Metropolitan District Council (2002) *One landscape many views: The Bradford District Community Strategy 2002–2007*, Bradford: Bradford Metropolitan District Council.

Bradford Metropolitan District Council (2006) *Bradford Unemployment Bulletin*, April, Bradford: Bradford Metropolitan District Council.

Bradford Vision (2000) 'What do we know about 2020?', *Bradford 2020 Vision* (www.bradford2020.com/bradford2020/vision_detail.html).

Bradford Vision (2001) 'Living without fear', *Community pride: Making diversity work in Bradford*, July, Bradford: Bradford Vision.

Bradford Vision (2002) *The Bradford District outline community cohesion plan*, Bradford: Bradford Vision.

Bradford Vision (2003) *Directory of community cohesion activities*, Bradford: Bradford Vision.

Bradford Vision (2004) *Community cohesion in the Bradford District: A guide to community cohesion activities*, Bradford: Bradford Vision.

Bradford Vision (2005) *One landscape many views: Delivering the 2020 Vision*, Bradford: Bradford Vision.

Bradford Vision Active Citizenship Working Group (2004a) *Active citizenship in Bradford District*, draft for consultation, Bradford: Bradford Vision.

Bradford Vision Active Citizenship Working Group (2004b) *Active citizenship continuum*, Bradford: Bradford Vision.

Brenner, N. and Theodore, N. (2002) 'Cities and the geographies of "actually existing neoliberalism"', *Antipode*, vol 34, no 3, pp 349–79.

Bourne, J. (2007) *In defence of multiculturalism, IRR Briefing Paper no. 2*, London: Institute of Race Relations.

Bühler, U., Bujra, J., Carling, A., Cumming, L., Hannam, M., Lewis, P., Macey, M., Nias, P., Pankhurst, D., Pearce, J., Samad, Y. and Vine, I. (2002) *Bradford one year on: Breaking the silences*, Bradford: Programme for a Peaceful City, University of Bradford.

Bunyan, T. (2005) 'While Europe sleeps …', in T. Bunyan (ed) *The war on freedom and democracy: Essays on civil liberties in Europe*, London: Spokesman Books for the European Civil Liberties Network.

Burnett, J. (2004) 'Community, cohesion and the state', *Race and Class*, vol 45, no 3, pp 1–18.

Burnett, J. (2005) 'Hearts and minds in the domestic "war on terror"', *Campaign Against Racism and Fascism*, 18 October, (http://www.carf.org.uk).

Burnett, J. (2007) 'Community cohesion: A new framework for race and diversity', *Race and Class*, vol 48, no 4, pp 115–18.

Cameron, D. (2007) 'No one will be left behind in Tory Britain', *The Observer*, 28 January.

Campaign Against Criminalising Communities (2003) 'Terrorising minority communities: "Anti-terrorism" powers: their use and abuse', submission to the Privy Council Review of the 2001 Anti-Terrorism Crime and Security Act (ATCSA 2001), full statement of August 2003 (www.cacc.org.uk).

Campaign Against Criminalising Communities, in Association with Index on Censorship (eds) (2003) *A permanent state of terror?*, London: Campaign Against Criminalising Communities in Association with Index on Censorship.

Campaign Against Racism and Fascism (2002) 'Community cohesion … Blunkett's new race doctrine', *Campaign Against Racism and Fascism*, no 66, February/March, pp 3–6.

Cantle, T. (2005) *Community cohesion: A new framework for race and diversity*, Basingstoke: Palgrave Macmillan.

Cantle, T. (2006) 'Parallel Lives', *Index on Censorship*, vol 35, no 2, pp 85–90.

Chan, W.F. (2006) 'Planning Birmingham as a cosmopolitan city: Recovering the depth of its diversity', in J. Binnie, J. Holloway, S. Millington and C. Young (eds) *Cosmopolitan urbanism*, London, Routledge.

Clarke, T. (2001) *Burnley Task Force*, Burnley: Burnley Borough Council.

Colborn, C. (2003) 'The state of the District', *Bradford Info*, 6 August, (www.bradfordinfo.com/District/district.cfm).

Community Cohesion Independent Review Team (2001) (Cantle Report) *Community Cohesion: A report of the Independent Review Team, chaired by Ted Cantle*, London: Home Office.

Darlow, A., Bickerstaffe, T., Burden, T., Green, J., Jassi, S., Johnson, S., Kelsey, S., Pucell, M., South, J. and Walton, F. (2005) *Researching Bradford: A review of social research on Bradford District*, York: Joseph Rowntree Foundation.

Denham, J. (2004) 'Time to get to grips with Britishness', *Guardian Unlimited*, 26 February (www.society.guardian.co.uk).

Eaton, M. (2002) 'Foreword', in Bradford Metropolitan District Council, *One landscape many views: The Bradford District Community Strategy 2002–2007*, Bradford: Bradford Metropolitan District Council.

Fekete, L. (2001) 'The emergence of xeno-racism', *Race and Class*, vol 43, no 2, pp 23–40.

Fekete, L. (2004) 'Anti-Muslim racism and the European security state', *Race and Class*, vol 46, no 1, pp 3–29.

Giddens, A. (1998) *The third way – The renewal of social democracy*, Cambridge: Polity Press.

Goudie, A. and Ladd, P. (1999) 'Economic growth, poverty and inequality', *Journal of International Development*, vol 11, no 2, pp 177–99.

Greenhalf, J. (2004) 'Caught in the poverty trap', *Bradford Telegraph and Argus*, undated.

Grice, A. (2001) '"Parallel lives" of blacks and whites blamed for riots', *The Independent*, 11 December.

Home Office (2003) *Section 17 in action: Lessons from the first policing priority areas*, London: Home Office.

Home Office (2004) 'Prince of Wales to attend first citizenship ceremony', Home Office Press Release 066/2004, London: Home Office.

James, D. (1990) *Bradford*, Halifax: Ryburn Publishing.

Johnston, P. (2007) 'Brown's manifesto for Britishness', *The Daily Telegraph*, 13 January.

Jones, M. and Ward, K. (2002) 'Excavating the logic of British urban policy: Neoliberalism as the "crisis of crisis-management"', *Antipode*, vol 34, no 3, pp 474–94.

Jowitt, J.A. (1991) 'Preface', in *Mechanization and misery: The Bradford woolcomber's report of 1845*, Halifax: Ryburn Publishing.

Kundnani, A. (2001) 'From Oldham to Bradford: The violence of the violated', *Race and Class*, vol 43, no 2, pp 105–10.

Kundnani, A. (2007a) *The end of tolerance: Racism in 21st century Britain*, London: Pluto Press.

Kundnani, A. (2007b) 'Integrationism: The politics of anti-Muslim racism', *Race and Class*, vol 48, no 4, pp 24–44.

Marshall, M. (2003) 'Could this be Bradford?', in Bradford Centre Regeneration *Masterplan for the city centre*, Bradford: Bradford Metropolitan District Council (www.bradford.gov.uk/NR/rdonlyres/CE753F10-7847-4970-99DD-F9501029A99C/0/extra_city_centre_masterplan.pdf).

Miraftab, F. and Wills, S. (2005) 'Insurgency and spaces of active citizenship: The story of Western Cape anti-eviction campaign in South Africa', *Journal of Planning Education and Research*, vol 25, no 2, pp 200–17.

Oaten, M. (2005) Speech by Mark Oaten MP, Liberal Democrat Shadow Home Secretary, Liberal Democrats, 21 September (www.libdems.org.uk/conference/conferencedoc.html?id=7679).

The Observer (2005) 'What does it mean to be British?', 31 July.

Odekon, M. (2006) 'Globalization and labor', *Rethinking Marxism*, vol 18, no 3, pp 415–31.

Office for National Statistics (2001) *National statistics: Bradford*, London: Crown Copyright (www.statistics.gov.uk/census2001/profiles/00CX-A.asp).

Office for National Statistics (2004) *Neighbourhood statistics: Neighbourhood profile*, London: Crown Copyright (www.neighbourhood.statistics.gov.uk/dissemination).

Oldham Independent Review Panel (2001) *One Oldham, one future, Panel report chaired by David Ritchie*, Oldham: Oldham Metropolitan Borough Council and Greater Manchester Police.

Ouseley, H. (2001) *Community pride not prejudice: Making diversity work in Bradford*, Bradford: Bradford Vision

Ouseley, H. (2007) 'Bradford and the northern towns', *Race and Class*, vol 48, no 4, pp 77–81.

Pascoe-Watson, G. (2001) 'Riot report backs Blunkett on race', *The Sun*, 11 December.

Phillips, D. (2001) 'The changing geography of South Asians in Bradford', supplementary report in H. Ouseley *Community pride not prejudice: Making diversity work in Bradford*, Bradford: Bradford Vision.

Ramamurthy, A. (2006) 'The politics of Britain's Asian youth movements', *Race and Class*, vol 48, no 2, pp 38–60.

Runnymede Trust (2000) *The future of multi-ethnic Britain: The Parekh Report*, London: Profile Books.

Simms, A. (2007) *Tescopoly: How one shop came out on top and why it matters*, London: Constable.

Simpson, L. (2004) 'Statistics of racial segregation: Measures, evidence and policy', *Urban Studies*, vol 41, no 3, pp 661–81.

Singh, R. (1997) 'Understanding Bradford's South Asian Community', in C. Rank (ed) *City of peace: Bradford's story*, Bradford: Bradford Libraries.

Singh, R. (2002) *The struggle for racial justice from community relations to community cohesion: The story of Bradford 1950–2002*, Bradford: Ramindar Singh.

Sivanandan, A. (2006) 'Attacks on multicultural Britain pave the way for enforced assimilation', *Guardian Unlimited*, 13 September (commentisfree.guardian.co.uk/a_sivanandan/).

Sivanandan, A. (2007) 'The global context', *Race and Class*, vol 48, no 4, pp 46–50.

Stiglitz, J. (2003) *The roaring nineties: A new history of the world's most prosperous decade*, New York: W.W. Norton & Company.

Travis, A. (2003) 'New Britons to pledge loyalty to country', *The Guardian*, 26 July.

Walker, K. (2001) 'Segregation blamed for the inner-city race riots', *The Express*, 11 December.

West Yorkshire Economic Partnership (2004) *West Yorkshire investment plan 2004: Strategic economic analysis*, Wakefield: West Yorkshire Economic Partnership.

Williams, G. (2001) '"Parallel lives" are blamed for race riots', *Daily Mail*, 11 December.

THREE

Connectivity of place and housing market change: the case of Birmingham

Ian Cole and Ed Ferrari

Introduction

In his foreword to the seminal British study of race and housing, *Race, community and conflict*, J.B. Rose noted: 'The city is a crucible into which we pour the most disparate elements in our modern industrial society vaguely expecting that given time they will fuse into an acceptable amalgam' (Rex and Moore, 1967, p v). Rex and Moore's groundbreaking research was adequate testament to how far this 'vague expectation' could be confounded by the operation of social and economic processes, notably the dynamics of the local housing market. This was crystallised in their observation that the 'competition for the scarce resource of housing leads to formation of groups very often on an ethnic basis and one group will attempt to restrict the opportunities of another by whatever sanctions it can' (Rex and Moore, 1967, p 16). In this chapter we revisit the city that was the focus of their study, Birmingham, more than 40 years on, and explore how market dynamics are continuing to shape patterns of mobility and settlement among different minority ethnic communities in two parts of the city.

Rex and Moore's Weberian approach subsequently attracted a great deal of attention and prompted a lively debate on their notion of 'housing classes' (Haddon, 1970; Saunders, 1981). This approach was evident in their focus on the struggle for control over parts of the local housing market by different groups, their attention to the role of 'urban gatekeepers' and their emphasis on market change, in response to the new pressures brought by immigration in the 1950s and early 1960s.

While the backdrop is very different now, we want to keep the notion of market change in focus in our account of the present-day Birmingham housing market. There is now extensive evidence on the different housing circumstances of minority ethnic groups in terms of housing quality, type, tenure and location. This has been the recurrent theme of research that has charted racialised inequalities in access, dwelling condition, overcrowding and housing wealth. In debates on community cohesion, it has also led some to argue that minority ethnic communities are 'self-segregating', forming distinct enclaves within urban systems (although see Phillips et al in Chapter Four, this volume). Yet this approach is essentially concerned with housing outcomes and can say little about the intervening influence of market processes on these outcomes. The outcomes may simply reflect the 'working through' of different starting points for different groups, and it is not possible to identify processes of convergence or divergence between the groups as a result of market pressures and opportunities.

Our concern is therefore to explore the structure of the housing market in a specific case, to establish if there are inherent reasons why the market produces different outcomes for different groups, and to establish the pattern of change this reveals. Are there distinctive ethnic 'sub-markets' in cities like Birmingham, which constrain or channel access to housing for different groups? Or are differences between minority ethnic groups simply the 'expression', in housing terms, of underlying demographic, economic and social differentiation, or even the desire for 'separateness'? The empirical evidence reviewed here does not allow a conclusive response to such questions, but it does suggest some possible trends and sets out future challenges for policy and research into mobility, settlement and housing market change.

There are potential policy messages for community cohesion in assessing these trends. Rex and Moore's may have been an explicitly sociological study, but it also paid due attention to the policy implications emerging from their research. They were writing in the immediate post-Rachman period of the 1960s, when a great deal of attention was focused on the regulation of the private rented sector, the improvement or clearance of poor-quality private sector dwellings and allocation policies in the burgeoning local authority sector. Forty years on, the policy landscape has changed in many ways, but the need for public intervention to ease market pressures and improve housing quality has remained.

For example, part of Birmingham is now covered by the Housing Market Renewal (HMR) programme (Cole and Nevin, 2004; Leather et al, 2007), which seeks to adjust the balance between housing supply and demand to combat market fragility or dysfunctionality in particular sub-regions. For our purposes, if the evidence suggests that market discontinuities exist, policies may be required that seek to 'bridge the gap' between different markets. If, on the other hand, market processes appear to be working through for each group – even though they produce very unequal outcomes – then adjustments may be more about giving particular groups additional support, or selectively increasing access and opportunity to produce more convergence in housing outcomes.

In this chapter we therefore consider whether the differences in housing outcomes between different minority ethnic communities are converging or diverging over time, and whether it makes sense to refer to distinct ethnic housing sub-markets being created as a result of increasing residential segmentation. The chapter then moves on to consider patterns of settlement among minority ethnic communities in two parts of Birmingham – the 'Eastern Corridor' and the north-west of the city. It suggests that there may be potentially different processes at work in these two areas, requiring in turn a different set of policy responses. Any locally sensitised approach, it is suggested, needs to focus on different kinds of 'critical arenas' at the neighbourhood level that may be the source of actual or potential tensions between different minority ethnic communities. In relatively 'self-contained' and discontinuous markets, policies may point in the direction of supply-side measures; in more 'continuous' markets, on the other hand, demand-side measures may be more appropriate in order to ameliorate housing outcomes for specific groups.

Ethnicity and housing market outcomes

We have suggested that a snapshot of a housing market may tell us little about its underlying dynamics. A case in point is the introduction of housing market assessments at a local level, supported by central government (Office of the Deputy Prime Minister, 2005). These documents can provide a more or less comprehensive picture of market conditions at the point of survey (although many still rely on the census as an information source) but policymakers may still struggle to identify processes of market change and the messages this carries for future policy intervention. A study of housing market intelligence undertaken by Housing Market Renewal pathfinders, for example, confirmed that many of these exercises were insufficiently dynamic and disaggregated to neighbourhood level to inform decisions on interventions (Robinson et al, 2005).

However, a stocktake of housing market characteristics will at least demonstrate the impact of the changing demographic, social and economic terrain of urban Britain on housing outcomes, even if the speed and direction of travel cannot be discerned. Ethnicity is one of the key dimensions of such differences, alongside factors such as income and age, and a brief note on the nature and scale of these inequalities between different minority ethnic communities is perhaps the best starting point for an understanding of market segmentation and inequality.

The housing market in England is pitted by difference and division – between the wealthy and the poor, between the socially mobile and the socially excluded, between the equity rich and the pension poor, and between different communities in different cities (Dorling, 2006). Members of minority ethnic communities may share some of the concerns that have recently penetrated the living rooms of white, middle-class households: concerns about interest rate rises, the potential erosion of their housing wealth to meet future commitments, or the difficulties that younger household members have in gaining a foot on the housing ladder. They are much more likely to face more acute difficulties as well.

Some enduring housing problems, such as the lack of decent quality accommodation, or overcrowding, are much more prevalent in minority ethnic communities. A minority ethnic household in 2005 was more than five times more likely to live in overcrowded circumstances than one headed by a white person.[1] In some tenures, the difference is even greater: 1% of White owner-occupiers in England are living in accommodation below the 'bedroom standard' – the official measure of overcrowding – while nearly 8% of minority ethnic owner-occupiers are in this position.[2] Ethnicity is also a source of marked difference in both housing condition and the quality of living environments. Of minority ethnic households, 31% live in a non-decent home (compared to 26% of White households); 13% live in a home in 'serious disrepair'; and nearly twice as many minority ethnic households live in a poor-quality environment.[3]

This précis of differential outcomes may tend to suggest that households start out in the housing market at the same point, only for their future path to be shaped by different economic or social circumstances so they end up at different points in the housing market. Clearly this is not the case: outcomes are shaped by historical patterns across the generations, and the starting point of households from different minority ethnic groups will show systematic differences. The more pertinent question is therefore whether the housing outcomes of different communities are converging or diverging over time. In all likelihood both processes occur simultaneously, although the relative strength of convergence and divergence will vary according to locality, market vitality and the minority group(s) concerned. A consideration of these trajectories turns our attention to the journey, rather than the point of destination, in housing careers – to market processes rather than outcomes.

Later in this chapter we explore two different local markets in Birmingham and consider whether market continuities are apparent, and whether housing market outcomes are widening, or narrowing, between different minority ethnic groups. In order to introduce a more dynamic framework to account for observable differences in housing circumstances, we need to consider first patterns of residential mobility among different minority ethnic communities and its impact on outcomes.

Mobility and housing market processes

Residential mobility is at the heart of housing market change, and is clearly important in understanding how differentials in housing market position are reproduced. One key test is whether households in minority ethnic groups tend to operate in different parts of the housing market, compared with white British households with a similar level of income and wealth. If the market is segmented to the extent that different patterns of price formation and appreciation occur (that is to say, ethnic sub-markets exist) then the propensity for, and ability of, minority ethnic households to make good historic deficits and move up the housing ladder may be disproportionately hindered by such barriers.

One way to express this dilemma is therefore to assess whether the market is 'continuous' or 'segmented'. Does it provide a range of products and price points that permit relatively easy trading up and down, or is it more segmented, with clear breaks between product and price groups? Are members of some minority ethnic communities unduly constrained by visible or invisible barriers between different parts of the market, which prevents them from expressing, as it were, any change in economic circumstances in housing terms? If so, how can the position be ameliorated by public policy? There is at present little evidence either way to this question, partly due to the formidable methodological difficulties involved in answering the question. Any response to such issues will have important implications for policy intervention; it would suggest whether policy would be better directed to restructuring the supply side of the market, to 'dissolve' such barriers and thereby assist minority ethnic communities, or be focused instead on facilitating demand and enhancing opportunity.

One relevant measure for the existence of discrete housing markets is the notion of self-containment. If a high proportion of moves have both their origin and destination in the same area, then it can be said to constitute a determinate housing market area. Nominal thresholds such as 70% are often used to specify self-containment. Such tests may be helpful in determining the spatial extent of housing markets and, by extension, the diversity of supply- and demand-side characteristics within them, but they have little normative value. The tests do not specify what constitutes a housing market area in any qualitative sense. The theory of spatial arbitrage, upon which self-containment tests are based, does not allow for the fact that some markets may exhibit little spatial coherence: the global market for extremely high-value apartments, for example, would not be captured by any self-containment measure. And, finally, the measure underplays the extent to which differences between housing markets may reproduce opportunities and constraints for specific groups. This last point is developed further below, in the context of ethnic mobility and settlement patterns and the implications for community cohesion.

One of the recurrent concerns of macroeconomists about the housing market is the tension between the economic benefits of market transactions and the potential dampening effects of owner-occupation on workforce mobility (Henley, 1998). There is a key link between housing market activity and social mobility, which takes two main forms. First, equity appreciation and the capital gains made through property transactions allow frequent movers who are owner-occupiers to benefit financially from their mobility when housing market conditions permit. Second, mobility potentially allows households to trade up in property and neighbourhood terms, such as allowing access to higher-quality services and amenities, notably education.

Given this, the notion of self-containment requires some important qualification. Moving in and around a large, diverse housing market (such as that in London) may do little to dampen social mobility. On the other hand, a very tightly defined housing market (which nonetheless has a similar level of self-containment) may be significantly more internally homogeneous, for example the housing market of a depressed, de-industrialised town. The extent to which households have the means and opportunity to move outside this housing market is arguably the principal factor underpinning social mobility. Any differentials between groups in how these means and opportunities are distributed will materially affect how the housing market either aids or hinders their wider social mobility.

Essentially, efforts to measure and describe housing markets will have limited value in explaining relationships between different ethnic communities unless (1) the market can be contextualised, so that the balance of opportunities for households within and outside it can be scoped; and (2) significant breaks or discontinuities exist in the market, which might impact differentially on specific groups.

The identification of such trends presents immense challenges in terms of data analysis and interpretation. One relatively crude (and periodically out-of-date) approach would be to refer to migration data from the census to consider which minority ethnic groups are more successful in moving to a higher-priced (local authority) area than the one where they formerly lived. Information drawn from the 2001 Census and shown in Figure 3.1 shows differences in the propensity for different ethnic groups to move to 'higher-priced' areas. Of course, this basic analysis ignores the substantial internal heterogeneity of most local authority districts in price terms. Nevertheless, just under one fifth (19.6%) of all households who moved went to a higher-priced area than where they had lived. This propensity was significantly higher for households from Indian and Chinese communities (25.6% and 27.9% respectively). Households from Pakistani and Bangladeshi communities had a lower propensity to move to a higher priced area (15.9%), and members of Black (African and Caribbean) communities were also less likely to do so (18.5%) than average.

This analysis needs to be set alongside the work by Ludi Simpson and colleagues, which suggests that apparently different rates of migration

Figure 3.1: Proportion of moves to a higher-priced district, by ethnicity

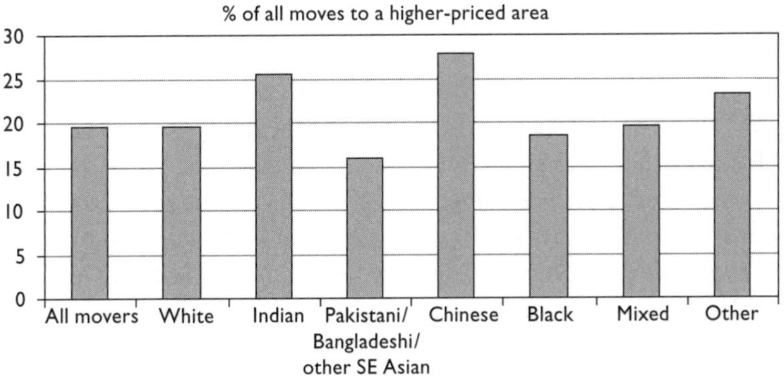

Base = all people moving in the year preceding the 2001 Census.

Source: 2001 Census.

among minority ethnic communities can be largely explained by the socio-economic and demographic composition of the groups, rather than any inherent tendencies to 'self-segregation', as is often alleged. Common trends of counter-urbanisation and dispersal from areas of co-ethnic concentration are observable across communities. One difference Simpson does note, however, is that Bangladeshi and Pakistani households will tend to make shorter distance moves than other groups (Finney and Simpson, 2007). This type of analysis underlines the extent to which overall categorisations of black and minority ethnic (BME) households mask considerable variation between communities – not just in housing market terms but in economic resources as well.

However, given that most residential mobility takes place within 'localised' geographical boundaries and that sub-areas within any single district, town or city can comprise large differences in housing market characteristics, it is perhaps most telling to look for evidence, one way or another, of distinct ethnic sub-markets operating at this level. We therefore explore this question by turning our attention to two parts of the city that was the focus of Rex and Moore's research more than 40 years ago – Birmingham.

Birmingham: one city, two case studies

Birmingham provides an instructive case study to assess how patterns of residential settlement and housing market change can interact. In 2001, the city had a population of 977,000, of which just under 30% defined themselves as belonging to a 'non-White' minority (Census, 2001). Over the course of the next two decades, the total minority ethnic population is likely to become larger than the total White British population, although White British people will remain the city's largest single ethnic group (Finney and Simpson, 2007).

Birmingham's minority ethnic population has a distinctive pattern of settlement in the city. Since Rex and Moore's pioneering study, waves of 'succession' have concentrated on a 'middle ring' of neighbourhoods such as Sparkbrook, Small Heath and Handsworth. Each of these has, over time, become associated to some extent with particular minority groups. Abbas, for example, refers to Rex's later work in the 1980s, and its description of 'Sparkbrook [as] a largely Pakistani area, the Handsworth area as the Caribbean centre of Birmingham, and the Soho area as overwhelmingly Indian' (2005, p 5). This portrayal is largely justified if one looks at the results of the 1991 Census (Figure 3.2). One would, however, need to be cautious in deploying terms like 'overwhelmingly': there were actually comparatively few neighbourhoods in the city in 1991 (or 2001 for that matter, see Figure 3.3) where non-White groups were the numerical majority. However, a more complex picture of settlement and mobility can be discerned among those groups who are the most strongly represented in a specific neighbourhood.

Despite the apparently stark representation of different minority ethnic communities in sections of the two maps shown in Figures 3.2 and 3.3, it would be misleading to think the picture in Birmingham is unusual compared with other cities with high non-White populations. Using the Index of Dissimilarity, *The state of the English cities* report (Office of the Deputy Prime Minister, 2006) ranked cities and major towns according to their score (ranged from 0 to 1, with higher scores showing more dissimilarity or 'segregation'). Birmingham scored 0.58 on the White/non-White distinction (the 11th highest score out of 56 cities and major towns), 0.63 on White/Asian comparisons (also 11th highest) and 0.52 on White/Black comparisons (17th highest). While Birmingham is therefore not unusually segregated by ethnic group, this overall figure can disguise marked differences at the local level. Therefore, in the following sections, we contrast two segments of the city, both with relatively high representations of minority ethnic settlement: the 'Eastern Corridor' and the north-west.

The 'Eastern Corridor'

The 'Eastern Corridor' is a term that has been applied to a broad swathe of east Birmingham running outwards from the city centre. It has recently been the focus of a regeneration and housing programme developed by the two local authorities involved, Birmingham City Council and Solihull Borough Council (Ecotec, 2006). Stretching from the city centre eastwards to Birmingham Airport, it encompasses neighbourhoods such as Small Heath, Duddeston, Washwood Heath, Sparkbrook, Tyseley, Hodge Hill and Yardley. The area also includes at its easternmost point the peripheral systems-built estate at Chelmsley Wood, which lies in the neighbouring district of Solihull. The Eastern Corridor is a highly diverse area, containing 105,700 households in 2001. Just over 40% of the population were members of minority ethnic communities, heavily concentrated in the older neighbourhoods closer to the city centre (Centre for Regional Economic and Social Research, 2006). The evolution of this segment of the conurbation can be broadly described in terms of three phases of development: the Victorian inner city; a 'planned' middle ring consisting mainly of inter-war housing

Figure 3.2: Majority ethnic group representation by neighbourhood, 1991

Note: Census output areas, the smallest unit of statistical geography in use in the UK, are used as a proxy for 'neighbourhoods'. Data have been assigned to output areas on the basis of their closest geographic fit, which may lead to a small number of inaccuracies. 'Majority' refers to the largest ethnic group by share of population.

Source: 1991 Census Small Area Statistics (England and Wales). Map contains portions © Crown Copyright/database right 2007. An Ordnance Survey/ EDINA supplied service.

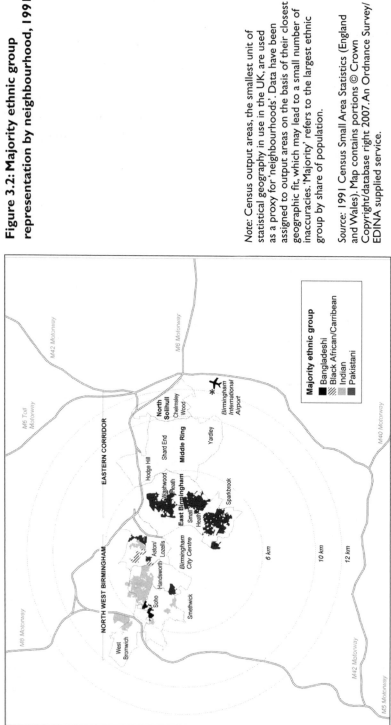

Figure 3.3: Majority ethnic group representation by neighbourhood, 2001

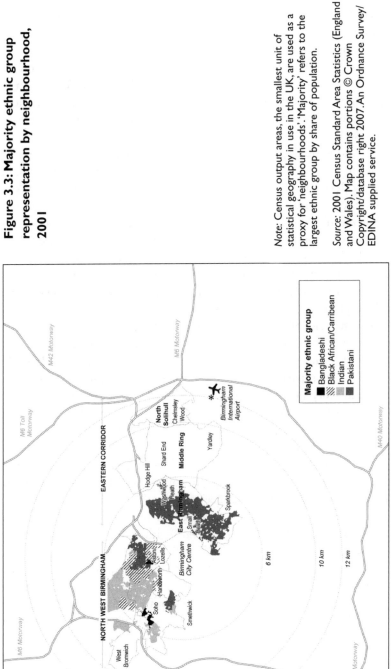

Note: Census output areas, the smallest unit of statistical geography in use in the UK, are used as a proxy for 'neighbourhoods'. 'Majority' refers to the largest ethnic group by share of population.

Source: 2001 Census Standard Area Statistics (England and Wales). Map contains portions © Crown Copyright/database right 2007. An Ordnance Survey/ EDINA supplied service.

estates; and the post-war overspill developments around Chelmsley Wood (Lee et al, 2003).

The population of the Eastern Corridor increased by 0.6% between 1991 and 2001 (compared with an increase in the city as a whole of 1.7%). This masked considerable internal variability. The population of the inner ring of the Corridor increased by 6.7% during this period, compared with a decrease of 2.3% in the middle ring and a decrease of fully 10.8% in North Solihull (Ecotec, 2006, p 26). The estimates of future households produced for the regeneration partnership suggested that the number of White households in the Eastern Corridor would fall by 1,449 between 2001 and 2031, while the number of BME households would increase by 22,457 (Ecotec, 2006). The overall challenge for the regeneration prospectus was to assess whether, in an area of widespread social and economic disadvantage, it would be possible to 'smooth' the market, by easing pressures in the congested inner ring, and encouraging outward migration towards the middle and outer rings. As yet, however, there is little evidence of this process taking place.

The majority of Birmingham's Pakistani population live in the Eastern Corridor, specifically in and around the inner-ring neighbourhoods of Small Heath and the focus of Rex and Moore's study, Sparkbrook. Unlike other parts of inner-city Birmingham, there is relatively little diversity in the ethnic composition of the population in these neighbourhoods, aside from a small Bangladeshi presence. The Black African, Black Caribbean, and Indian communities are a much more significant presence in the north-west of the city, as shown in Figures 3.2 and 3.3. Between 1991 and 2001, this picture changed little, and market processes have largely consolidated Pakistanis' residential pattern in the city. There has been no significant growth of Pakistani representation in the neighbourhoods further east, despite additional indigenous household growth, in line with the demographic profile of the community.

The contrasts between the different rings in the Eastern Corridor are exemplified by the fact that in 2001 in east Birmingham (the inner ring), 45% of the population were Pakistani, compared to a mere 3.3% of residents in the adjacent middle ring and 0.1% in the outer North Solihull ring (Centre for Regional Economic and Social Research, 2006, p 5). Where growth has occurred, it has largely been compressed in the existing areas of Small Heath, Sparkbrook and Sparkhill, resulting in growing problems of poor housing quality and overcrowding. The apparent result is a community that is 'hemmed in' against a set of local housing markets into which residents have been unable to make significant headway. A study of housing aspirations among members of minority ethnic communities in the Eastern Corridor seemed to confirm this syndrome:

> Segregation and ethnic enclaves was the reality in the Eastern Corridor, ... peripheral housing estates in the middle and outer ring were seen as monolithically white and were associated with harassment ... Inner ring neighbourhoods were viewed as monolithically Pakistani and were associated with crime and poor public services. (Goodson et al, undated, para 8.4.2)

There was evidence of very modest dispersal among the Pakistani communities into the Eastern Corridor's 'middle ring' (largely inter-war settlements like Stechford, Yardley and Shard End) and affluent south-eastern suburbs like Olton, Hall Green and Moseley. Only in the neighbourhood of Aston, where there is a significant Bangladeshi population, is there evidence of more substantial migration from the Pakistani communities.

There are several possible explanations for this pattern. The relatively deprived circumstances of many Pakistani households (Platt, 2007) makes it difficult for them to compete in the housing market in more affluent neighbourhoods (as, for example, many Indian households have done). The Pakistani community has been established more recently and they tend to occupy housing – often in poor condition – in neighbourhoods with relatively low housing market values and thus have a comparatively poor equity base on which to build.

A second explanation, put forward by Abbas (2005), is that Pakistani Muslims have demonstrated strong preferences to remain in the same geographic locations as their parents and their religious networks. Pakistani settlement in Birmingham has carried through very strong kinship networks from Mirpur, a rural district of Kashmir. This rationale is contested, however, by others. A study by Bains (2006), although largely impressionistic, suggested that young Pakistanis were increasingly searching for housing beyond their families' neighbourhoods:

> Indications are that middle class Pakistani and Bangladeshi groups will seek to follow a similar path worn by their Indian peers. While living with people of a shared cultural background and proximity to place of worship was highlighted these issues were of less priority and importance

than the quality of the environment, housing and schools.
(Bains, 2006, p 8)

Bains also suggests that the pooling of family income and adherence
to traditional (extended) family structures were diminishing practices
among younger South Asians. The mobility path might not, however,
extend along a tract running outwards in an easterly direction away
from the city centre. Instead, he suggests, younger households wish to
remain within easy access of the 'buzz' of the city centre rather than
the more peripheral locations in the Eastern Corridor, bucking the
trend of counter-urbanisation. Furthermore, their perceptions of the
more peripheral areas were unfavourable:

> In east Birmingham, where demand has considerably
> outstripped supply, inflating local house prices to
> unreasonable levels, people are still prepared to buy. The
> eastern periphery provides opportunity for social rented and
> home ownership, however there is little interest from the
> overspill South Asian communities … the primary reason
> is that some of these traditional white areas are perceived as
> hostile and have a reputation for organised racist activities.
> (Bains, 2006, p 35)

A third potential reason is that the structure of the housing market in
the Eastern Corridor is discontinuous, thereby 'distorting' the expected
trajectories of migration. It might consist of sub-markets, which while
not necessarily spatial may have the effect of constraining the locational
choices that households can make, hence contributing to spatial
segregation or concentration. Movement within these sub-markets
might be relatively easy. Movement between them, on the other hand,
might be more difficult because of price differentials or other barriers
(such as fear of harassment or cultural isolation, see Phillips et al in
Chapter Four, this volume).

The sub-markets hypothesis, together with Bains' evidence of
changing perceptions and attitudes, suggests segregated housing
outcomes are likely to be more powerfully explained by constraint
and competition between different ethnic groups than by active 'self-
segregation'. These housing market processes would therefore appear
to be broadly consistent with Simpson's (2004) robust challenge to the
recent orthodoxy about the (voluntary) 'self-segregation' of minority
ethnic communities.

North-West Birmingham

North-West Birmingham contains neighbourhoods that have a significant minority ethnic population and high levels of poverty and deprivation. Problems of social exclusion and of physical blight have both been a concern, and the area has been for many years a focus of local authority and central government regeneration activity. In numerical terms, the Handsworth area is dominated by the Indian population. But the various neighbourhoods in the north-west of Birmingham are home to a number of different minority ethnic groups, and there are areas of majority Black African, Black Caribbean, Pakistani and Bangladeshi communities. Unlike the Eastern Corridor, this part of the city witnessed considerable change in residential patterns between 1991 and 2001.

Media reports of violent disturbances in the area in 2005 focused on the perceived tensions between different groups, particularly black and Asian youths (see Flint in, Chapter Eight, this volume). These disturbances echoed those of 20 years earlier and suggested that relatively little progress had been made to combat the lack of economic opportunity, the legacy of discriminatory housing decisions and other factors underpinning the comparative disadvantage suffered by residents in neighbourhoods like Handsworth (Cohen, 2005). They highlight the comparative intractability of cohesion issues in areas of greater diversity and co-location of different minority ethnic communities.

There are clear signs of quite rapid and far-reaching change in the residential patterns of minority ethnic households at the neighbourhood level in the north-west. There is a clear spread in the number of neighbourhoods that are majority Indian, mainly to the north of Handsworth but also to some areas of Smethwick. There has also been a significant expansion in the number of areas where Black African and Caribbean and Pakistani population are the majority, principally centred on Aston and Lozells. The question arises whether the structure of the market in North-West Birmingham is fundamentally different to that in the Eastern Corridor. While they are both relatively low-value markets, one can postulate that the housing market in the north-west exhibits fewer discontinuities and works in a more 'fluid' and dynamic way than in the east.

Although at this stage we can only proffer suggestions rather than definitive conclusions about the structure of the Birmingham housing market, it is instructive to examine potential links between house sale prices and the pattern of population mobility. Property sales in North-West Birmingham generally achieve lower prices than those in the inner ring of the Eastern Corridor. A more detailed analysis is needed to compare the structure of property types and sizes in the two areas, but an initial assessment does not suggest that there are significant differences in property styles, sizes or types. Terraced houses, for example, account for 68% of sales in the inner ring of the Eastern Corridor and 66% in North-West Birmingham.

A household moving from the inner ring of the Eastern Corridor to an adjacent area (the middle ring) would have to find an additional £3,000 for an average property. On the other hand, a household moving from North-West Birmingham to its closest adjacent area would find that the average property is nearly £4,000 cheaper (Table 3.1). This tends to suggest that households in certain parts of the city face greater price constraints if seeking to move to a nearby area, even where there are few significant differences in the overall 'housing offer'. More systematic tracking of mobility chains over time in the two areas, however, would be needed to put this to a more robust statistical test.

Analysis of population mobility is more difficult because of the paucity of reliable data. However, it is possible to use information from the 2001 Census on the previous address of respondents to determine the relative 'propensity' for households to move from one area to another. Table 3.2 presents an analysis of various scenarios of geographic mobility as they relate to the two study areas. It shows that people from minority ethnic communities in the Eastern Corridor are substantially more likely to remain in the same area than those from North-West

Table 3.1: Average property sale prices implicated in moves to adjacent areas

Origin	Destination	Average house sale price 2006 in origin £ (A)	Average house sale price 2006 in destination £ (B)	Absolute price difference £ (B-A)	% Price difference (B-A)
Eastern Corridor inner ring	Eastern Corridor middle ring	£126,875	129,994	3,119	2.5
North-West Birmingham	West Bromwich/ Smethwick	£118,339	114,377	-3,962	-3.3

Source: Land Registry data analysed as part of research projects in Eastern Corridor and North-West Birmingham.

Table 3.2: Propensity to move

		Number of movers		Combined number of movers in origin and destination		Propensity to move[c]	
		BME	White	BME	White	BME	White
Propensity to remain in the area	Eastern Corridor inner ring	5,703	1,462	15,662	8,652	36.4%	16.9%
	North-West Birmingham	2,150	1,061	8,329	6,185	25.8%	17.2%
Propensity to move to adjacent area[a]	Eastern Corridor inner ring	405	693	9,433	10,753	4.3%	6.4%
	North-West Birmingham	196	94	6,321	5,286	3.1%	1.8%
Propensity to move to the rest of Birmingham (outside the Eastern Corridor/North-West Birmingham)	Eastern Corridor inner ring	1,768	2,421	19,531	4,7512	9.1%	5.1%
	North-West Birmingham	1,575	1,618	15,730	4,5715	10.0%	3.5%
Propensity to move to the adjacent local authority[b]	Eastern Corridor inner ring	114	292	9,366	16,746	1.2%	1.7%
	North-West Birmingham	427	343	8,759	17,264	4.9%	2.0%

Notes: [a] Adjacent area for Eastern Corridor inner ring is the Eastern Corridor middle ring. Adjacent area for North-West Birmingham is West Bromwich and Smethwick housing market renewal area.
[b] Adjacent local authority for Eastern Corridor is Solihull. Adjacent local authority for North-West Birmingham is Sandwell.
[c] The measure of propensity used is the number of movers divided by the combined total of movers in both the origin and destination areas. This standardises for mobility rather than population. These propensities therefore control for uneven rates of mobility among population groups and areas.

Source: 2001 Census Special Migration Statistics.
(Note: Areas are based on Electoral Wards current at the time of the 2001 Census.)

Birmingham. Furthermore, it is possible to discern differences between the BME population and the white population. White households from the Eastern Corridor are more likely to move to an adjacent area than those of minority ethnic origin. The converse is marginally true in North-West Birmingham. Finally, although the percentages are small, a higher percentage of minority ethnic households in North-West Birmingham moved to an adjacent area than did those in the more constrained market in the Eastern Corridor.

Together these data do not present conclusive evidence, but they do suggest that there are potentially different processes at work in the two case study areas that may reflect structural differences in the housing market. These in turn may be related to physical or geographic constraints or, of more importance for our own analysis, the nature of housing opportunities and population characteristics in adjacent neighbourhoods. At the very least, we would suggest that a micro-level analysis of housing market structure and patterns of mobility is an important component of any endeavour to understand how community cohesion issues will change over time at the neighbourhood level. We would also suggest that 'context-free' discussions of cultural preferences or differing demographic profiles will have limitations if they are insufficiently attentive to local market variations.

It has been possible for us in this chapter to pose questions about the way in which the treatment of residential mobility and settlement patterns among minority ethnic communities needs to be alive to market context to a greater degree. This, we suggest, could lead to more nuanced views about the mainsprings for change than could purely 'cultural' explanations or arguments that rely on assumptions about 'maturity of settlement' among different groups (see Reeve in Chapter Nine, this volume). In assessing this evidence, the significant literature on housing market economics – and on sub-markets specifically – suggests that there is merit in pursuing this line of inquiry, in different cities, and over different periods. In the UK at least, attempts to integrate cohesion issues into formal housing economics have been very poorly developed. There may be quite different policy implications arising in a 'continuous' market, as opposed to a 'discontinuous' market, as discussed later. It is also suggested that policy responses need to be developed selectively at neighbourhood level, focused on what we term 'critical arenas' of actual or potential tension between different communities.

Policy responses to housing market change

Our main purpose in this chapter has been to advance the case for a better appreciation of relatively localised housing market processes to inform an understanding of patterns of mobility and settlement among different minority ethnic communities. We have suggested that an important ingredient here may be the existence or otherwise of distinct sub-markets that may distort the typical pattern of dispersal away from city-centre locations towards more suburban environments as communities become more established. There is nothing inevitable about this process: it is contingent on market characteristics, the profile of housing tenure and the dwelling stock, and perceptions and anticipated reactions among the 'host' communities in the outer areas. But what of the policy implications of this form of analysis and the argument that underpins it?

The foregoing suggests that district-wide or city-wide 'programmes' for community cohesion are likely to be insufficiently sensitive to local variation in market circumstances. In their 2006 analysis of the Eastern Corridor, the Centre for Regional Economic and Social Research (CRESR) suggested that, while many of the neighbourhoods in the Eastern Corridor may be stable and self-sustaining, any community cohesion strategies need to be focused on localities that were termed 'critical arenas'. These areas are marked by actual or potential tensions between different ethnic groups. In some cases, local authorities and other agencies would need to adopt proactive measures that anticipate negative consequences of neighbourhood change and in others they would need to adopt reactive measures to mitigate the impact of overt conflict and tension.

The CRESR report outlined different types of 'critical arena' and suggested that each might require a different suite of interventions:

- *Reception localities* – points of initial arrival for households, and often low-value yet highly pressurised housing markets.
- *Turbulent localities* – marked by high levels of residential mobility, often associated with a relatively large private rented sector. These areas may be functioning well, as an important lubricating part of the wider housing market, where qualities such as ready access and high turnover are at a premium. The neighbourhoods are not necessarily problematic, but the key aspect is that the character of such areas may change relatively quickly, if the pattern of in-movers and out-movers alters.

- *Transforming localities* – marked by a systematic shift in their ethnic profile, especially if they become sites of new settlement for groups, or as new generations of households move out from established areas of settlement.
- *Contested localities* – distinguished by sporadic or continuous tensions and conflicts between different ethnic groups, which may experience 'flashpoint' incidents that focus attention on issues that often develop from longstanding resentments or suspicions.
- *Eroding localities* – stable, usually white-dominated, neighbourhoods with low household turnover and household formation, often high levels of residential satisfaction and established local amenities. However, the areas may be dominated by a large cohort of ageing households that may not be replaced organically once residents leave or die. As property values start to fall, they may then become attractive locations for those households living in pressurised localities seeking more affordable options. This does not necessarily betoken a smooth transition to a more mixed community than before: the process of transition can be problematic.

This five-fold designation of critical arenas is indicative rather than definitive or universally applicable, but it suggests that the combination of different localities within a larger segment of a town or city may lead to different policy instruments being developed to enhance community cohesion or minimise conflict. In terms of the earlier discussion, the extent to which there are identifiable sub-markets carries important messages for policy. A 'discontinuous' market may point policies in the direction of market restructuring and supply-side interventions. A 'continuous' market, on the other hand, may suggest the introduction of demand-side measures to ameliorate the housing outcomes for different communities. This may not necessarily involve 'housing' initiatives per se so much as measures to enhance the economic resources of minority ethnic households so that they are able to compete more effectively in the market. The difference between these two approaches is not just about focus; it also affects timescales. A programme to reconfigure the 'housing offer' at neighbourhood level would need to be developed over a long time frame; initiatives to stimulate demand, by improving access to the labour market for example, might bring returns more quickly.

Conclusion

In their research, undertaken in the early 1960s, Rex and Moore identified the housing market in Birmingham as a source of inequality of access and outcome, and charted its differential effects on ethnic groupings, focused on one area of the city, Sparkbrook. They suggested that analyses concerned only with labour market position, economic power and social-class formation needed to incorporate a clearer understanding of how the housing market offered different types of access to ethnic groups, and thus could become a crucial and 'independent' arena of competition and conflict.

In this chapter, we have suggested that, 40 years on, universalising prescriptions about housing, community cohesion, cultural preference and patterns of mobility also need a keener sensibility of housing market processes and functions. The local housing markets in two different areas of the same city – Birmingham, again – may have markedly different impacts on minority ethnic communities; we speculate that these are partially explicable by different market constraints, rather than purely by reference to the descriptive characteristics of the communities affected (such as ethnicity, length of residence or household composition).

The boundaries around any ethnic sub-markets may themselves be the distillation of a host of influences: antipathy from host or dominant communities, racialised inequalities, defensive strategies by those with little economic power to penetrate new markets, changing locational preferences and so on (see Burnett in Chapter Two, this volume). This approach in turn suggests that for policymakers a more locally sensitised approach to 'community cohesion' will be necessary, attuned to the dynamics of neighbourhood change. Explanations of patterns of residential mobility and settlement – whether 'self-segregating' or 'out-migrating' – also need to be aware that local housing sub-markets can shape these processes in quite different ways in the same city.

Notes
[1] Housing in England 2004/05, p 34.

[2] Ibid.

[3] English House Condition Survey 2005 Annual Report, p 48.

References

Abbas, T. (2005) 'Muslims in Birmingham, UK', Background paper for *Muslims and Community Cohesion in Britain*, Oxford: Centre on Migration, Policy and Society (www.compas.ox.ac.uk/publications/papers/Birmingham%20Background%20Paper%200206.pdf).

Bains, J. (2006) *Futures housing 2020: Housing needs, choices and aspirations of South Asian communities in the West Midlands*, Birmingham:, Ashram Housing Association.

Cohen, N. (2005) 'Politics of the ghetto', *The Observer*, 30 October.

Cole, I. and Nevin, B. (2004) *The road to renewal: The housing market renewal programme*, Sheffield: Centre for Regional Economic and Social Research. Sheffield Hallam University.

Centre for Regional Economic and Social Research (2006) *An approach for promoting community cohesion through housing market renewal in the Eastern Corridor of Birmingham*, Sheffield: Centre for Regional Economic and Social Research.

Communities and Local Government (2007) *English housing condition survey 2005 annual report*, London: Communities and Local Government.

Department for Communities and Local Government (2006) *Housing in England 2004–05*, London: Department for Communities and Local Government

Dorling, D. (2006) 'Inequality in Britain 1997–2006: The dream that turned pear-shaped', *Local Economy*, vol 21, no 4, pp 353–61.

Ecotec (2006) *Eastern Corridor housing market assessment and evaluation tool*, Birmingham: Ecotec.

Finney, N. and Simpson, L. (2007) *Internal migration and ethnic groups: Evidence from the UK from the 2001 census, CCSR Working Paper 2007–04*, Manchester: Cathie Marsh Centre for Census and Survey Research.

Goodson, L., Beider, H., Joseph, R. and Phillimore, J. (undated) *Black and minority ethnic communities in the Eastern Corridor: Aspirations, neighbourhood 'choice' and tenure*, Birmingham: Centre for Urban and Regional Studies.

Haddon, R. (1970) *A minority in a welfare state society: West Indians in the London housing market*, Padua: Atlantis.

Henley, A. (1998) 'Residential mobility, housing equity and the labour market', *Economic Journal*, vol 108, no 447, pp 414–27.

Leather, P., Cole, I., Ferrari, E. with Flint, J., Robinson, D., Simpson, C. and Hopley, M. (2007) *National evaluation of the HMR pathfinder programme: Baseline report*, London: Communities and Local Government.

Lee, P., Barber, A., Burfitt, A., Collinge, C., Ferrari, E., Hall, S., Murie. A. and Roberts, J. (2003) *The housing market and economic function of the Eastern Corridor of Birmingham & Solihull*, Birmingham: Centre for Urban and Regional Studies.

Office of the Deputy Prime Minister (2005) *Housing market assessment: Draft practice guidance*, London: Office of the Deputy Prime Minister.

Office of the Deputy Prime Minister (2006) *The state of the English cities: A research study volume*, London: Office of the Deputy Prime Minister.

Platt, L (2007) *Poverty and ethnicity in the UK*, Bristol: The Policy Press.

Rex, J. and Moore, R. (1967) *Race, community and conflict: A study of Sparkbrook*, London: Institute of Race Relations and Oxford University Press.

Robinson, D., Ferrari, E. and Coward, S. (2005) *Housing market intelligence in the HMR pathfinders*, Sheffield: Centre for Regional Economic and Social Research.

Saunders, P. (1981) *Social theory and the urban question*, London: Hutchison.

Simpson, L. (2004) 'Statistics of racial segregation: measures, evidence and policy', *Urban Studies*, vol 41, no 4, pp 661–81.

FOUR

Shifting geographies of minority ethnic settlement: remaking communities in Oldham and Rochdale

Deborah Phillips, Ludi Simpson and Sameera Ahmed

Introduction

This chapter explores the way in which young British Asian and white adults living in the Pennine towns of Oldham and Rochdale understand ideas of 'community' and how these affect their decisions and aspirations about where to live. The image of community relations in the multi-ethnic, former industrial towns of northern England was tarnished by the urban disturbances of 2001 in Oldham, Burnley and Bradford. Press reports at the time sensationally referred to the existence of 'no-go areas', ethnic territories and ghettoisation in these localities. The ethnic residential segregation evident here was widely thought to be indicative of social separation, cultural difference and divided communities. This gave rise to a racialised political discourse on urban segregation, through which minority ethnic clustering was constructed as problematic. The ensuing debates about 'parallel lives' brought calls for policy interventions to break down segregation and rebuild cohesive communities, which took shape through the community cohesion agenda.

The government's vision of moving towards more socially and spatially integrated communities through the implementation of community cohesion strategies is particularly challenging in places like Oldham and Rochdale. Ethnic tensions here continue to be fuelled by Far Right political activity, particularly in Oldham, and are readily sustained by racialised national discourses on asylum and immigration, minority ethnic citizenship and belonging. Long histories of racial exclusion in the workplace and housing market in these localities have brought a legacy of racialised divisions, suspicions and resentment, which may prove difficult to disrupt. Indeed, when reporting on community relations in Oldham five years after the disturbances, a review team, led by Ted Cantle, observed that progress towards the development of more socially mixed communities could well be hindered by 'continuing entrenched divisions' and the 'sheer scale of Oldham's problems' manifest in fractured communities, segregated neighbourhoods and separate schooling. While noting some evidence of change, the team were 'struck by the extent to which divisions between, and polarisation within, Oldham's many communities continue to be a feature of social relations' (Cantle et al, 2006, pp 4–5).

Despite this rather pessimistic assessment, there is evidence of a desire for greater social and spatial mixing among young British Asian and white adults living in Oldham and the neighbouring town of Rochdale. In-depth qualitative research conducted by the authors in 2006 explored young Asians' and whites' views on community and their housing and neighbourhood aspirations. Focus groups and interviews were used to examine their willingness to live in areas beyond those traditionally associated with their ethnic group, their views on ethnically mixed neighbourhoods, factors shaping their housing decisions/aspirations and perceived barriers to achieving their goals. Like Cantle and his team, we observed obstacles to achieving greater social mixing at the neighbourhood level; housing affordability and fear of racist harassment both emerged as significant dimensions of young Asian adults' housing decision-making process. There is, nevertheless, an optimistic story to be told as well, which points to the capacity for remaking multi-ethnic communities in these localities.

Oldham and Rochdale have much in common. Both have sizable populations of Asian heritage, mainly of Pakistani and Bangladeshi origin. According to government estimates for 2004, the black and minority ethnic population of Oldham stands at 33,000 (15% of the total population) and in Rochdale it is 26,000 (13% of the population). Groups of Asian heritage are characterised by spatial clustering, predominantly within the inner-city areas of older housing. A statistical analysis of the levels of residential clustering shows this to be slightly greater in Oldham than in Rochdale, although, significantly, levels of ethnic clustering had decreased in both localities over the 1991–2001 period (Simpson and Gavalas, 2005). Migration and new household formation is, however, constrained for many families by poverty, housing affordability and the structure of housing choices available to them. A Housing Market Renewal (HMR) pathfinder scheme was established in 2002 with the aim of regenerating the housing market and opening up new housing opportunities in both towns. While many HMR pathfinders have shown a variable level of engagement with the community cohesion agenda, Oldham and Rochdale have placed the goal of building cohesive communities at the core of their regeneration strategy. They seek to widen housing options and provide greater equality of opportunity in order to enable residential mobility and present better prospects for building more sustainable multi-ethnic neighbourhoods.

There are also differences between Oldham and Rochdale that present specific challenges to the community cohesion agenda. Most obviously, Oldham has a special place in the national discourse on citizenship and belonging in 21st-century Britain. Along with places like Bradford, Blackburn and Burnley, it has come to epitomise what are seen to be the failings of multiculturalism in the public imagination; a town divided by racial tensions and mistrust, and a lack of community cohesion stemming from the limited spatial and cultural integration of a so-called self-segregating 'other' (Phillips, 2006). While these interpretations of inter-cultural relations in these places have been contested (eg Simpson, 2004; Phillips, 2006), they now form part of the local history of Oldham and help to frame British Asians' sense of identity, community and belonging. Ethnic relations in Rochdale, meanwhile, were described by some young men and women in our focus groups as 'not like Oldham', and 'better than Oldham', partly because of the different histories of 'rioting' and because of an active British National Party (BNP) presence in the latter. While racialised tensions were evident in Rochdale, barriers to social and spatial integration were perceived by its residents to be lower and more permeable than in Oldham.

The research presented in this chapter was conducted as part of a wider project undertaken for the Oldham and Rochdale HMR pathfinder to investigate racial segregation in the housing markets of the two towns, the processes underlying this and the potential for change across the generations (see Simpson et al, 2007, 2008). It is not the purpose of this chapter to evaluate the specific housing or community cohesion objectives of the pathfinder, nor their strategy for achieving them. Rather, we aim to give voice to the young Asian and white people of Oldham and Rochdale who participated in a series of focus groups and interviews for this project and to present their accounts of 'community' and the potential for remaking multi-ethnic spaces in these particular places. A total of 100 British Asian (of Pakistani and Bangladeshi origin) and white men and women, mostly aged between 18 and 30, participated in the research. The focus groups were constructed on the basis of housing tenure and living arrangements, and included young single people living with their parents as well as people who were married and living independently. These data were supplemented by interviews with key stakeholders in the community cohesion and regeneration programme.

The chapter begins with a critical look at the discourses on segregated and ethnically divided communities that underpin the community cohesion agenda and the policy response to concerns about minority ethnic segregation and integration in multicultural Britain. It then moves on to investigate the capacity for building more ethnically diverse residential areas in places like Oldham and Rochdale, as well as real and imagined barriers to change. The findings highlight the importance of locality-based initiatives that are sensitive to the particularities of place and local history, as well as commonalities of experience across localities. The chapter argues that many young people, irrespective of ethnic group, share similar housing and neighbourhood concerns and aspirations. While the obstacles to change should not be underestimated, our research points to a foundation for inter-cultural cooperation, inclusion and community development.

Discourses on ethnic segregation and the loss of community

Recent politicised anxieties about the fragmentation of communities along ethnic and religious lines have promoted a discourse that is infused with racially coded notions of ethnic segregation, community and integration. It is claimed that levels of minority ethnic segregation in Britain are increasing and that this is leading to tensions between ethnic groups that threaten the stability and cohesion of the nation. This concern has triggered calls for strategies to 'break down' ethnic segregation as part of a move towards remaking communities and building common values (Community Cohesion Panel, 2004, p 17), a policy that was endorsed by Cantle and his team in their 2006 review of Oldham.

The justification for a policy approach that focuses on 'breaking down' segregation is, we would argue, rather shaky. Furthermore, the community cohesion agenda is underpinned by a number of dubious assumptions about 'community'. In this section we highlight the key features of a critique of the link between segregation and cohesion that has been explored in depth by the authors elsewhere (eg Harrison et al, 2005; Phillips, 2006; Phillips et al, 2007; Simpson, 2007).

First, the residential segregation of ethnic groups is not increasing. Statistical indices show countervailing trends, that is, minority ethnic populations living in established community areas (usually in the inner city) are growing as a result of demographic change, but minority ethnic households are also dispersing away from these clusters to new areas (Simpson, 2007). Furthermore, politicised debates about segregation are not informed by any objective definition of 'intense' segregation or 'acceptable' segregation, and there is often no appreciation of the fact that ethnic clusters can have a transient population: as some households move out they are replaced by others.

Second, what is meant by ethnic segregation in this policy context? The term has multiple meanings, both in a scholarly and in a political sense. As Massey and Denton (1989), writing about the US, and Simpson (2007) in the British context have signalled, segregation is a multidimensional construct and the complexity of experiences embedded within it is often missing from policy debates. Simpson's (2007) conceptualisation of segregation builds on Massey and Denton's distributional measures of 'evenness', 'exposure' and locational measures of 'concentration', 'centralisation' and 'clustering' to capture minority ethnic group mobility as well. Crucially, he sheds light on the dynamic processes associated with population change (that is, growth *in situ* through natural increase and immigration) as opposed to population movement towards, or away from, one's own ethnic group. Political and policy anxieties about minority ethnic segregation seem to be grounded in concerns about 'exposure' or 'isolation', as is evidenced by the 'parallel lives' debate, and movement. The latter has important implications for debates about 'white flight' and 'self-segregation', and the process of withdrawal from social mixing implicated within it. The statistical evidence for both of these processes of separation is, however, debatable (Simpson, 2007).

Third, it is presumed that minority ethnic residential segregation is a problem. Peach (1996), however, has drawn a distinction between 'good' and 'bad' segregation, reminding us that ethnic and racial clustering may arise through communality, or through discrimination, inequality and exclusion. This suggests that there may be different forces at work in different contexts, and that it is the continuing association between segregation and deprivation that should be of concern.

Fourth, there is an assumption that residential segregation hinders the 'normal' process of integration; an understanding shaped by the pathways of white immigrant groups in the US. This, however, does not stand up to scrutiny, either empirically or conceptually. There is a long history of empirical research that has attempted to measure minority ethnic integration into the receiving society. Most commonly, socio-economic variables have been used as indicators of structural integration, while social interaction indices have been used as a proxy for ethnic difference (eg Musterd, 2003; Dekker and Bolt, 2005). As Castles et al (2002) note, however, the implications of such research findings are contentious. Policy discourses on integration tend to be highly politicised and rest on shifting, multiple meanings of what it means to be integrated. Furthermore, the link between spatial desegregation and social integration is uncertain. There is ample research to suggest that living in spatial proximity to other groups is not a sufficient condition for overcoming ethnic, racial and class divisions (Atkinson and Kintrea, 2000; Amin, 2002; Atkinson, 2006).

Finally, the 'parallel lives' discourse, and ensuing community cohesion debates, have led to a reinvigoration of the salience of 'community' for everyday experiences and the project of nation building. But what is meant by community? An extensive literature highlights the multifaceted and contested nature of this concept (eg Stacey, 1969; Cater and Jones, 1989; Rose, 1990). Contributors to this body of work have argued that while communities may be represented in many positive ways, and can be a source of social capital and support, they can also be intolerant of difference and exclusionary (Young, 1990). Community cohesion strategies, which focus largely on the reconstruction of community at the neighbourhood scale (see Robinson, 2005 for a critique), are founded on an idealised notion of the neighbourhood community as cohesive (rather than differentiated along the lines of class, age, lifestyle and so on), cooperative and inclusive. Multi-ethnic neighbourhood communities could potentially be important social spaces that help to shape people's sense of inclusion, citizenship and belonging. However, different people are likely to experience the neighbourhood 'community' in different ways. For some people, the neighbourhood and its residents are integral to their everyday experiences. For others, they are peripheral and, providing they are safe spaces, may have little meaning for them.

It could be argued that the agenda outlined in government documents (eg Home Office, 2001, 2005; Department for Communities and Local Government, 2006) is not only inspired by communitarianism, but also by the goal of assimilation. The political vision, which is replete with normative values about the nature and virtues of community, constructs the neighbourhood as a place where minority ethnic or 'micro-communities' can 'gel or mesh' into the wider population (Home Office, 2001, p 70). However, a political discourse that focuses on the 'problems' associated with black minority ethnic segregation, as opposed to white, serves to racialise this agenda (Phillips, 2006). Policy-related solutions to ethnic segregation are primarily couched in terms of the need for black minority ethnic households to move. Indeed, the fracturing of 'community', and the problems believed to be associated with this, is largely constructed in terms of ethnic difference. A recent review of HMR pathfinders' approach to community cohesion, for example, found that most officers understood their task to involve the remaking of 'multi-ethnic' communities (personal communication, David Robinson, 2007). Few embraced any other social dimensions, such as social class or lifestyle, in their conceptualisation of community in this context.[1] Similarly, the segregation of white groups is overlooked. Thus, although levels of residential segregation for Jewish minorities are in fact higher than for any black minority ethnic group in the UK (Dorling and Thomas, 2004), we do not hear calls for Jewish residential segregation to be broken down in the name of community cohesion. In fact, Jewish communities are more likely to be referred to as successful models of integration.

This critique of the prevailing political discourses on ethnic segregation and community casts doubts on the vision for community cohesion espoused in policy documents. It also raises questions about how progress towards building a more cohesive nation might be measured. But what are the views of those living their everyday lives in the racialised spaces of our cities? The chapter now turns to look at the changing ethnic geographies in Oldham and Rochdale and explores understandings of ethnic segregation, neighbourhood and community from the perspective of young adults living in these localities.

Shifting geographies of 'race' in Oldham and Rochdale

The development of distinct Asian and white areas in Oldham and Rochdale has its roots in historical immigration to central parts of each locality. This ethnic geography has been sustained by demographic growth and the importance placed – by both Asian and white people – on family networks, community support structures and a sense of attachment and belonging to particular neighbourhoods. Clustering has also been reinforced by negative factors, including the disadvantage experienced by minority ethnic groups in the labour market (increasing their poverty), racist attitudes and stereotypes (rooted in national political and media discourses as well as local events) and a dysfunctional local housing market, which reinforces racial segmentation through barriers to housing choice and mobility.

Although it is commonly thought that ethnic segregation in places like Oldham and Rochdale is firmly entrenched and needs special policy measures to 'break it down', evidence from the census indicates that some important shifts in the pattern of segregation are already under way. An analysis of changing ethnic distributions between 1991 and 2001 reveals two key trends: populations of Asian heritage living in the central areas are continuing to grow, mainly because of their young demographic structure, but Asian households are also moving out from these traditional areas of community settlement (Simpson et al, 2008). This migration is contributing to the decrease in ethnic residential clustering noted earlier. The pattern of dispersal, however, has been uneven and there has been some re-clustering of migrants in areas attractive to, or more accessible to, Asian households. Many of the new growth areas are relatively close to the established community areas and are in relatively low-status neighbourhoods, albeit with better housing and neighbourhood amenities than the inner city. As yet, no distinct Asian clusters have emerged in the most prosperous areas of either locality.

The dispersal of households from the Asian inner areas of Oldham and Rochdale is thus clearly under way. Simpson et al (2008) calculate that the rate of out-migration between 2000 and 2001 was in the region of 2%–3% and this is likely to grow in the future. This outflow includes white as well as Asian households, although a detailed analysis of migration data suggests that the level of so-called 'white flight' from 'Asian' areas is probably relatively small (Simpson et al, 2007). The net outward movement of white households in 2000–01 was not much greater in percentage terms than for Asian households and, at the time of the last census, even the most Asian ward in Oldham was 40% white. However, since the remaining white population will not experience the same high level of demographic growth as the Asian population, the overall impression is one of whites moving out.

There was certainly a perception among both the Asian and white young adults in our focus groups that 'white flight' was helping to sustain ethnic residential divisions in both towns. The following quotes are typical of Asian perceptions:

> '... as Asians are moving into Belfield, the white people are moving out and that's what happened in Wardleworth and when you start seeing Asian families, you want to go. So I think that's going to be the trend. Whether we'd want that or not ...' (Bangladeshi man, Rochdale)

> 'As soon as the Asians start moving in, the white people move out ...' (Pakistani woman, Oldham)

While the young white people we interviewed suggested that the changing ethnic mix of an area might not worry them, they recognised that some of the older generations did have negative reactions to ethnic change:

> 'My grandparents have said that [white people are moving out].They have their perceptions about Asians ... They said if anyone moves up here with a black face, we're off, and I used to say "are you serious?"' (white man, Oldham)

The process of 'white flight' was generally thought to be more subtle than in the past, but it was nevertheless still seen as a barrier to creating and sustaining ethnically mixed areas. Stereotyped views that property values might decline as neighbourhoods changed and fears that neighbourhoods would be 'taken over' by 'other' groups were articulated. It may well be that white flight is not a major force in the changing composition of an area; it may simply be that fewer white families are moving in. Nevertheless, the perception that white flight is occurring might well affect people's decisions (both Asian and white) on where to move and may pose challenges to the remaking of multi-ethnic communities.

So, what is the potential for further residential change in towns with such a legacy of separation? The picture is mixed. It was evident that some neighbourhoods were still considered to be 'no-go areas' for people of certain ethnic groups, but these sentiments tended to be focused on specific areas with poor reputations for anti-social behaviour. Overall, there appeared to be a growing confidence among young Asians that they could venture into areas that were previously seen as 'white'. A trend towards Asian out-migration from the inner-city areas reflects a desire for better-quality housing in less run-down areas offering better prospects in terms of schools, environment and infrastructure. By no means all of the young Asians wished to make the move outwards, but a growing gap in the housing aspirations of the different generations was widely recognised.The comments of one young Pakistani woman in Oldham were not untypical: '... I would look for different things than my mum and dad would look for. ... We want a nice area. My mum and dad, they want an Asian community. I would want nice scenery, a nice spacious garden or something like that.' Similarly, a focus group discussion with young Bangladeshi women in Rochdale referred to their generation 'spreading out' and 'making a go of it' in other areas.

While most Asian young people talked about this outwards migration in terms of short-distance moves to the edge of the established ethnic clusters, a few had aspirations to move to more distant urban or rural localities. Some felt that ethnic mixing would be easier if they lived alongside middle-class white people rather than in working-class housing estates, but affordability was clearly an issue. Both Asian and white focus group participants nevertheless recognised the growing importance of income and class differences within the Asian population and its likely impact on wider housing choices and outwards movement.

Building multi-ethnic communities

The shifting ethnic geographies of Oldham and Rochdale were not only driven by changing housing needs and aspirations, but also by a desire by some Asian and white young people for greater social mixing between ethnic groups. Their experiences and imagining of community and the potential for residential change in Oldham and Rochdale were nevertheless framed by historical and contemporary tensions. Some young people were thus sceptical that the distinctive geographies of separation could be changed significantly. Most had, however, observed the trend towards greater residential mixing and thought that this would grow in the future. Importantly, this development was generally welcomed by the young people participating in our research as a step towards better integration. Whites, however, tended to see mobility as a one-way process; most could not envisage living in areas they identified as 'Asian'. This reticence was partly due to the unappealing physical environment of the older Asian areas, but some aversion to moving into areas of new-build labelled as 'Asian' was also expressed.

There are certainly barriers to building multi-ethnic neighbourhood communities, especially in terms of safety, fear of racist harassment and affordability. Nevertheless, the general view to emerge from the focus groups and the stakeholders was that there is potential for further change, particularly through widening housing choices for young people. A number of young Asians talked about the benefits of social integration that might accompany a move to a more ethnically mixed area. They saw this as important for themselves and their children.

Such views were not universally held; the social capital that could be drawn upon by living in, or close to, 'Asian areas' was still valued by many. Nevertheless, there was a feeling, expressed by the young Asian men and women in both towns, that it was 'good for the kids to mingle' and that ethnic mixing at the neighbourhood level could enrich their lives. One Pakistani woman in Rochdale summed up her feelings on ethnic mixing by saying: 'Your life's a lot more richer because you obviously learn things that you just wouldn't in predominantly Asian areas.' Another in Oldham expressed remarkably similar sentiments when she asked: 'Why can't we have a mixed balance of Asians and whites and appreciate each other's cultures? You know you learn from each other and it can only make us richer.'

Such observations provide some support for the idea of the neighbourhood as a place where groups might, under the right circumstances, 'gel' (Home Office, 2001). The legacy of ethnic segmentation within the housing markets of Oldham and Rochdale will nevertheless be difficult to surmount. There will be geographical inertia; both young whites and Asians commonly expressed loyalties to their respective neighbourhoods, and many young women in particular aspired to live within easy access of their families, which may draw them back to the divided spaces. Young Asian people's views were also divided on whether they would move to an 'all-white area' as some observed that they might feel isolated or vulnerable. Most would prefer to see some other Asians living in a neighbourhood before deciding to move there; as few as three or four families was sufficient for some. The expression of such anxieties picks up on the earlier critique of community as possibly exclusionary and unwelcoming rather than inclusive.

Social housing providers in Oldham and Rochdale have responded to such concerns through their supported tenancies schemes, which assist minority ethnic households wanting to move into traditionally white areas of social housing. There was much praise from both young Asian and white people for the Community Induction Project operating in Rochdale, which had facilitated the social transformation of a particular housing estate. One Pakistani woman described this estate as now having 'a fair mix – you haven't got too much of one [group] or too much of the other'. Another group saw the potential for creating new inter-cultural spaces, free from a history of ethnic tension, through the construction of new-build housing that was not associated with the territory of a particular group. Referring to a specific new development in Oldham, one Asian woman observed:

> '... there's no set nationality or culture settled there, so all
> sorts of people are buying houses there. Nobody's asking
> "what kind of area is it? who lives there?", because nobody
> lives there. It is [a] completely new area ... we have got a
> mix of Pakistanis, whites, Bangladeshis, Indians, Chinese,

black people all speaking when you walk around. It's a good mix.'

The picture presented by both quantitative and qualitative data is thus one of changing patterns of ethnic clustering in Oldham and Rochdale. There is also a desire for ethnic mixing, which suggests that this trend will grow. However, while increasing minority ethnic household mobility and exposure to other ethnic groups might present opportunities for inter-cultural contact and community building, it is not sufficient a condition for this to take place. Our research thus explored how young Asians and whites in these towns conceptualised 'community', particularly in the context of neighbourhood change.

There was wide agreement among focus group participants on what is necessary for building a successful community; both whites and Asians talked about wanting ties and connections to other people and to their neighbourhood, good neighbours and a focus for the community (eg in terms of local amenities), a sense of belonging, and mutual respect and tolerance from those in the immediate area. The ethnic composition of an area was often raised in the course of these discussions. Asian young people observed that their parents would be most likely to construct 'community' in terms of people from the same ethnic background. The young people were more willing, however, to express a more inclusive concept of community, arguing that 'good' people from any ethnic background were the key to successful community relations. White people expressed ambivalence when talking about communities constructed along ethnic lines. When discussing the closeness of Asian families in Oldham and Rochdale and the strength of their 'tightly knit' communities, they expressed both feelings of envy and exclusion. Several also expressed regret about the loss of community spirit in many white areas, which they wished could be rekindled, possibly along multi-ethnic lines.

There was, however, a strong feeling by both Asians and whites that ethnic mixing and community building could not be socially engineered. Typical comments included 'you can't force community cohesion ...' and that '... community cohesion is for the community and not for politicians'. Perceived stumbling blocks to the development of cohesive multi-ethnic communities were encapsulated in discussions about feelings of belonging and security. Myths about one ethnic group not wanting to mix with another surfaced in both Asian and white focus groups. Some Asians suggested that ethnic mixing in Oldham and Rochdale was inhibited by whites not wanting to interact with them, and vice versa. Both whites and Asians raised anxieties about their sense of belonging in particular areas and communities. Some suggested that they might feel 'out of place' in the areas traditionally associated with other ethnic groups. This made Asian women in particular feel vulnerable, as illustrated by the comments of a Pakistani woman who had considered moving to a white rural area of Rochdale: 'You go there, and people just look at you funny … just the thought of moving there, and people staring at you and everything, it was just like we're not gonna go there. They look at you like you're an alien or something.'

For some, this feeling of unease was expressed more strongly in terms of anxieties about safety, racism and racist harassment. In Rochdale, young Bangladeshi men described how they felt that their housing options in white areas were constrained by the risk of harassment. Similarly, a Pakistani woman commented: 'I think, being Asian, we've always got the fear that if we move into a white area where there are no Asians, we are going to get racially harassed.'

Women in both Oldham and Rochdale spoke of their fears and experiences of harassment on social housing estates. While recognising that patterns of residence were changing for Asian families, one argued that 'ideally nobody wants to move there'. Some white people also spoke of feeling 'intimidated' by groups of Asian youths in certain areas. Both Asian and white young people emphasised the importance of anti-social behaviour in their assessment of areas that they would favour or avoid.

It is important to recognise that racialised tensions persist in both Oldham and Rochdale, presenting barriers to mixing and community building. Nevertheless, people often qualified their comments on ethnic tensions with examples of friendship and neighbourliness across the ethnic groups, and many Asian young people could recount positive experiences of 'friendly' or 'good' white neighbours. The potential for greater social interaction in a supportive environment, in which anxieties and anti-social behaviour are addressed, would thus seem to exist.

Conclusion

The national guidelines issued by the Local Government Association (LGA, 2002) define a cohesive community as one where people hold 'a common vision and sense of belonging' and develop 'strong and positive relationships … between people from different backgrounds'. The young people participating in our research in Oldham and Rochdale did express a 'common vision' of their ideal neighbourhood, but their 'sense of belonging' to neighbourhood communities was still racialised. The LGA guidance also refers to the importance of 'those from different backgrounds having similar life opportunities'. The goal of promoting equality of opportunity in Oldham in particular is demanding, given its specific history of ethnic tension, but racist harassment clearly presents a challenge to progress in both localities.

Our research indicates that many white and Asian young adults still identify and favour areas partly in terms of their ethnic composition in ways that might maintain clustering. Since demographic processes will in themselves maintain residential clustering, it may be argued that this clustering should not be of concern to housing and community cohesion policies. Clustering itself need not be considered a negative phenomenon. Loyalty to family and locality are positive aspects to a thriving neighbourhood, which sustain cultural development, maintain facilities including shops and religious facilities, and provide support from one generation to the next. Cultural and family clustering is also positively helpful to the integration of new immigrants and their families, who develop social networks that can support them in the search for work and housing. We would argue that the benign and often positive aspects of residential clustering have not been given sufficient recognition in reports on community cohesion for the government in this decade. Indeed, ethnic clustering of this nature is no more worrying than clustering that separates social classes and tenure types into observable residential clusters.

Successful integration and community cohesion cannot therefore be measured by the absence of residential clustering. Clustering will continue for positive reasons. Of greater concern are distortions of the housing market; residents need to be able to choose where to live on an equal basis, and there should be provision of appropriate quality services to all neighbourhoods irrespective of ethnic composition. Issues of housing type and tenure, affordability and security are all important to achieving greater residential mixing and community cohesion. Our research suggests that there is potential for change. While older generations are unlikely to move, and ties of proximity to work, availability of affordable housing, family/community, facilities and a sense of security do still underlie Asians' decisions to settle in the 'traditional' areas, these factors are becoming less binding. There are also increasing pressures from overcrowding in central Oldham and Rochdale to relocate. Many younger Asian families are contemplating moving out of areas in which their parents live and have the competence and 'cultural capital' to do so. Communities are thus likely to be refashioned by ethnicity, social class and generation, as more mobile households move in search of different lifestyles and better housing.

Thus we do not find that young Asian and white residents have different values that require negotiation and trimming to find a common denominator, as the community cohesion agenda proposes. Social values and housing aspirations are remarkably similar. The same high priority is put on safe neighbourhoods with a good environment, close to other family members and friends. Anti-social behaviour is singled out consistently as the main deterrent for all residents considering where to make their next move. The separation of communities is based partly on benign causes, which do not cause worry, and partly on racialised attitudes to what constitutes a safe neighbourhood. These results chime with previous studies. For example, Alam and Husband's (2006) interviews with Muslim men in Bradford uncovered widespread concerns for children's education and a crime-free environment, in common with the general population. Young families – especially those who could afford to do so – were moving from inner Bradford, but the same young men talked of a 'comfort zone' in the areas of diversity where they had grown up, which they knew well and were loyal to. Similar views were expressed by young Asian people moving from the inner ethnic areas of Leeds (Phillips et al, 2007). As in Oldham and Rochdale, Asians in Leeds and Bradford felt that there were some barriers to mixing because of the exclusionary practices of some white communities.

The challenge to the community cohesion agenda is therefore not that the tensions associated with 'parallel lives' do not exist. It is that the tensions do not arise from parallel lives, from isolation or from a divergence of values. They seem to come more from a not universal but quite common racialised view of safety, in which some neighbourhoods are labelled not only as belonging to a particular ethnic group but also as dangerous spaces, places where anti-social behaviour is expected from some people against those of a different ethnic background. This is a safety and an educational issue, which could be tackled through support for civility and firm action against racism. In practice this may not only mean resident 'induction' schemes, such as those praised by some of the interviewees in Rochdale, but community action and criminal prosecutions of racially hateful behaviour, and more cross-cultural meeting points – already supported by the cohesion agenda. These would complement and build on the common aspirations of young people of all backgrounds and provide positive potential for building sustainable communities.

Note

[1] Yet, as Dorling and Rees (2003) explore, social clustering on the basis of employment state is increasing in Britain, while ethnic group clustering is on the decrease.

References

Alam, M.Y. and Husband, C. (2006) *British-Pakistani men from Bradford: Linking narratives to policy*, York: Joseph Rowntree Foundation.

Amin, A. (2002) 'Ethnicity and the multicultural city: Living with diversity', *Environment and Planning A*, vol 34, no 6, pp 959–80.

Atkinson, R. (2006) 'Padding the bunker: Strategies of middle-class disaffiliation and colonisation in the city', *Urban Studies*, vol 43, no 4, pp 819–32.

Atkinson, R. and Kintrea, K. (2000) 'Owner-occupation, social mix and neighbourhood impacts', *Policy & Politics*, vol 28, no 1, pp 93–108.

Cantle, T., Kaur, D., Athar, M., Dallison, C., Wiggans, C. and Harris, J. (2006) *Challenging local communities to change Oldham: Review of community cohesion in Oldham*, Coventry: Institute of Community Cohesion.

Castles, S., Korac, M.,Vasta, E. andVertovec, S. (2002) *Integration mapping the field*, London: Home Office.

Cater, J. and Jones, T. (1989) *Social geography: An introduction to contemporary issues*, London: Edward Arnold.

Community Cohesion Panel (2004) *The end of parallel lives? The report of the community cohesion panel*, London: Home Office.

Dekker, K. and Bolt, G. (2005) 'Social cohesion in post war estates in the Netherlands: Differences between socioeconomic and ethnic groups', *Urban Studies*, vol 42, no 13, pp 2447–70.

Department for Communities and Local Government (2006) *Strong and prosperous communities: The local government White Paper*, Cm 6939-1, London: HMSO.

Dorling, D. and Rees, P. (2003) 'A nation still dividing: The British census and social polarization 1971–2001', *Environment and Planning A*, vol 35, no 7, pp 1287–313.

Dorling, D. and Thomas, B. (2004) *People and places: A 2001 census atlas of the UK*, Bristol: The Policy Press.

Harrison, M., Phillips, D., Chahal, K., Hunt, L. and Perry, J. (2005) *Housing, 'race' and community cohesion*, Coventry: Chartered Institute of Housing.

Home Office (2001) *Building cohesive communities: Report of the ministerial group on public order and community cohesion*, London: Home Office.

Home Office (2005) *Improving opportunity, strengthening society: The government's strategy to increase race equality and community cohesion*, London: Home Office.

Local Government Association (LGA) (2002) *Guidance on community cohesion*, London: LGA.

Massey, D. and Denton, N. (1989) 'Hyper-segregation in US metropolitan areas: Black and Hispanic segregation along five dimensions', *Demography*, vol 26, no 3, pp 373–93.

Musterd, S. (2003) Segregation and integration: A contested relationship, *Journal of Ethnic and Migration Studies* vol 29, no 4, pp 623–41.

Peach C. (1996) 'Good segregation, bad segregation', *Planning Perspectives*, vol 11, no 1, pp 1–20.

Phillips, D. (2006) 'Parallel lives? Challenging discourses of British Muslim self-segregation', *Environment and Planning D: Society and Space*, vol 24, no 1, pp 25–40.

Phillips, D., Davis, C. and Ratcliffe, P. (2007) 'British Asian narratives of urban space: Changing geographies of residence in multi-cultural Britain', *Transactions of the Institute of British Geographers*, vol 32, no 2, pp 217–34.

Robinson, D. (2005) 'The search for community cohesion: Key themes and dominant concepts of the public policy agenda', *Urban Studies*, vol 42, no 8, pp 1411–28.

Rose, G. (1990) 'Contested concepts of community: Imagining Poplar in the 1920s', *Journal of Historical Geography*, vol 16, no 4, pp 425–37.

Simpson, L. (2004) 'Statistics of racial segregation: Measures, evidence and policy', *Urban Studies*, vol 41, no 3, pp 661–81.

Simpson, L. (2007) 'Ghettos of the mind: The empirical behaviour of indices of segregation and diversity', *Journal of the Royal Statistical Society A*, vol 170, no 2, pp 405–24.

Simpson, L. and Gavalas, V. (2005) *Population dynamics within Rochdale and Oldham: Population, household and social change*, CCSR working paper, Manchester: University of Manchester.

Simpson, L., Phillips, D. and Ahmed, S. (2007) *Housing, race and community cohesion in Oldham and Rochdale*. Oldham: Oldham and Rochdale Housing Market Renewal Pathfinder.

Simpson, L., Gavalas, V. and Finney, N. (2008) 'Population dynamics in ethnically diverse towns: The long-term implications of immigration', *Urban Studies*, vol 45, no 1, pp 163–83.

Stacey, M. (1969) 'The myth of community studies', *British Journal of Sociology*, vol 20, no 20, pp 134–47.

Young, I. (1990) 'The ideal of community and the politics of difference', in L.J. Nicholson (ed) *Feminism/Postmodernism*, London: Routledge.

FIVE

Employment and disconnection: cultures of worklessness in neighbourhoods

Del Roy Fletcher

Introduction

The labour market is a key arena in which the cohesiveness of society is shaped. It is where the economic well-being of individuals and families is determined and their social values and relationship to society are, in part, moulded. It follows that long-term unemployment may have a disintegrative effect leading to economic marginalisation, poverty and social exclusion. Tackling unemployment and economic inactivity are integral to the UK government's strategy for increasing prosperity and reducing social exclusion: 'Work is the best route out of poverty. It strengthens independence and dignity. It builds family aspirations, fosters greater social inclusion and can improve individuals' health and well being' (Department for Work and Pensions (DWP), 2006, p 2).

UK policymakers have increasingly endorsed a 'workfare' agenda in relation to labour market policy, drawing heavily on the US model, emphasising individual responsibility in the quest for self-dependency rather than income maintenance. Welfare dependency and passivity are viewed as the primary cause of worklessness, which necessitates a compulsive strategy to enforce work habits. In the UK benefit recipients have, for example, more often been required to attend compulsory work-focused interviews as a condition of benefit receipt. This new regime places a strong emphasis on the work ethic, and citizenship rights are made conditional on a willingness to participate in paid employment.

The number of people in employment in the UK has risen steadily over recent years, so that by July 2006 there were a record 28.97 million in work, with an employment rate of 74.6% (Office for National Statistics (ONS), 2006). At the same time, the level of unemployment has fallen. In July 2006 the International Labour Organisation (ILO) unemployment rate was 5.5% and the Jobseeker's Allowance (JSA) claimant count stood at historically low levels (ONS, 2006). However, not all groups have benefited from recent improvements in the economy and labour market. Unemployment and economic inactivity (or 'worklessness') have become progressively concentrated within some households, groups and communities. The Social Exclusion Unit (SEU) (2004) identified 16,000 concentrations of worklessness in England at a census super output level and raised concerns about the attitudes and culture of people living in such communities:

> The most worrying aspect of this problem is the existence of unemployment affecting two or three generations in the same families and neighbourhoods, which means children and young people do not have role models with jobs. This can damage children's aspirations for education and work and their understanding of them. (SEU, 2004, p 36)

It is in this context that cultural explanations of unemployment have begun to flourish. The Working Neighbourhoods Pilot, launched in April 2004, sought to combat a 'culture of worklessness' in 12 selected localities across Britain by offering intensive support to help people move into and retain local jobs. The pilot programme was predicated on the view that: 'Rising concentrations of worklessness have led to the emergence of communities in which worklessness is no longer the exception, but the norm. Households that have experienced generations of unemployment often develop a cultural expectation of worklessness' (HM Treasury and DWP, 2003, p 76).

The current association of 'culture' with the attitudes and behaviour of marginalised groups owes much to the 'culture of poverty' debate in the US in the late 1960s, when Oscar Lewis (1968, cited in Dean and Taylor-Gooby, 1992) deployed cultural criteria to help explain the lack of social mobility among some of the poor, with cultural patterns (family structure, interpersonal relations, value systems, sense of community and spending patterns) inter-generationally transmitted to reinforce a recurring cycle of poverty. Conservative theorists and eugenicists emphasised a hereditary dimension to poverty and a pathology, not only of poor individuals, but also of poor families (Dean and Taylor-Gooby, 1992). In the UK, Keith Joseph delivered a number of speeches in the early 1970s in which he developed the idea of a 'cycle of deprivation' that was inter-generationally transmitted. During the 1980s US theorists such as Murray (1990) identified the existence of an 'underclass', a culturally distinct deprived minority that included both the delinquent and the dependant whose culture was seen as undermining social cohesion. Illegitimacy, violent crime and non-participation in the labour market were deemed to be key indicators of the 'underclass'. This stands in stark contrast to Lewis's original work, which maintained that the culture of poverty was characteristic of an inadequate stage of capitalist development and reflected a failure of capitalism, not the poor (Dean and Taylor-Gooby, 1992). This chapter examines the historical evidence for cultural explanations of worklessness through a case study of the Manor Estate in Sheffield. Several key dimensions of the contemporary worklessness problem are identified and contrasted with the situation on the estate in the 1930s.

The evolution of a Sheffield council estate

The Manor Estate is a particularly useful case study. First, it has been the focus of a number of regeneration and employment initiatives over the past 25 years, culminating in its designation as a Working Neighbourhoods Pilot. Second, it is a large estate and residents have a strong sense of local identity. This may be more conducive to the development of an estate 'culture'. Finally, a number of local source materials are available, which means that it is possible to gain an insight into life on the estate from the 1930s. It is my contention that a focus on a small community over such a long time horizon may be particularly illuminating, given the ahistorical nature of much contemporary unemployment and community cohesion policy development.

Sheffield City Corporation was keen to make use of the 1919 Housing and Town Planning Act's subsidies for state-provided housing to address the city's slum areas, where: 'Cobbled courtyards and dimly lit alleys were lined with row upon row of back-to-back houses: dirty, overcrowded, insanitary hovels' (Bean, 1981, p 5; see also Hey, 1998). The growth of the city's population, which was rising by approximately 5,000 individuals per year, and the marriage of ex-servicemen were also putting additional strain on the housing stock (Mercer, 1999). In September 1919 the city acquired land from the Duke of Norfolk for a new housing estate to be situated between two and three miles east of the city centre. The plan for a new working-class suburb was submitted by the city architect for approval in February 1921. The design incorporated principles of the 'Garden City' movement and was distinguished by its geometrical street patterns and tree-lined avenues (Mercer, 1999). Most of the planned homes had two or three bedrooms and were grouped in two, fours and sixes. All had generous gardens, and space for shops, schools and churches was also designated for the new suburb.

Construction began in 1923, and 3,600 homes had been completed by 1932, with the population rising to 15,952 people by the end of the decade (Mercer, 1999). The Manor Community Centre, the first to be built by a municipal authority in Britain, was opened in 1933. The new residents were largely young working-class families from the 19th-century alleys, courts and yards of the inner city and the industrial east end. The new low-density estate with its gardens, tree-lined avenues and purpose-built facilities was perched high on a hill surrounded by open country. A resident of the 1930s described moving from the slums of Attercliffe into 'our mansion on the circle' (George Bunting in the Manor Memories Group, 1990, p 5).

The post-war period saw the rise of home ownership and the motor car, which facilitated the removal of the more able residents to newer council and private developments, which Mercer (1999) notes as a partial explanation for the falling church membership on the estate during this period. The poor-quality construction of many homes on the Manor, which meant that they were expensive to heat, appears to have been a significant contributory factor to movement from the estate, along with high transport costs associated with living on the fringes of the city (Mercer, 1999).

This process was further intensified by the decline of Sheffield's traditional industries, coupled with reductions in council house building and the take-up of 'right to buy' in the 1980s. Pedler et al (1990) note that job losses averaged 1,000 per month in the four years to 1983; the steel industry alone shed 21,000 jobs in the city during this period. This prompted the *Morning Telegraph* newspaper to publish a series of articles exploring the impact on the estate, describing a community 'overwhelmed' and 'demoralised' by the scale and speed of job losses. A resident of 28 years was quoted as saying that: 'the emergence of mass unemployment over the last few years has been a major factor in the deterioration of the estate' (quoted in Holloway, 1983). Local youth and adult unemployment rates were 60% and 39% respectively (Holloway, 1983).

Housing allocation policies also had the unintentional effect of making the Manor an estate with a bad reputation, with tenants arriving in the area from necessity rather than choice (City of Sheffield Metropolitan District Council Department of Planning and Design, 1983). Many residents interviewed by Holloway in 1983 felt that the local authority was dumping problem families on the estate: 'If families with problem children come to Manor it is because the estate has the shortest waiting list in Sheffield' (Holloway, 1983, p 11). Some residents also drew attention to the growing problems of social cohesion within the estate in terms of the conflict between older residents and young people proud of their tough image. More recently, some of the worst dwellings have been demolished and new private and social housing has been built.

An historical analysis of employment and unemployment on the estate

The 2001 Census shows that the Manor ward has a predominantly White (over 95%) population. Table 5.1 indicates that most working neighbourhood pilot areas had economic activity rates around 20 percentage points lower than the national figure and unemployment rates up to three times higher. The Manor ward had less than half of its residents economically active and an unemployment rate in excess of three times the national average. Directly comparable data from previous historical periods is unfortunately not available.

The defining feature of most of these areas is the very high level of economic inactivity, especially as a result of sickness and disability; the

Table 5.1: Economic activity, 2001 (% of 16- to 74-year-olds)

Pilot area	Economically active	Employed	Unemployed	Student
Aston	54	38	13	3
Birkenhead	46	35	9	1
Castle	62	53	7	2
Hutchesontown	38	27	10	1
Lansbury	51	40	8	3
Manor	**48**	**37**	**10**	**1**
Monkchester	48	38	8	2
Northwood	41	30	10	2
Parkhead	39	30	7	2
Penderry	47	38	7	2
Regent	59	47	11	1
Thorntree	48	37	9	1
England and Wales	67	61	3	3
Scotland	65	58	4	3

Source: Census of Population (2001)

Manor ward had 15% of its residents in this category (see Table 5.2). The Manor ward is also notable for the fact that the economically inactive are just as likely to be retired as permanently sick or disabled.

Table 5.2: Economic inactivity, 2001 (% of 16- to 74-year-olds)

Pilot area	Econo- mically inactive	Retired	Looking after home and family	Perman- ently sick or disabled	Econo- mically inactive student	Other
Aston	46	9	9	12	7	9
Birkenhead	54	13	11	20	4	7
Castle	38	13	7	11	3	5
Hutchesontown	62	15	8	25	3	11
Lansbury	49	13	12	9	8	9
Manor	**52**	**14**	**12**	**15**	**4**	**7**
Monkchester	52	14	11	17	4	6
Northwood	59	10	14	19	6	9
Parkhead	61	16	10	22	3	11
Penderry	53	11	13	18	4	7
Regent	41	12	9	12	3	5
Thorntree	52	11	14	15	4	8
England and Wales	33	14	6	5	5	3
Scotland	35	14	6	7	4	4

Source: Census of Population (2001)

The next section presents a historical analysis of the worklessness problem focusing on four key themes:

- poor health
- low human capital
- low pay and in-work poverty
- undeclared work and criminal activity.

Poor health

There has been a great deal of recent discussion about the growth of sickness and disability as key causes of economic inactivity. People living in concentrations of worklessness are three times more likely to report that their general health is 'not good' compared with those resident in areas with the lowest rates (SEU, 2004). In the Manor ward 17% of residents aged 16 to 74 years are 'not in good health', compared to just 9% in England and Wales (Census of Population, 2001). A study by Jobcentre Plus (2003) found that many Manor residents claim Incapacity Benefit, Disability Benefit and Carer's Allowance and that mental health problems are a significant labour market barrier.

An earlier study found a high incidence of ill-health among residents, particularly chest complaints and respiratory disorders, and identified three contributory factors: the stress placed on families as a result of long-term unemployment, damp caused by the difficulties heating inadequate homes, and insufficient income to afford adequate clothing and nourishment (City of Sheffield Metropolitan District Council Department of Plannning and Design, 1983). The role played by the local authorities in concentrating individuals suffering from serious health problems on the estate is less well known. In the 1930s many tuberculosis suffers and those with other serious respiratory problems were directed to the area as a matter of policy: 'There were a lot of chest problems and they used to bring them higher up away from the works and industry' (Manor Memories Group, 1989, p 14).

The SEU (2004) suggests that drug and alcohol abuse is a key labour market barrier for many individuals in deprived areas. It notes that such communities have many residents with multiple disadvantages including drug misuse and physical and mental health problems. Jobcentre Plus (2003) also found that a drug culture existed on the Manor Estate. There are no historical references to drug misuse on the estate, although anecdotal evidence suggests that some young residents became hard-drug users during the early 1980s. The concern of policymakers with the adverse effects of alcohol on the morals and work ethic of the working class has a long history. At the local level these sentiments were reflected in the design of the Manor Estate. The corporation was, for example, careful to allot sites to various denominations to build churches, but banned the construction of licensed premises (Mercer, 1999); it was not until 1939 that the first public house was built. However, this policy had the unintended effect of stimulating the development of three very large working men's clubs along the main road linking the estate with the city centre.

Low human capital

The SEU (2004) found that people living in concentrations of worklessness were three times more likely to have no qualifications than people in areas with the lowest rates. Nearly two thirds (60%) of Manor ward residents aged between 16 and 74 years have no qualifications, compared to 29% in England and Wales (Census of Population, 2001). Similarly, Jobcentre Plus (2003) found a widespread perception among local people that education and training was not for them. The roots of this particular problem can be traced to the earliest days of the estate. Mercer (1999) shows that the city council were initially slow to respond to the demand for new school places; when new places were forthcoming some children were reported to have been reluctant to attend on a regular basis. Negative attitudes towards school and learning often persisted into adulthood. Mercer (1999) identifies a widespread aversion to 'book learning' among adult male residents of the Manor in the 1930s. Similarly, many residents were reported to be reluctant to attend night school as a means of getting a better job, and: 'Many turned their back on anything that resembled schooling and its implied authority' (Mercer, 1999, p 120).

Poverty meant that many families could not afford to let their children proceed to secondary education. School uniforms, books and travel were expensive and implied parents would keep children financially. Preference was often given to able boys as future breadwinners if family resources allowed. The *Manor and Woodthorpe Review* (1934a, p 17) acidly noted that: 'Many parents still regard the rearing of children as a good investment, on which they want to realise as soon as possible, and for this are anxious to see them starting work at an early age.' It went on: 'Even the shockingly low wages paid to adolescents in the northern towns are eagerly sought, for the smallest additional contribution to the family exchequer is very welcome.'

The legacy of a lack of engagement with education and training places many residents at a distinct disadvantage in the contemporary labour market. In particular, low human capital constrains the type of jobs that they can secure. The opportunities available to many will be low paid, short term, temporary or part time. Many jobs will be insecure and offer only a modest improvement in their financial circumstances. Breaking a benefit claim for a short period of work can lead to financial strains that are intolerable for those living in poverty.

Low pay and in-work poverty

The shift to a service-dominated economy over the past 30 years has generated new forms of employment-centred poverty. Sassen (1996) has shown that economic restructuring has polarised labour markets between 'knowledge- and information-intensive' and 'labour-intense and low-productivity' sectors. Lash and Urry (1994) argue that the British economy has been a prodigious creator of 'junk jobs' in occupations such as cleaning, fast food and bar work. Over half (52%) of British children in poverty live in a household where one adult is in paid work (cited by Macnicol in Smith [2005]). It is in this context that UK policymakers have introduced the national minimum wage and tax and benefit changes intended to 'make work pay'. The SEU (2004) shows that those resident in concentrations of worklessness tend to be over-represented in low-paying employment sectors. Of written consultation responses to the SEU report, 32% also mentioned the quality of jobs (mainly the level of pay and conditions as well as the skills required) as a cause of high rates of worklessness. It is, perhaps, surprising then that the local Working Neighbourhoods Pilot design document for the Manor failed to mention job quality. It does, however, find that debt is a key labour market barrier for many (Jobcentre Plus, 2003).

During the 1980s the Manor was identified as one of the city's worst areas of poverty (City of Sheffield Metropolitan District Council Department of Planning and Design, 1983). One report found that the number of households receiving welfare benefits had reached 60% and was increasing rapidly (City of Sheffield Metropolitan District Council Department of Planning and Design, 1983). Moreover, it also suggested that high unemployment was forcing residents to take poorly paid work. The result was that poverty was endemic and not confined to the unemployed.

The parallels with the situation in the 1930s depression are striking. High unemployment and poverty were also defining features of the Manor at this time. Mercer (1999) characterises life on the estate in the 1930s as an 'unremitting struggle', with many residents unable to afford basic foodstuffs such as meat, dairy produce and fresh fruit. Some local children had no footwear. A special shop on Staniforth Road provided shoes that were stamped so parents would not 'pawn' them for money (interview with Mr Dolby, Manor Memories Group, 1990, p 8). The *Manor and Woodthorpe Review* (1934b, 1934c, 1935) also carried several readers' letters complaining that the journal did not reflect the concerns of residents: 'One feels after reading it [the

Manor and Woodthorpe Review] that there is nothing wrong on this estate, but it is simply a modern utopia' (*Manor and Woodthorpe Review*, 1934c, p 77). Furthermore, poverty reached beyond the large ranks of the unemployed to embrace many residents who were in work. In particular, a combination of short-time working and lay-offs meant that many believed that they were only half a crown better off working than on the dole (Mercer, 1999).

Undeclared work and criminal activity

The notion of a culture of worklessness suggests that the problem cannot be understood simply in terms of individual attributes and barriers. Rather it emphasises broader family and community-level influences that conflict with 'mainstream' social values. It may be, for example, that the persistence of worklessness across several generations has created a situation where undeclared work and criminal activity are viewed as acceptable ways of making ends meet. It is in this context that the SEU (2004) suggests that 'cash-in-hand' or undeclared work when combined with benefits can act as a disincentive to leaving welfare for regular employment.

Previous research has suggested that a lack of opportunities in the formal labour market can lead to participation in the informal economy. Leonard's (1998) research in Belfast found that 49% of unemployed men and 27% of economically inactive women interviewed on the Newbury Estate had some type of informal work. Smith (2005) also discovered widespread participation in undeclared employment among residents of the St Helier Estate in London. However, such work was usually intermittent and short term and was more commonly used to supplement formal wages rather than benefits. MacDonald's (1994) study of benefit fraud ('fiddly jobs') in Cleveland has identified the importance of social networks in determining access to such opportunities. He concluded that those 'who did not live a public life on the streets and in the pubs of particular estates, but instead lived a life of isolation, boredom and home-centred tedium became excluded from avenues into fiddly work' (MacDonald, 1994, p 525).

Jobcentre Plus (2003) suggested that the informal economy has been a long-term feature of the Manor Estate. There are, however, no historical references to its existence. This may simply reflect a gap in the historical record. Alternatively, it might indicate that the informal economy has recently flourished in response to the decline of traditional work. This is consistent with the 'marginality thesis' that argues that undeclared work is undertaken primarily for profit and is concentrated in deprived communities. Williams (2004) has, however, found that higher-income populations not only used and supplied undeclared work to a greater extent than lower-income populations but also received a disproportionate share of the income from it. He concluded that the vast majority of undeclared work was not conducted for profit but was likened to a 'moral economy' of paid favours between friends, kin and neighbours.

The SEU (2004) suggests that criminal activities can have a damaging effect on local economies by diverting people from legal work., The Jobcentre Plus (2003) study of the Manor found that crime and the 'drug gang culture' thrives, and it describes the 'negative hold' that a small number of families have on the community. Criminal activity and gang culture is not new, however; rather it has been a recurrent feature of the area. In the 1980s crime and anti-social behaviour on the Manor received more comment that any other area covered by a council grassroots survey (City of Sheffield Metropolitan District Council Department of Planning and Design, 1983). In the 1930s, gangs of juveniles were breaking and entering local shops and homes (Mercer, 1999); in the 1920s, gang warfare in the Park District resulted in five years of shootings and knifings that left one man dead, two others hanged for murder and Sheffield being dubbed Britain's 'Little Chicago' (Bean, 1981).

Behavioural explanations of economic marginality have often focused on the criminal behaviour of particular 'culturally deprived' social groups (Auletta, 1982; Murray, 1990). Auletta (1982) estimated that nine million Americans were unable to overcome their poverty. His taxonomy included both the dependant in the guise of the 'passive poor' and the delinquent, including 'hostile street criminals' and 'hustlers' who earned their livelihood in the underground economy. Similarly, Murray (1990) argued that the criminal is the classic member of the 'underclass'. The roots of the earlier period of gang warfare in Sheffield are instructive to these debates.

The mass unemployment characterising Sheffield in the 1920s meant that street bookmakers flourished. Huge profits were made on a daily basis. Gambling was not limited to horse racing: pitch and toss, where three coins were placed on the end of the first two fingers and tossed and bets placed on the outcome, was very popular. Poverty and desperation rather than cultural values were at the root of the phenomenon: 'To the working classes, without jobs, without prospects, and with very little money, gambling provided perhaps the last vestige of hope' (Bean, 1981, p 6).

The principal tossing rings in Sheffield were at Wadsley, Five Arches, Tinsley and Sky Edge, and were run on strict business lines (Bean, 1981). The bosses or 'tollers' employed a small army of men to ensure that business was not disrupted by police raids. The deployment of the army to help combat street bookmaking in Sheffield provides a dramatic indication of the scale of the problem. Bean concludes that:

> Gang warfare in Sheffield began as a result of violent competition for the exclusive and lucrative rights to the Sky Edge tossing ring. The chief protagonists were men known for their criminal behaviour and disinclination towards honest toil, men whose company the law abiding citizens eschewed – mainly out of fear. (Bean, 1981, p 133)

Building local solutions to local problems?

The targeting of small defined areas and a focus on local effects is a defining feature of the government's approach to tackling unemployment and economic inactivity. Yet the historical evidence shows that the underlying causes comprise a complex mixture of local and predominantly national factors. In terms of the latter, the fortunes of the Manor have always been closely tied to the national economy. The post-war economic boom meant that full employment prevailed, with the result that the estate ceased to be a focus for the attention of policymakers for three decades. The link between macro-economic trends and the prevalence of social problems has long been known. In the US, Kershaw (1970, cited in Alcock, 2005) found that after five years of the programme's existence most poor people had not heard about the 'War on Poverty' and in terms of the move from welfare to work the investments made in the Vietnam War had been more effective. In the UK Stedman-Jones concluded that: 'Middle class anxiety about the position of casual labour in London ... disappeared in the First World War. All "surplus" labour was absorbed by the needs of the wartime economy. The workhouses emptied and the casual wards shut down' (1971, p 336).

Similarly, the contemporary pattern of worklessness in Britain primarily reflects 'the loss of jobs in manufacturing and mining, which has not only been very large overall, but has also clearly been concentrated in the cities and coalfields' (Webster, 2000, p 124). In Sheffield the contraction of the steel, coal and engineering industries has effectively removed the economic *raison d'être* of the Manor Estate. Personal recollections are full of references to once-famous steel and engineering companies such as English Steel, Firth Browns, Davy United, Hadfields, Brown Bayleys, Vickers and Shardlows (Manor Memories Group, 1989). Most men were manual wage earners; salaried workers were rare. Women, on the other hand, were expected to leave formal employment on marriage to become homemakers (Mercer, 1999).

The class position of residents made them particularly vulnerable to economic change. Gallie (1994) notes that long-term unemployment disproportionately affects the manual working class and, in particular, non-skilled manual workers. These are precisely the groups that the Manor Estate was built to accommodate. In recent years new job opportunities have arisen, but these have mainly been in the service sector and have not been on the same scale as the earlier manufacturing work. Increasingly, it is low-level service jobs that present the most accessible route out of unemployment for poorly educated men. However, such employment is unattractive to male residents because of low wages and the nature of the work. Hogarth and Wilson (2001) have also shown that the demand for physical and technical skills has been superseded by the requirement for interpersonal and customer-handling skills.

At the same time, broad social processes have concentrated the most vulnerable on the Manor Estate. Brennan et al (2000) have highlighted the interaction between the provision of low-cost, often poor-quality housing and the characteristics of particular groups of residents who are among the least competitive in the labour market. This process began in the 1930s with the rise of home ownership and the motor car. Reductions in council house building and the take-up of 'right to buy', which decimated council portfolios, intensified the residualisation process in the 1980s. The Manor had been devised for the two-generation family with father in full-time work and mother at home with the children. However, since the early 1980s it has increasingly been 'called upon to accommodate the very thing that it had been devised to avoid: idle populations dependent on welfare, with high concentrations of unsupported youth and children' (Ravetz, 2001, p 194).

The tough reputation of the estate, which has regularly been featured in the tabloid press and has just been declared a 'no-go zone' by the RAC, is an important area effect. The indications are that it may underpin employer discrimination, which further constrains the ability of some residents to find employment. Similarly, the enduring sexual division of labour characterising work and family life in the area has depressed female labour market participation rates. Stereotypical expectations are also likely to mean that partners are less willing to share domestic responsibilities. This restricts the amount of time that women can dedicate to paid employment and determines the type of work that they are able to undertake. The experience of long-term unemployment may have reinforced these traditional roles (Gallie, 2004).

Nevertheless, policymakers should not place undue emphasis on area-based approaches. First, deprived communities are not homogeneous but are comprised of a range of groups with different attributes and needs. Second, many people living in the pilot areas are not unemployed or economically inactive, and most of those without work live outside such areas. Third, the underlying causes are primarily of a structural nature and are, therefore, external to the local communities where the effects are most acute. This means that area-based approaches, whatever their achievements, are incapable of challenging the root causes of worklessness. Moreover, in focusing on cultural explanations of unemployment they may contribute to the pathologisation of such problems.

Combating a poverty of aspirations?

The prime ministerial foreword to the SEU (2004) report noted that: 'There is a danger that children grow up in families and neighbourhoods with little contact with the world of work – detached from the opportunities and aspirations of most people.' There are two main theses about the influence of attitudes and behaviour on labour market marginality (Gallie, 1994). The 'conservative view' attributes long-term unemployment to personal characteristics and work attitudes. Family breakdown or being brought up in a deprived community may mean that individuals fail to assimilate a conventional work ethic in their formative years. Behavioural instability may also make it difficult for some individuals to retain employment. This thesis is accompanied by a pessimistic attitude towards the role of public policy. Welfare assistance may, for example, be counter-productive because it contributes to a 'dependency culture'.

This chapter has provided little support for such views. Residents of the Manor Estate have exhibited a strong work ethic rooted in manual employment. Negative attitudes towards schooling have, in part, reflected the desire of many parents to get their children into paid work at the earliest opportunity. However, the decline of traditional industries has broken the transmission of jobs and skills from father to son. The lack of appropriate openings in the contemporary labour market has led to some to participate in the informal economy and criminal activities. Drug gangs now thrive on the estate. Yet it is possible to draw parallels with an earlier period. The mass unemployment of the 1920s led to a notorious period of gang warfare in the Park area as rivals fought for control of the huge profits to be gained from street bookmaking. This did not, however, prevent the community from realising full employment when the national economic climate improved in the post-war period.

The 'radical view' sees the unemployed as victims of circumstances. Myrdal (1963, cited in Gans, 1996) was the first to use the term 'underclass', but saw its roots in structural changes that would force increasing numbers to the margins of the labour force. The growth of dual or segmented labour markets suggested by Giddens (1973, cited in Gallie, 1994) is another example. In the latter, the exclusion of secondary workers from work and their dependence on state support combine to generate a consciousness that is markedly different from the rest of the working class. The decline of Sheffield's traditional industries has locked male manual workers into a position of disadvantage in the labour market. However, evidence that purports to show a lower cultural commitment to work among such groups remains elusive (Gallie, 2004). Similarly, Dean and Taylor-Gooby (1992) found that the long-term unemployed are not separated culturally from the rest of society but follow a value orientation in which material dependency upon the wage relation is seen as natural to personal identity.

Conclusion

This chapter has shown that concerns about the cultural patterns of residents and declining social cohesion are nothing new but have been reflected in recurring cultural collisions between professionals and local residents over much of the 20th century. During the 1930s, for example, many residents refused to take part in the educational activities planned for them in the Manor Community Centre. Furthermore, the activities chosen were not always what professionals hoped; the warden of the community centre promptly removed the billiard table and turned the recreation room into a reading and debating room. This policy led to a series of expulsions and a centre that, although a 'social and cultural outpost in a wilderness of ignorance', was empty (Ravetz, 2001, p 142).

In April 1934 the *Manor and Woodthorpe Review* was launched as a means of developing the cultural and educational life of the area. A letter printed in the second issue exemplifies the views of those behind the enterprise. 'Your provocative articles should surely lead to a welcome revival in the art of discussion and debate, and shake some people out of the deadly lethargy which has stolen across them and made them seek nothing more enlightening than the pictures and the sex-ridden dope of the baser of the newspapers' (*Manor and Woodthorpe Review*, 1934a, p 24). The pictures and 'sex-ridden dope' were apparently more appealing since the *Review* folded in little over a year. A civilising mission was again evident, with features such as 'Philosophic philanderings' and 'Salt for the socialist egg'. A reader tellingly complained: 'Why has there been no article dealing with the cause of high rents, and the possibility of their reduction? Why not an article as to the advantage or otherwise of moving families further away from the centre of the city?' (*Manor and Woodthorpe Review*, 1934b, p 37).

During the 1980s the Manor Employment Project was established to stimulate the creation of community businesses. From the outset some viewed it as 'the brainchild of middle-class do-gooders' (Pedler et al, 1990, p 203). A guiding principle was the belief that local women were central to the creation of alternatives to 'men's work'. However, project staff were continually frustrated by an enduring sexual division of labour (Pedler et al, 1990). Furthermore, it appears to have come as a nasty surprise when it was discovered that local residents wanted jobs rather than cooperatives and resident businesses.

However, the significance of the cultural explanations is that they cast attitudes and behaviour of marginalised groups – rather than a lack of access to appropriate jobs – as the underlying problem. This legitimises the supply-side policies currently favoured by UK policymakers while deflecting attention away from the structural causes of poverty and worklessness that encompass the demand side of the labour market. The lack of attention paid by UK policymakers to demand-side factors has been highlighted by many commentators (see, for example, Turok and Edge, 1999; Sunley et al, 2001). The low human capital characterising many residents means that the available opportunities are invariably insecure and offer only a modest improvement in financial circumstances. Furlong and Cartmel (2004) have shown that the main problem faced by vulnerable young men in deprived communities is not in finding work, but in keeping it. Many are caught in a cycle of unemployment and casual work that offers few opportunities for training and advancement.

The failure of many residents in communities like the Manor to benefit from improvements in the economy partly reflects the precarious nature of employment that a deregulated labour market is creating. Yet a key purpose of UK welfare reform is to expand the labour supply to meet this requirement. It is in this context that deprived communities have been problematised. The deployment of cultural explanations of unemployment in recent years should be viewed in this context. Moreover, focusing on the alleged deficient work ethic of particular communities provides justifications for further erosions of the British welfare state, arguably a key pillar of national cohesion during the 20th century, and provides the ground for a more punitive approach to poverty and worklessness.

There are echoes of early 20th-century views of slum dwellers as a morally defective race apart. In the 1930s at the Conference of New Estates Community Committee, Dr Scott-Wilkinson drew attention to an important 'biological principle' that could be applied to the new council estates. 'Whenever large numbers of similar individuals are grouped and segregated from those of a different type they are bound to show retrogressive development' (quoted in *Manor and Woodthorpe Review*, 1934a, p 17). The attendant danger is that in failing to learn from the past the growing ascendancy of cultural explanations of unemployment may legitimise an increasingly punitive policy response. It is, perhaps, appropriate that a local resident has the last word: 'The attitude is that Manor is a place where problem families live, therefore if you live on the estate you are regarded as a problem' (City of Sheffield Metropolitan District Council Department of Planning and Design, 1983).

References

Alcock, P. (2005) 'Maximum feasible understanding: Lessons from previous wars on poverty', *Social Policy and Society*, vol 4, no 3, pp 321–9.

Auletta, K. (1982) *The underclass*, New York: Random House.

Bean, J.P. (1981) *The Sheffield gang wars*, Sheffield: D&D Publications.

Brennan, A., Rhodes, J. and Tyler, P. (2000) 'The nature of local area social exclusion and the role of the labour market', *Oxford Review of Economic Policy*, vol 16, no 1, pp 129–46.

Census of Population (2001) (www.neighbourhood.statistics.gov.uk).

City of Sheffield Metropolitan District Council Department of Planning and Design (1983) *Areas of poverty in Sheffield: A report to the Urban Strategy Panel*, 13 September, Sheffield: City of Sheffield Metropolitan District Council.

Dean, H. and Taylor-Gooby, P. (1992) *Dependency culture: The explosion of a myth*, London: Harvester Wheatsheaf.

Department for Work and Pensions (DWP) (2006) *A new deal for welfare: Empowering people to work*, Cm 6730, London: DWP.

Furlong, A. and Cartmel, F. (2004) *Vulnerable young men in fragile labour markets: Employment, unemployment and the search for long-term security*, York: York Publishing Services Ltd.

Gallie, D. (1994) 'Are the long-term unemployed an underclass? Some evidence from the Social and Economic Life Initiative', *Sociology*, vol 28, no 3, pp 737–57.

Gallie, D. (ed) (2004) *Resisting marginalisation: Unemployment experience and social policy in the European Union*, Oxford: Oxford University Press.

Gans, H. (1996) 'From underclass to undercaste: Some observations about the future of the post-industrial economy and its major victims', in E. Mingione (ed) *Urban poverty and the underclass*, Oxford: Blackwell.

Hey, D. (1998) *A history of Sheffield*, Lancaster: Carnegie Publishing.

HM Treasury and Department for Work and Pensions (2003) *Full employment in every region*, London: Stationery Office.

Hogarth, T. and Wilson, B. (2001) *Employers' skill survey: Skills, local areas and unemployment*, London: Department for Education and Employment.

Holloway, M. (1983) 'Portrait of the Manor', *Sheffield Morning Telegraph*, 12 September.

Jobcentre Plus (2003) *Sheffield District local worklessness pilot approach document*, Sheffield: Jobcentre Plus.

Lash, S. and Urry, J. (1994) *Economies of signs and space*, London: Sage.

Leonard, M. (1998) 'The long-term unemployed, informal economic inactivity and the underclass in Belfast: Rejecting or reinstating the work ethic?', *International Journal of Urban and Regional Research*, vol 22, no 1, pp 42–59.

MacDonald, R. (1994) 'Fiddly jobs, undeclared working and the something for nothing society', *Work, Employment and Society*, vol 8, no 4, pp 507–30.

Manor Memories Group (1989) *Manor memories*, no 1, July, Sheffield: Manor Memories Group.

Manor Memories Group (1990) *Manor memories*, no 2, July, Sheffield: Manor Memories Group.

Manor and Woodthorpe Review (1934a) '"The way of the world": Comments on current events', *Manor and Woodthorpe Review, the Organ of the Manor Community Association*, vol 1, no 2, May.

Manor and Woodthorpe Review (1934b) 'Readers' letters', *Manor and Woodthorpe Review, the Organ of the Manor Community Association*, vol 1, no 4, July.

Manor and Woodthorpe Review (1934c) 'Readers' letters', *Manor and Woodthorpe Review, the Organ of the Manor Community Association*, vol 1, no 9, December.

Manor and Woodthorpe Review (1935) 'Readers' letters', *Manor and Woodthorpe Review, the Organ of the Manor Community Association*, vol 2, no 2, June.

Mercer, M. (1999) *A portrait of the Manor in the 1930s: The evolution of a council estate*, Sheffield: Mediac.

Murray, C.A. (ed) (1990) *The emerging British underclass*, London: Institute of Economic Affairs.

Office for National Statistics (ONS) (2006) 'Labour market statistics' (www.statistics.gov.uk).

Pedler, M., Banfield, P., Boraston, I., Gill, J. and Shipton, J. (1990) *The Community Development Initiative: A story of the Manor Employment Project in Sheffield*, Aldershot: Avebury.

Ravetz, A. (2001) *Council housing and culture. The history of a social experiment*, London: Routledge.

Sassen, S. (1996) 'Service employment regimes and the new inequality', in E. Mingione (ed) *Urban poverty and the underclass*, Oxford: Blackwell.

Smith, D.M. (2005) *On the margins of inclusion: Changing labour markets and social exclusion in London*, Bristol: The Policy Press.

Social Exclusion Unit (SEU) (2004) *Jobs and enterprise in deprived areas*, London: Office of the Deputy Prime Minister.

Stedman-Jones, G. (1971) *Outcast London: A study in the relationship between the classes in Victorian society*, Oxford: Oxford University Press.

Sunley, P., Martin, R. and Nativel, C. (2001) 'Mapping the New Deal: Local disparities in the performance of welfare-to-work', *Transactions of British Geographers*, vol 26, no 4, pp 484–512.

Turok, I. and Edge, N. (1999) *The jobs gap in Britain's cities: Employment loss and labour market consequences*, Bristol: The Policy Press.

Webster, D. (2000) 'The geographical concentration of labour market disadvantage', *Oxford Review of Economic Policy*, vol 16, no 1, pp 114–28.

Williams, C. (2004) 'Beyond deterrence: Rethinking the UK public policy approach towards undeclared work', *Public Policy and Administration*, vol 19, no 1, pp 15–30.

SIX

Beyond 'social glue'? 'Faith' and community cohesion

Robert Furbey

Introduction

Religion has been conspicuous in the recent development of social and community cohesion discourse in the UK and other nation states. Religion is seen simultaneously as problem and solution, a cause of social division and bloody conflict, but also a resource in building civic 'partnership', inclusive local governance, 'strong communities' and a vibrant civil society. This public prominence of 'faith' and 'faith communities' is a relatively recent development, a cause, variously, for surprise, dismay, celebration and often for febrile debate.

Secularisation, the draining of social significance from religious thinking, practice and institutions (Wilson, 1966), had been regarded as irreversible and ultimately universal. A defining feature of modernity in the West has been the ascription of religion to the private realm and to issues of personal religious practice and spirituality, distinct from the public, secular, sphere of the state and politics. In England, despite the established status of the Church of England, this division has been particularly pronounced. Academic marginalisation has also been evident, with religion often reduced to an epiphenomenon, a surface manifestation beneath which the 'real' causes of human development and conflict (specified in terms of such concepts as ethnicity, class and gender) can be uncovered (McTernan, 2003). Relatively little public research funding in the UK has been assigned to religion, while social policy debate in the decades after 1945 was preoccupied by the scope and delivery of state-funded welfare, with religious organisations accorded a subordinate role.

The secularisation thesis continues to draw strength from the sharp decline in participation at formal worship in the main UK Christian denominations (see, for example, Brierley, 2000; Bruce, 2002). But other commentators point to the persistence, and indeed revival, of religion across the globe, with 'only secular Western Europe and Australasia … appear[ing] to be conforming to the demise of the public deity so confidently pronounced by the founding fathers of modern social science' (Ruthven, 2004, p 196). Parekh goes further, arguing that 'the kind of inexorable and comprehensive secularisation predicted and hoped for by secular writers has not occurred even in advanced western societies' (2006, p 323).

Moreover, although it remains a personal matter for many, religion also refuses to remain confined to the private realm. Many Christians in the UK act in the 'public square', giving contemporary expression to longstanding social and political engagement, motivated by religious belief. Furthermore, the western distinction between public and private is liable to be less firmly drawn by the growing numbers of people of non-Christian religion in the UK:

> [Although] there was always recognition within Muslim societies of distinction between the public and private leading to a *de facto* division of powers, … the Divine Spirit touches all of man's actions whether this worldly or other worldly – in fact God is the Guide in all affairs [and] Muslim societies saw a fusion of religious, political, economic and social life. (Hussain, 2004, pp 92–3)

Much of this global religious resurgence is associated with separation and conflict, reflecting a defensive reaction to the uncertainties and risks of a globalised and 'liquid' world (Sennett, 1998; Bauman, 2004). The UK government's community cohesion agenda has developed in a context punctuated by the attacks on New York and Washington in 2001, the London bombings of July 2005 and subsequent attempted bombings in UK cities. Perhaps most immediately significant in the development of UK community cohesion policies were the disturbances in northern British cities and towns in 2001. Here religion was implicated, together with ethnicity and social class, in socio-spatial segregation and the development of what the influential Cantle Report termed 'parallel lives' (Community Cohesion Independent Review Team, 2001). Yet, despite these negative associations, the UK government has emphasised the positive social impact of religion.

This chapter explores policy assumptions about faith and social cohesion. The first section explores the officially prescribed role of faith as 'social glue', and documents the government's support for the social engagement of 'faith', followed by an assessment of the contribution of religious organisations, communities and their members to social cohesion on the government's terms. The chapter then provides a critical account of the complexity of 'religion' and 'faith' and their capacity to present an independent challenge to the state. The concluding section draws on empirical research to assess the potential of faith communities and organisations to question the official definition of 'social glue' and to move beyond it, working with others in a freer civil sphere marked by cross-boundary association, deliberation and empowered citizenship.

Faith's prescribed role

For centuries, the Church of England was both an instrument of social care and social control, reaching down into every locality. Churches and religious bodies were, after the family, the major source of welfare support. Christian social thought, campaigning and philanthropic action (Nonconformist and Catholic as well as Anglican) have been important in shaping social policy and practice (Farnell et al, 1994). Even at the high point of secular welfarism in the decades after 1945, this religious influence persisted through the legacy of figures such as R.H. Tawney and Archbishop William Temple.

Nevertheless, the post-1945 welfare state was embraced, popularly as well as officially, as 'an effective guardian of the common good [that] should be the principal provider of welfare' (Forrester, 1985, p 14), reducing the role in public policy of religious and indeed other voluntary organisations. It is only in the last 15 years that 'faith' appears to have 'come in from the cold'.

The recent governmental 'turn to faith' in the UK pre-dates the advent of New Labour. The Inner Cities Religious Council (ICRC) was established in 1992 during the Major Conservative administration. Since 1997 the Labour government has been consistent in enagaging with 'faith communities', retaining the ICRC as a forum where faith representatives 'can work together on urban renewal and social exclusion' (Department of the Environment, Transport and the Regions (DETR), 2001, p 1). In 1997, a report by the DETR made a positive case for faith community involvement in urban regeneration:

> They can help regeneration partnerships to understand the needs and concerns of people living in particular areas, or groups of people with particular needs ... In terms of their active membership, churches, mosques, temples, synagogues and gurdwaras are often among the most substantial

> community-based organisations within an area. They have
> as much right to contribute to discussions concerning
> regeneration as residents' or tenants' organisations. (DETR,
> 1997, p 149)

In the wake of the 2001 urban disturbances and 9/11 attacks,
government partnership with faith communities was explicitly linked
to community cohesion and became increasingly consolidated within
the Home Office and its Cohesion and Faiths Unit within the Race,
Cohesion and Faiths Directorate. In April 2006 the government
combined the ICRC and the Home Office's Working Together Steering
Group in a new Faith Communities Consultative Council (FCCC).
The council is a non-statutory body, including representatives of major
world faiths, which:

> aims to provide a national forum, chiefly concerned with
> issues related to cohesion, integration, the development of
> sustainable communities, neighbourhood renewal, and social
> inclusion. [It also has] general oversight on engagement
> between central government and faith communities [and has
> the overarching aim of] giving faith communities a strong
> role and clear voice in improving cohesion, regeneration and
> renewal in local communities. (www.communities.gov.uk/
> communities/racecohesionfaith/faith/faithcommunities/
> faithcommunitiesconsultative/)

The place of faith in public policy and cohesion strategies has been
defended at regular intervals by senior politicians and key official
documents. Tony Blair gave his strong endorsement early in his
premiership: 'Our major faith traditions – all of them more historic and
deeply rooted than any political party or ideology – play a fundamental
role in supporting and progagating values which bind us together as
a nation' (Blair, 2001).

In 2002 the Local Government Association (LGA) collaborated with
the Home Office and the government-supported Inter Faith Network
to produce a guidance manual for local councils working with faith
groups, commending the latter as sources of community cohesion (LGA,
2002). In 2005 an interim report on the third sector included a positive
assessment of the potential of faith communities in building networks
and trust within civil society (Office of the Deputy Prime Minister
(ODPM)/Home Office, 2005). Soon afterwards, faith communities were
identified in a local government White Paper as having an important part

to play in achieving 'strong and prosperous communities' (Department for Communities and Local Government (DCLG), 2006, p 54).

However, the overall tone of these policy documents is instrumental. Faith communities are groups to be harnessed in order to address government objectives. Moreover, religion is seen in essentially functional and consensual terms: as a social glue to be pulled out of the toolkit to bind community and society. Before critiquing this simplistic view, which neglects the complexity and independence of religion, the following section explores the contribution of faith in the government's own terms.

Contributions of faith

The 2001 Census of Great Britain included a question asking people: 'What is your religion?'. People assigning themselves to the category of 'Christian' constituted a large majority (71.82%), while the non-Christian religious population constituted 5.56%. The largest groups within the latter were Muslim (2.78%), Hindu (0.98%), Sikh (0.59%), Jewish (0.47%) and Buddhist (0.26%) (Office for National Statistics (ONS), 2004). People stating 'no religion' constituted 15.05% and 7.76% did not enter any response. However, these broad categories can mask a complex 'range of diversities' and 'create an unhelpful abstraction that is not adequate to historical reality' (ODPM, 2006, pp 8–9). Moreover, the census question sheds little light on the significance that people attribute to religion in their lives and the extent to which it influences their personal and social practice. When the European Values Survey asked respondents about the importance of religion in their life only 12.6% of respondents in Great Britain said 'very important' and 24.8% said 'quite important', while 33% said 'not important' and 29.7% said 'not important at all' (Halman, 2001, p 33, cited in ODPM, 2006, p 7).

This gap between affiliation and the significance that people attach to religion varies across the major faith traditions. The fourth Policy Studies Institute (PSI) survey found that 95% of Muslims, 89% of Hindus and 86% of Sikhs regarded religion as 'very' or 'fairly' important in their lives. The comparable figures for white members of the Church of England and white Roman Catholics were 46% and 69% respectively (Modood, 1997, p 301, cited in ODPM, 2006, p 7).

When assessing the contribution of 'faith communities' and 'people of faith' to social cohesion and its perceived component elements, this division between passive affiliation and positive commitment is underlined. Thus, the Home Office Citizenship Survey of 2001 found that religious affiliation made little difference to levels of informal and formal volunteering (Home Office, 2001). The Citizenship Survey of 2005 found a similar pattern in relation to participation in civic activities and charitable giving (DCLG, 2005). However, volunteering and civic participation were, in general, above the national average among people claiming to practise a religion, as shown in Tables 6.1 and 6.2.

Table 6.1: Formal volunteering in 12 months before interview, by whether respondent currently practises a religion within ethnic group (%)

Ethnic group	Percentage of people who have engaged in formal volunteering
White	
Practises a religion	58
Others	41
Asian	
Practises a religion	36
Others	34
Black	
Practises a religion	51
Others	34

Source: National Council for Voluntary Organisations (NCVO) (2007), drawing on the Citizenship Survey of 2005 (DCLG, 2005)

Table 6.2: Participation in civic activities, by whether respondent practises a religion within ethnic group (%)

Ethnic group	Percentage of people who have participated in civic activity (civic activism, civic consultation or civic participation)		
	Civic activism	Civic consultation	Civic participation
White			
Practises a religion	13	25	45
Others	8	9	37
Asian			
Practises a religion	8	16	27
Others	8	18	29
Black			
Practises a religion	13	22	29
Others	9	18	29

Source: NCVO (2007), drawing on the Citizenship Survey of 2005 (DCLG, 2005)

A similar pattern emerges in the context of charitable giving. Religious affiliation correlates positively with giving, but the active practice of religion is associated with a further increase in levels of donation (DCLG, 2005). These data require further exploration. There is some unevenness between groups and in the forms in which 'contributions of faith' are made. Variations between religions and broad ethnic groupings are likely to reflect differences and inequalities in material, human and social capital; religious and cultural histories; and diversity in theology and tradition. Overall, however, religious commitment is associated with above-average levels of volunteering, civic activity and financial giving that address issues of social and community cohesion.

In relation to the role of collective activity through faith organisations, it was estimated that there were over 54,000 places of worship in the UK in 2005 (Christian Research, 2005). In addition, there are many and diverse organisations that are prompted and shaped by faith but not necessarily engaged in explicitly 'religious' activity. In August 2006 over 23,000 organisations stated in their returns to the Charity Commission that they engaged in religious activity. Many more organisations do not classify themselves formally as religious even though they are based on religious principles. Furthermore, faith community members engage in a multitude of social activities on varying scales that are not found on official registers. The National Council for Voluntary Organisations concluded that: 'the institutional manifestations of faith are embedded in society, in the fabric of the voluntary and community sector' (NCVO, 2007, p 16). In terms of social cohesion, however, much depends on what these faith communities and organisations actually do. There can be negative social, and indeed 'spiritual', capital that, in extremity, may ultimately be expressed in terrorism and murder.

An accumulation of recent research evidence indicates that many of the activities undertaken by faith groups may reasonably be seen as contributing implicitly to social and community cohesion. One study, notable for its scale and scope, was made in North-West England (Northwest Development Agency, 2003). This research surveyed over 2,300 faith groups and organisations, encompassing nine religions (and including nine Christian traditions). The researchers found over 5,000 social projects, involving over 45,000 volunteers across the region. These initiatives addressed diverse issues, including homelessness, asylum, racism, crime, drug and alcohol abuse, health, skills development, art, music and the environment. Studies in other regions and in specific cities have produced similar findings (see, for example, Yorkshire Churches, 2002; Cairns et al, 2005; Lovatt et al, 2005).

This research confirms the significance of individual action by faith group members and the provision by faith communities and organisations of charitable local social care and welfare. However, a closer reading of this research also suggests engagement at a more structural level. Thus, a study commissioned by the Church of Scotland concluded that '[Church of Scotland] congregations make important contributions to the *institutional infrastructure* and social cohesion of many Scottish communities' (Flint and Kearns, 2004, p 18, emphasis added). This prompts an assessment of the contribution, present and potential, of faith groups in a wider official project of civic renewal, working explicitly across boundaries to achieve community cohesion as distinct from 'parallel' social cohesion. Research for the Home Office (Lowndes and Chapman, 2005) and studies funded by the Joseph Rowntree Foundation (Farnell et al, 2003; Furbey et al, 2006) found evidence for a substantial contribution of faith in these contexts. They also identify obstacles, misunderstandings and tensions. Any simple view of faith as handy 'social glue' is challenged by the complexity and independence of Britain's faith communities.

Misunderstanding faith – complexity and independence

The instrumental tone of much official policy discourse and its underestimation of the complexity and independence of religious faith have already been noted. With regard to complexity, if religions indeed 'grow out of experiences, just like all other kinds of human knowledge' (Taylor, 2003, p 27), then the faith landscape will be highly diverse (see also Armstrong, 1999). This places major demands on the 'religious literacy' of government policymakers, all actors in local and regional governance – political, official, academic, community and indeed faith. There are few who are able currently to meet these challenges. 'Faith communities' exist at different spatial scales from global to local, with policy tending to focus on the local when religion is also a primary carrier of globalisation. World faiths are all marked by internal differences of belief, interpretation, tradition and practice. Local 'faith communities' that may seem homogeneous can exhibit significant internal diversity. Failure to recognise this can lead to false assumptions regarding such issues as the identity of 'faith leaders', their legitimacy in representation, the establishment of 'faith seats' on regional assemblies and local partnership boards, and the existence of a discrete 'faith sector' view within a wider, similarly diverse, voluntary and community sector.

Complexity is related to independence. Although government ministers have approved the 'values' that faiths bring to civic renewal and community cohesion programmes and have sought the moral validation of faith, the main official endorsement of faith involvement in public policy is with regard to the resources and organisational capacity that they can offer as a distinctive part of the voluntary sector. At a local level it is faith communities themselves that are more likely to stress the distinctive significance of both values and beliefs (Lowndes and Chapman, 2005), not only the concrete actions and institutional commitment of 'religious capital' but also 'spiritual capital' defined as: 'the motivating basis of faith, belief and values (sometimes expressed in tangible forms as worship, credal statements and articles of faith, or more intangibly as one's own "spirituality") that shapes the actions of faith communities' (Baker and Skinner, 2006, p 5).

Of course, faith communities and their members have no monopoly of values, or indeed of faith and belief, although secular organisations may not readily use these words. Yet participation in a worshipping community accords a particular centrality and regular reminder of ultimate sources of motivation. Baker and Skinner observe that: 'Some of the contributions of spiritual and religious capital naturally overlap with the practices and values of secular civil society – others are more distinctive and can create dissonance and discomfort' (Baker and Skinner, 2006, p 9). While not universal, therefore, it is in the nature of faith members, communities and organisations to assert varying forms and directions of independence from official agendas and vocabularies of 'regeneration', 'well-being' and 'prosperity' (see for example, Commission on Urban Life and Faith, 2006).

An earlier article on urban regeneration and faith (Furbey and Macey, 2005) risked the very over-simplification just signalled by drawing upon a typology used by Castells to explore responses to globalisation and its challenge to personal and collective identity (Castells, 1997). Castells refers first to those who seek to assume the 'legitimising' identities offered and approved by dominant institutions. The evidence presented earlier in this chapter confirms the relative strength of engagement by faith communities, organisations and their members in voluntary action and varying 'legitimate' civic activities. However, even here independence is soon evident and what, from the state's perspective, might seem the 'cuddlesome' virtues of faith in assisting the 'delivery' of official policies and programmes is joined by 'troublesome' challenge. Thus, competing with their commitment to engagement with the state, faith communities and their members also experience (often in common with secular organisations) a sense of 'capture' and mission compromised (as argued strongly by Bretherton, 2006), pressed to redirect limited capacity to public initiatives that disappoint in their outcomes and involve contrasting understandings, priorities, processes and timescales to their own (Farnell et al, 2003; Baker and Skinner, 2006; Furbey et al, 2006). These experiences, refracted by the doctrines, beliefs, values and collective knowledge of faith communities themselves, can prompt critique and resistance.

Resistance is the second of Castells' types, a response that he sees as essentially defensive. In these terms, 'resisting' religious community offers strong internal bonding, separation from 'the world' and an emphasis on personal spirituality, piety and experience. Resistance can also involve the digging of 'trenches' of 'survival' (Castells, 1997, p 9), designed to hold on to physical, cultural and, in the case of faith, theological turf. Such responses place more emphasis on internal social cohesion than on 'bridging' community cohesion.

But these fortifications can, in time, become bridgeheads, a basis for more active advance back into society. Re-engagement may take various forms, including the proselytising of individuals as well as social and political action. Whether they have a 'spiritual' or a 'social' emphasis or elements of both, such outwardly directed activities can begin to connect with Castells' final type, the 'project' identity. Here, the community or group goes on the offensive to empower people as subjects, transform society and to achieve a different life. People may be prepared for projects of this kind by the negative experiences and the capacity building stemming from 'legitimising' activity, or by frustration with retreat as a mode of resistance.

Of course, much project activity, as well as resistance, is inimical to the boundary crossing associated with community cohesion, not least in a religious setting and particularly in a religious fundamentalist context. Ruthven underlines the origins of the term 'fundamentalist' in Christian Protestantism in North America and is careful to recognise the differences between world 'fundamentalisms'. Nevertheless, he identifies what he terms their shared 'family resemblances': 'Put at its broadest, it [religious fundamentalism] may be described as a "religious way of being" that manifests itself in a strategy by which beleaguered believers attempt to preserve their distinctive identity as a people or group in the face of modernity and secularisation' (Ruthven, 2004, p 8). But religious fundamentalism rarely involves only the resistance of retreat, because: 'For the activist fundamentalist (as distinct from the passive traditionalist) the quest for salvation cannot be realised by withdrawing into a cultural enclave' (Ruthven, 2004, p 57).

The consequences can certainly be 'troublesome', and not only for governments. A key question is therefore whether in terms of social and community cohesion, faiths must either be the 'cuddlesome' instruments of government or divisively troublesome, or whether they have a more independent and positive potential.

Faith in civil society – 'admirably troublesome'?

Shortly after the London bombings of July 2005, Bernard Crick, a vice-president of the British Humanist Society, used the phrase 'admirably troublemaking' in reference to the East London Tenants Organisation (TELCO). This organisation (now part of the wider London Citizens network) is a coalition of faith and secular groups, whose beliefs, values and collective experiences motivate campaigns on issues of poverty, citizenship and empowerment. TELCO, Crick observes, 'stretched their ecumenicity' by electing him as an honorary fellow. He explains his reason for acceptance in these terms:

> I risked a humanist blasphemy trial gladly, because all their practical actions were motivated by a morality of social justice. That is what they had in common … their real religious differences, if insisted on at every turn, would render impossible their common commitment to concrete objectives of justice and human rights. (Crick, 2005)

This example serves to question the assignment of 'faith' to a Durkheimian role as social glue with which to 'stick the teapot back together' – a source of 'binding' values, a stock of physical and human resources, a compliant 'partner' in governance, an agent of a 'responsibilised' moral community and a means to restored neighbourhood 'governability' (Atkinson, 2003). Rather, we see here a particular expression of the 'independence' of faith as a critical and oppositional presence and its detachment from a purely civic role to one in the freer 'space' of civil society.

An influential advocate of an 'associational politics' of civil society was Paul Hirst, who came to advocate a decentralised liberal politics, with 'associations' working with government to secure better services based on local democratic involvement and enabling social groups to build their own social worlds in civil society. He makes this particular reference to religion: 'At present [writing in 1994], it is not the old political forces of the left – who continue to advocate failed collectivist solutions – but *religious* and community groups who see the need for activism and co-operation to build a "civil society" for the poor and excluded' (Hirst, 1994, p 10, emphasis added).

The idea of 'associationalism' has been developed more recently by Chapman (2005) in relation to Christian theology and social practice in the age of New Labour. He contrasts the communitarianism, managerialism and nationalism of New Labour and 'its depoliticized public sphere' with a much more bottom–up pluralist society composed of participative communities characterised by the willingness and skill to resolve conflicts through deliberation and negotiation. Chapman refers to the 'premature harmony' of official 'partnership' and draws a parallel with what he regards as the oppressive notion, influential in Christian social theology, of a 'common good' as an end state. With Hirst, he prefers to focus on a process that involves communities that recognise the rights of others to be different and have a willingness to learn through dialogue, recognise complexity and develop the qualities and skills of deliberation and negotiation (Chapman, 2005, ch 7). These attributes seem highly congruent with those identified by Parekh for cohesion in a multicultural future: 'Our task today is to encourage this process of *unplanned* social and cultural integration by creating conditions in which our different communities can carry on their formal and informal conversation and help to evolve a shared but plural way of being British' (Parekh, 2005, emphasis added). Similarly, Amin contrasts the frequently exclusionary, defensive, divisive and reactive character of the politics of 'community' with a more open life in the wider public realm, which demands the negotiation of difference and a willingness to 'transgress' the normal boundaries of interaction (Amin, 2002).

A faith contribution to such deliberation, conversation and transgression demands of faith communities and organisations, not the fix of social glue, but an ability to contribute as a lubricant in the outworking of what Modood terms 'an inclusive and work–in–progress concept of national identity' (Modood, 2007). In order to examine the potential and the limitations of faith organisations and their members in such a devolved and exploratory politics, the following discussion draws on evidence from two recent research studies (Farnell et al, 2003; Furbey et al, 2006).

With regard to the limitations of faith, earlier discussion has referred to assertive world religious fundamentalisms that define themselves in terms of boundaries. Further religious traditions involve a socially and politically passive retreat from 'the world'. In the language of social capital, both embody strong 'bonding' but exhibit very limited 'bridging' and 'linking'.

Many faith groups are not internally democratic; democracy may co-exist or conflict with scripture, tradition and charisma as principles of authority, reflected in internal exclusion and inequality on lines of gender, generation, ethnicity, class and sexuality. While such divisions and inequalities are not unique to 'faith' and may often have cultural rather than scriptural origins, barriers can arise that test the trust and understanding of other faith and non-religious groups and create tensions in the use of faith buildings for common civil endeavour.

Further, there is substantial inequality between faith communities in their capacity to engage across boundaries. The declining membership, the increasing average age of many 'mainstream' Christian congregations and the poor state and limited adaptability of religious buildings across the main traditions all raise issues of sustainability in civil engagement. The allocation of resources to external networking activities often has to be balanced against members' need for care. Non-Christian and Christian black-majority faith communities and organisations vary greatly in size and material resources. However, compared with the Church of England, for example, capacity in terms of physical capital, organisational development and training is typically much lower. In all faith communities and organisations, leaders may lack the awareness and training required for boundary-crossing encounter and deliberative politics.

More positively, however, faith communities can be important contexts that develop the motivation, skills and qualities needed for 'lubricating' activity in civil society. First, 'bonding' within a faith community can provide the individual with the required confidence, purpose, identity and ongoing sustenance, as many distinguished public lives confirm (the connections between Methodism and the Labour Party provide one example). Second, although faith communities may seem homogeneous to the outsider, many are internally very diverse compared with other voluntary and community groups. This provides a context for the practice of deliberation, negotiation, conflict resolution and the exploration of other traditions and cultures. Third, faith communities are not just neighbourhood organisations. Rather, they are usually multilayered, linked in varying degrees to national and international organisations, giving them access to wider networks of knowledge and material resources. Hence, although there is considerable diversity between local faith communities, they are not to be understood simply as locally bonded and 'parochial' in vision. For example, Church Action on Poverty (CAP) is a national organisation that connects and supports local groups and, in turn, draws on their experiences in developing campaigns. CAP and a partnership of local churches established the Community Pride organisation, building networks with secular community groups to achieve a voice in the regeneration of Manchester and Salford.

Fourth, although we have seen that faith buildings can be regarded as alien to members of other faiths and those of no religious belief, there are multiplying examples of faith buildings that are being 'opened up' so that cross-faith and cross-cultural encounter and collaboration can occur. The importance of such physical 'spaces' is magnified in the many neighbourhoods that have become 'social deserts' through the closure of other contexts for civil activity. The Gujarat Hindu Society centre in Preston is adjacent to a magnificent temple and forms a major facility for Hindus in the city and well beyond. It serves to 'bond' and support local Hindu people through a range of services, but is also important in facilitating engagement with wider civil society and civic participation. The St Peter's Centre in Coventry and the St Mary's Church and Community Centre in Sheffield are two examples of finely adapted churches that permit inter-faith and faith–secular encounter and joint working in civil society (see Finneron and Dinham, 2002 for further discussion of faith buildings).

Fifth, faith organisations and their leaders are often (although by no means always) trusted. This trust, stemming often from long-term presence and commitment in the field, and the wider institutional capacity of faith communities and organisations, can create various non-physical spaces that serve to connect and support the associations of civil society. An example here is the Churches' Regional Commission for Yorkshire and the Humber, formed in 1998 with a particular focus on equipping people for confident engagement with public policy. This organisation has a good reputation and its resources permit the support and connection of both faith and secular groups. A more 'liquid' example of a 'space' is found in Together for Peace in Leeds (T4P), which has an institutional dimension in the form of a council of reference composed of individuals from a range of faith and secular backgrounds and ongoing links with the local authority. However, its overriding quality is that of a network, composed of individuals, often with no, or limited, connection with a formal religious congregation, but with beliefs that inform a 'vision for peace'. At the centre of T4P is a biennial cultural peace festival in Leeds. Between these festivals there is an ongoing programme of activity (theatre, film, music, sport, spiritual reflection and debate) on issues of peace and collaboration with others in events and campaigns.

Many of the preceding examples can be located in 'legitimate' and state-approved 'cuddlesome' activity. Yet they also signal the many contexts in which faith communities, organisations and their members are engaged with people of other faiths and of no religious faith in processes that can contribute to a stronger, more independent and yet cohesive civil society, marked by associational politics and the qualities of negotiation and deliberation. Such processes can 'mess up' the tidy 'finality' of governance and issue in troublesome campaigns, oppositional politics and, in Castells' term, 'projects', as in the cases of London Citizens, Church Action on Poverty and, on a national scale, Jubilee 2000. These activities, joined by the rapid growth of national and local inter-faith forums, all seem to contribute to a less programmatic understanding of 'social' and 'community' cohesion than that expressed in the idea of 'social glue'.

Conclusion

This chapter has identified both the potential divisiveness of religion and its complexity. The major faith traditions all have central beliefs that motivate activity that can build and sustain social and community cohesion, as reflected in the substantial commitment by faith communities, organisations and their members in voluntary action and civic and civil participation. A strong element of instrumentality is evident in the government's prescribed role for faith, presenting faith communities and organisations with both opportunities and dilemmas – a place at the table and an expanded role in service delivery, governance and civic and civil renewal, but at risk of capture and a compromise of mission.

Nevertheless, faith communities and organisations have not been reduced simply to the compliant applicators of consensual social glue. While they contribute substantially in 'legitimate' ways that accord with state priorities, they also operate in a freer mode in collaboration across faiths and with secular groups and organisations, contributing as lubricants and participants in the processes of associational politics in civil society that can challenge state and market and offer a more durable, if not easily measured, social and community cohesion.

Of course, not all faith actors are equally motivated, equipped or adept. If, as is so often stated, the practice of democratic citizenship has to be learned, then funding, substantially independent of government, must be found by faith communities to develop understandings, skills and qualities of deliberation, negotiation and wider democratic practice. Here we encounter the controversy at the heart of the debate on faith in the public realm. The 'strong' secularist argument is that – when allowed public expression – religion is liable to be divisive and destructive because communal religious allegiance runs counter to political loyalty to the secular liberal state; religions are inherently averse to compromise; a religious contribution to debate will be tied unhelpfully to closed belief systems that obstruct rational debate; and religion is concerned only with the transcendent, not the material. While this chapter has recognised religious traditions that display such characteristics, it has also identified very different expressions of faith, individual and collective, that contribute significantly to cohesion.

References

Amin, A. (2002) 'Ethnicity and the multicultural city: Living with diversity', *Enviroment and Planning A*, vol 34, no 6, pp 959–80.

Armstrong, K. (1999) *A History of God*, London: Vintage Books.

Atkinson, R. (2003) 'Addressing urban social exclusion through community involvement in urban regeneration', in R. Imrie and M. Raco (eds) *Urban renaissance? New Labour, community and urban policy*, Bristol: The Policy Press.

Baker, C. and Skinner, H. (2006) *Faith in action: The dynamic connection between spiritual and religious capital*, Manchester: William Temple Foundation.

Bauman, Z. (2004) *Identity*, Cambridge: Polity Press.

Blair, A. (2001) Speech to the Christian Socialist Movement, Westminster Methodist Central Hall, 29 March 2001 (www.pm.gov/output/Page3243.asp).

Bretherton, L. (2006) 'A new establishment? Theological politics and the emerging shape of church–state relations', *Political Theology*, vol 7, no 3, pp 371–92.

Brierley, P.W. (2000) *The tide is running out*, London: Christian Research.

Bruce, S. (2002) *God is dead: Secularisation in the West*, Oxford: Blackwell.

Cairns, B., Harris, M. and Hutchinson, R. (2005) *Faithful regeneration: The role and contribution of local parishes in local communities in the Diocese of Birmingham*, Birmingham: Centre of Voluntary Action Research, Aston Business School.

Castells, M. (1997) *The power of identity: The information age: economy, society and culture, volume 2*, Oxford: Blackwell.

Chapman, M.D. (2005) *Blair's Britain: A Christian critique*, London: SPCK.

Christian Research (2005) *Religious trends*, London: Christian Research.

Commission on Urban Life and Faith (2006) *Faithful cities: A call for celebration, vision and justice*, Peterborough and London: Methodist Publishing House/Church House Publishing.

Community Cohesion Independent Review Team (2001) (Cantle Report) *Community Cohesion: A report of the Independent Review Team, chaired by Ted Cantle*, London: Home Office.

Crick, B. (2005) 'This age of fanaticism is no time for non-believers to make enemies', *The Guardian*, 22 October (www.guardian.co.uk/politics/2005/oct/22/religion.world).

Department for Communities and Local Government (DCLG) (2005) *Citizenship survey*, London: DCLG.

Department for Communities and Local Government (DCLG) (2006), *Strong and prosperous communities: The local government White Paper*. London: DCLG.

Department of the Environment, Transport and the Regions (DETR) (1997) *Involving communities in urban and regional regeneration: A guide for practitioners*, London: DETR.

Department of the Environment, Transport and the Regions (DETR) (2001) *A forum for faith communities and government*, London: DETR.

Farnell, R., Lund, S., Furbey, R., Lawless, P., Wishart, B. and Else, P. (1994) *Hope in the city? The local impact of the Church Urban Fund*, Sheffield: Centre for Regional Social and Economic Research, Sheffield Hallam University.

Farnell, R., Macey, M., Shams al Haqq Hills, S. and Smith, G. (2003) *'Faith' in urban regeneration? Engaging faith communities in urban regeneration*, Bristol: The Policy Press.

Finneron, D. and Dinham, A. (2002) *Building on faith: Faith buildings in neighbourhood renewal*, London: Church Urban Fund.

Flint, J. and Kearns, A. (2004) *The role of Church of Scotland congregations in developing social capital in Scottish communities: Enabling and cohesive or irrelevant and divisive?* Centre for Neighbourhood Research paper 16, Glasgow: ESRC Centre for Neighbourhood Research.

Forrester, D. (1985) *Christianity and the future of welfare*, London: Epworth Press.

Furbey, R. and Macey, M. (2005) 'Religion and urban regeneration: A place for faith?', *Policy and Politics*, vol 33, no 1, pp 95–116.

Furbey, R., Dinham, A., Farnell, T., Finneron, D. and Wilkinson, G. with Howarth, C., Hussain, D. and Palmer, S. (2006) *Faith as social capital? Connecting or dividing?*, Bristol: The Policy Press.

Halman, L. (2001) *The European Values Study: A third wave, sourcebook of 1999/2000 European Values Study survey*, Tilburg: WORC, Tilburg University.

Hirst, P. (1994) *Associative democracy: New forms of economic and social governance*, Cambridge: Polity Press.

Home Office (2001) *Citizenship survey*, London: Home Office.

Hussain, D. (2004) 'British Muslim identity', in M.S. Seddon, D. Hussain and N. Malik (eds) *British Muslims between assimilation and segregation: Historical, legal and social realities*, Leicester: Islamic Foundation.

Local Government Association (LGA) (2002) *Faith and community: A good practice guide for local authorities*, London: LGA Publications.

Lovatt, R., Lyall-Grant, F., Morris, Z. and Whitehead, C. (2005) *Faith in the East of England*, Cambridge: East of England Development Agency/East of England Faiths Council/University of Cambridge.

Lowndes, V. and Chapman, R. (2005) *Faith, hope and clarity: Developing a model of faith group involvement in civil renewal*, Leicester: Local Governance Research Unit, De Montfort University.

McTernan, O. (2003) *Violence in God's name: Religion in an age of conflict*, London: Darton, Longman and Todd.

Modood, T. (1997) 'Culture and identity', in T. Modood (ed) *Ethnic minorities in Britain*, London: Policy Studies Institute.

Modood, T. (2007) 'Multiculturalism and nation building go hand in hand', *The Guardian*, 23 May.

National Council for Voluntary Organisations (NCVO) (2007) *Faith and voluntary action: An overview of current evidence and debates*, London: NCVO.

Northwest Development Agency (2003) *Faith in England's Northwest: The contribution made by faith communities to civil society in the region*, Warrington: Northwest Development Agency.

Office of the Deputy Prime Minister (ODPM) (2006) *Review of the evidence base on faith communities*, London: Office of the Deputy Prime Minister.

Office of the Deputy Prime Minister (ODPM)/Home Office (2005) *Stronger and connected communities: The future of the third sector in social and economic regeneration: Interim report*, London: ODPM/Home Office.

Office for National Statistics (ONS) (2004) *Focus on religion*, London: Office for National Statistics.

Parekh, B. (2005) 'Multiculturalism is a civilised dialogue', *The Guardian*, 21 January (www.guardian.co.uk/uk/2005/jan/21/islamandbritain.comment9)

Parekh, B. (2006) *Rethinking multiculturalism: Cultural diversity and political theory*, 2nd edn, Basingstoke: Palgrave Macmillan.

Ruthven, M. (2004) *Fundamentalism: The search for meaning*, Oxford: Oxford University Press.

Sennett, R. (1998) *The corrosion of character: The personal consequences of work in the new capitalism*, London: W.W. Norton and Company.

Taylor, J.V. (2003) *The Easter God and his Easter people*, London: Continuum.

Wilson, B. (1966) *Religion in a secular society*, London: Watts.

Yorkshire Churches (2002) *Angels and advocates: Church social action in Yorkshire and the Humber*, Leeds: Yorkshire Churches/The Regional Commission for Yorkshire and the Humber.

SEVEN

The third sector and community cohesion in deprived neighbourhoods

Peter Wells

Introduction

Policy and academic debate in the UK and internationally on the third sector has ascribed it myriad roles in, and emphasised its positive contribution to, public policy delivery, civil society, civil renewal, social inclusion, neighbourhood renewal and community cohesion. The aim of this chapter is to review some of these debates, with respect to community cohesion, to problematise certain policy and academic positions, and to outline future directions for investigation.

The focus of the chapter is on the contribution of the third sector to cohesion in deprived neighbourhoods. Clearly, the sector plays active roles in different policy domains and at different territorial levels. For instance, third-sector organisations such as Liberty and Searchlight operate in quite different ways in the field of community cohesion at a national (UK) level. These are not, however, the focus of this chapter, which examines organisations that operate within, and are often part of, local neighbourhoods.

Common themes around the contribution of the third sector include its roles in: promoting civic participation; providing forms of associative democracy as proxy representatives of different social, cultural, ethnic or faith groups; and, more recently, public service delivery. For Deakin (2001) these themes are outlined respectively as civil society and democracy, civil society and community, and civil society, charity and welfare. Policy statements by the UK government have reflected and promoted some of these themes, for instance in the *Cross-cutting review of the role of the voluntary and community sector in the delivery of public services* (HM Treasury, 2002) and more recently *The future role of the third sector in social and economic regeneration* (Office of the Third Sector,

2007). In this latter report, four common goals for government and the sector are defined: enabling voice and campaigning; strengthening communities; transforming public services; and encouraging social enterprise – echoing some of Deakin's themes.

Other chapters in this volume have documented and analysed the emergence of community cohesion as a policy discourse in the UK. Prima facie such discourse ought to be redolent of calls for community involvement and for voluntary action, the two cornerstones of the third sector and civic society. Moreover, the connections made between community cohesion and theories of social capital, drawn most strongly in the conceptual annex to the Cantle Report (Community Cohesion Independent Review Team, 2001), ought to provide a basis on which to set out a range of possibilities for the voluntary and community sector. Such possibilities from the Cantle Report through to the Department for Communities and Local Government's *Improving opportunity, strengthening society* (2007a) are, however, fleeting, vague or highly specific.

This chapter considers some of the different roles ascribed to the third sector in addressing a reported crisis in community cohesion in deprived neighbourhoods. These include: the funding of the third sector, civic participation and association, and partnership and associative democracy. Before turning to these issues, the chapter discusses two fault lines in debates on the third sector and neighbourhood cohesion: namely, the definition of the third sector and the nature of neighbourhood diversity and change.

Defining the third sector

The third sector has come to prominence in a range of policy areas such as health and social care, urban regeneration and housing. This is reflected in different academic debates and discourses as well as policy developments. These include: the emergence of new forms of political governance (Rhodes, 1996, 1997; Pierre, 2000; Jessop, 2002, 2004), changing relations between state and society (Gamble et al, 1996; Jessop, 2004), devolution and decentralisation (Keating, 2001; Loughlin, 2001; Hazell and Trench, 2004), social capital (Putnam, 1994), community and civil society (Bauman, 2001; Deakin, 2001) and communitarianism (Etzioni, 1995; Tam, 1998).

The third sector has also been construed as a key component of community cohesion, especially by advocates of social capital and communitarianism and for commentators who regard membership of associations as one element of cohesive societies (Putnam, 1994, 2007;

Etzioni, 1995; Tam, 1998). However, the third sector, as an embodiment of civil society, is much more complex and diverse than such advocates often portray. For instance, not only is civil society much more amorphous, but it is also a contested term. As Waltzer highlights: 'the words "civil society" name the space of uncoerced human association and also the set of relational networks – formed for the sake of family, faith, interest and ideology that fill this space' (1995, p 7).

Although the filling of this space is enacted through some form of common identity, the process of membership can take different forms. As Deakin (2001, p 5) shows, membership of civil society has different but overlapping meanings in republican, Marxist, liberal, religious and communitarian understandings. Gender, class and ethnicity can also form the basis for 'membership': and equally for exclusion. What appears to be the common feature is that different memberships are not mutually exclusive but plural and reinforcing. Defining the relations between cohesion and civil society is similarly complex. For cohesion, civil society is often defined along geographic (eg specific disadvantaged localities) and non-geographic (eg implicit or explicit exclusion of different groups from public services) lines.

The organisational basis for civil society has produced myriad terms and definitions. These include voluntary action and voluntary organisations (Knight, 1993; Deakin, 2001) where voluntary action is a 'form of energy, stemming from free will, having a moral purpose and undertaken in a spirit of independence' (Knight, 1993, p xii), but definitions also encompass terms such as the third sector, third system, not-for-profit sector, the social economy and non-governmental organisations. These terms typically have contextual and institutional baggage that can disrupt their use for comparative analysis. For example, the term 'non-governmental organisations' (NGOs) typically denotes bodies working in international development and relations, while 'the social economy' more commonly refers to a particular legal and cultural form – the *économie sociale* (Laville, 2004) – and the 'third sector' is usually applied to domestic voluntary and community sector organisations. Moreover, organisational boundaries can also blur and include more informal groups of individuals. In many respects these latter uncrystallised groups work at the boundary between informal networks of people and wider society. Salamon and Anheier have sought to address this 'terminological tangle' through defining the 'not-for-profit sector' as a collection of entities that are organised, private (institutionally separate from government), non-profit distributing, self-governing and voluntary (or at least involving some meaningful degree of voluntary participation) (1998, p 33, cited in Deakin, 2001, p 10). This broad definition is used for the purposes of this chapter.

The scope, scale and capacity of the third sector, and its variation between different areas, is often quickly passed over in pronouncements on what the sector can contribute. Similarly, authors such as Putnam (1994) and Etzioni (1995) often give insufficient attention to organisational complexities, the scale of associative activity and to local socio-economic contexts.

A stream of recent national and local studies in the UK has begun to measure the third sector and address the lacunae left by political and social theorists. One example of this work is by Macmillan (2006), who uses surveys in order to measure the voluntary and community sector in South Yorkshire. Macmillan presents an 'anatomy' of the sector that shows that at least 6,264 organisations exist in South Yorkshire, employing some 25,000 staff and having 112,500 volunteers, together with a further 50,500 management committee members. Given that the study area has a total population of around 1.3 million, these figures reveal some of the reach of the third sector in everyday lives in South Yorkshire. Macmillan also estimates that around 2,600 organisations are working at a neighbourhood level. Recourse to exemplars of good practice and funded projects in public policy (see for example Home Office (2005) *Improving opportunity, strengthening society*, and its two-year progress report: Department for Communities and Local Government, 2007a) is common, but little attention is given to the scale, scope and dynamics of the sector, the gap addressed by Macmillan.

Macmillan's study was not set objectives around community cohesion, and so there is little that can be drawn from it around the scope and scale of organisations working in this field. Figures on work at a neighbourhood level have already been given and an estimate is made of the number of church or faith organisations, which number just over 700. Interestingly, both categories of organisation form a significant, although overlapping, proportion of the third sector.

Other studies, especially within the social capital field, have highlighted that the scale of the third sector (total number of organisations) often increases in more ethnically diverse neighbourhoods. Evidence of this within the UK is somewhat limited. Anecdotal findings from the New Deal for Communities evaluation in England (Lawless, 2005) suggest that, similarly, neighbourhoods that are predominately comprised of a 'white British' population report a smaller voluntary and community sector. However, as Macmillan's study (2006) also reveals, variation in the scale and activities of the sector also varies markedly between prima facie similar local authority areas, suggesting that local factors other than the ethnic profile of local populations – and in particular local government funding decisions and policy – can be highly influential in shaping the development of the third sector.

Diversity and deprived neighbourhoods

A common thread in discourse on community cohesion is that greatest need for policy and institutional redesign is to be found in deprived neighbourhoods. It is also here that public policy requires most from the third sector. The report of the Commission on Integration and Cohesion, *Our shared future* (2007), drew on data that had been gathered for local best value performance indicators (BVPIs) and that were therefore collected at a local authority district level. These showed perceptions that cohesion was poor in areas in the 'M62 corridor' (in particular Hull, parts of West Yorkshire and East Lancashire) and 'around the Wash' (in particular West Norfolk, North Cambridgeshire and South Lincolnshire, an area approximating to the Fens). The report interprets these findings as responses to local issues and context: the legacy of the disturbances of 2001 and 'persistent challenges of parallel lives' in the M62 area, and recent migration into the fenland area from Portugal and more recently from A8 countries. The report also acknowledges the link between deprivation and cohesion, although qualifies this by evidence from high-cohesion/high-deprivation outliers to suggest 'local action can build resilience' (Commission on Integration and Cohesion 2007, p 27).

Data from the New Deal for Communities (NDC) evaluation suggests that the political elision between disadvantaged communities and (a breakdown in) community cohesion may be both overstated and require more subtle explanation; although it should be noted that NDC areas are not necessarily the most deprived areas, nor representative of all deprived areas in England (the focus of the programme). Figure 7.1 uses a simple indicator of ethnic diversity to show marked variation across the 39 NDC partnership areas.

Figure 7.1 reveals that the ethnic composition of NDC areas varies considerably, and these areas also show diversity in indicators such as the age profile and housing tenure composition. Moreover, a demarcation on the lines of age, ethnicity or housing tenure may oversimplify the lived experience of diversity and cohesion in deprived neighbourhoods, in which factors such as class, opportunities for association and the wider political and economic contexts of neighbourhoods should also be considered. However, building 'opportunities for association', as

Figure 7.1: Proportion of 'White' and 'non-White' populations in NDC areas

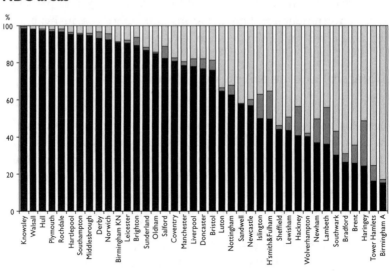

Data: NDC Household Survey (2006), undertaken by Ipsos-MORI for the national evaluation of NDC.

suggested throughout public policy on community cohesion, is unlikely to be such a straightforward task and is likely to be constrained by issues such as available resources and political legacies of past attempts to build cohesion.

It is the case that community cohesion in disadvantaged neighbourhoods may be affected by the finding that such neighbourhoods can be areas that are experiencing relatively high levels of population change. This may undermine opportunities for the state or the third sector to engage populations over a longer term or for socially cohesive relations to develop between residents. For instance, establishing third-sector organisations that work with a specific group may be undermined if that group is relatively mobile. Indeed many deprived neighbourhoods, especially those in London, appear to play specific transitory roles in the housing market. This is illustrated by Figure 7.2.

Population change appears to be high in these disadvantaged neighbourhoods, although for those areas to the left of the chart (showing over 25% change) this can be explained by the size of their student population (Newcastle and Nottingham) and/or by ongoing and NDC-funded demolition and new-build activities. Such local contextual factors are likely to be present in other deprived

Figure 7.2: Proportion of population moving (2002–04)

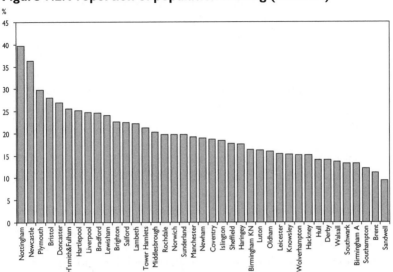

Note: The figure is based on data that show the proportion of the resident population who were no longer at the same address at the time of the repeat survey. It should be noted that a significant proportion of this change in Nottingham and Newcastle may be explained by both areas having large university student populations.

Data: NDC Household Surveys (2002, 2004), undertaken. by Ipsos-MORI for the national evaluation of NDC.

neighbourhoods. Despite this evidence, the Commission on Integration and Cohesion (2007) uses analysis at a local authority level to create a typology that places such neighbourhoods within localities that the Commission determines as having stable populations. The experience of population change at a neighbourhood level appears to be at odds with their classification within the Commission's typology in many cases.

Third-sector funding and the case of single group funding

The Cantle Report's main concerns with the third sector were primarily with the funding and role of community organisations with regard to community cohesion. Cantle highlighted that one factor driving community tensions was a perception that some communities had secured scarce funding resources in preference to others. In response, Cantle recommended that:

> Funding bodies should presume against separate funding
> for distinct communities, and require collaborative working,
> save for those circumstances where the need for funding is
> genuinely only evident in one section of the community
> and can only be provided separately. Funding should
> allow for this change to take place over a period of time.
> (Community Cohesion Independent Review Team, 2001,
> p 38)

The shorthand for this recommendation has been a presumption
against single group funding (SGF) where such groups represent
specific ethnic or faith communities. The report of the Community
Cohesion Panel (2004) picked up this theme in response to a ministerial
request for the panel to consider funding of voluntary organisations.
It concluded that 'SGF should be redirected to encourage cohesion in
communities in the long term, while still enabling and encouraging
new and isolated groups to build capacity prior to taking their place in
the wider community' (Community Cohesion Panel, 2004, p 50). This
conclusion forms the basis for the panel's main recommendation on
SGF. In other respects, the Community Cohesion Panel report simply
restated the government's main policy positions on the third sector, for
example that community cohesion should form a part of the compact
underpinning relations between government and the voluntary and
community sector.

The Commission on Integration and Cohesion report *Our shared
future* devotes an annex to 'The question of single group funding'
(2007, pp 160–4) and provides a more reasoned case for SGF. It
supports SGF only where there is a need to build the capacity of
a particular group (for example, an organisation that works with a
new group of migrants) and also recommends that awards should
be publicised and that any further or renewed funding require the
organisation to demonstrate that it is 'becoming more outward-
facing'. The rationale here draws explicitly from the social capital
literature and its emphasis on promoting 'bridging social capital'
between groups rather than continuing to strengthen 'bonding' social
capital within group memberships.

However, the consideration of SGF appears bereft of a close
understanding of the reported needs of third-sector organisations.
Returning to Macmillan's study (2006), one of his key findings is that
funding issues are a major concern for the majority of voluntary and
community sector organisations. Macmillan found that 'raising funds'
was regarded as a significant or major problem by 51% of respondent

organisations generally. In addition, having 'skills in being able to put in good quality funding bids' was also highlighted as a significant problem by organisations (Macmillan, 2006, p 7). Macmillan reports that these concerns are concentrated in organisations with a small number of paid staff (from one to four staff) and typically those with smaller annual incomes. Unfortunately, no data are presented on whether these problems are most apparent among organisations working at a neighbourhood level. However, both Macmillan (2006) and Shutt and Kumi-Ampofo (2005) suggest that this is most likely to be the case as regeneration funding in the UK undergoes a period of transition and reduction with changes to, or the ending of, European Structural Funds and Single Regeneration Budget funding for many disadvantaged areas.

The intentions of the policy towards SGF and its impacts on community cohesion are clear and in some cases undoubtedly necessary to address some localised community tensions. However, the policy also belies evidence that suggests that many third-sector organisations working in deprived neighbourhoods are highly reliant on public funding in the form of small grants, and that without this, such groups – without the financial capacity to support organisations through donations or fund raising – are unlikely to continue. Strong statements on SGF, coupled with ongoing regeneration funding changes in the UK, are therefore likely to have some unforeseen consequences in terms of the scope and scale of the third sector in deprived neighbourhoods – and with unintended detrimental consequences for community cohesion, including the demise of local organisations working with particular groups and/or promoting positive community relations between groups.

Civic participation

Beyond this focus on SGF, it is harder to define a clear set of public policy positions towards the role for the third sector in promoting community cohesion. For instance, the Denham Report (Home Office, 2001) is largely silent on the role of the third sector except for inferences that can be drawn from discussion of community leadership and the allocation of regeneration funding. These elements were reflected in a 2006 speech by Phil Woolas (then local government minister), who perceived the voluntary and community sector as being one of eight key elements of cohesive communities: 'a strong, active voluntary and community sector with good organisation behind it, recognising both the representational and service provider role' (Woolas, 2006). Perhaps this role is left intentionally vague and requires some reformulation from reading across different policy documents. It also appears to reflect a delegation of responsibility to local government and local strategic partnerships for addressing community cohesion and managing the consequences of different organisational capacities among various groups of the population and maintaining and building relations between them.

A further theme that emerges in policy documents is around the importance to community cohesion of community organisations and community premises. For example, the Commission on Integration and Cohesion (2007, p 121) highlights that 'smaller scale community facilities are an important resilience factor for cohesion'. However, the Commission, following the same argument it made around SGF, suggests that such facilities should not be solely for a single ethnic or faith group, but should rather provide a physical space for meeting and interaction across communities. Along with investment in community capacity-building activities, the emphasis here is on providing opportunities for both bonding and bridging social capital to emerge. This reflects the conceptualisation of community organisations and premises, alongside the workplace, schools and colleges, as spaces where association between groups and populations may emerge (Amin, 2002, p 969; Robinson, 2005, p 1424).

Similarly, the government also advocates volunteering, which is seen in the government strategies for race equality and community cohesion as a means of building cohesion. Implicit references to contact theory and bridging social capital abound here, with the focus on increasing volunteering among people from minority ethnic communities, people with a disability or long-term illness and people with no formal qualifications. As the two-year report on this strategy highlights, 'encouraging people from these groups to volunteer provides opportunities for those who might otherwise feel excluded to identify with wider society and come into contact with people from other communities' (Department for Communities and Local Government, 2007a, p 70).

Evidence from the New Deal for Communities evaluation casts some light on these rationales and anticipated outcomes, in terms of both their extent and the possible impact of public funding. Table 7.1 shows three neighbourhood attachment variables around community association, neighbour support and voluntary activity: these variables mirror those in the Home Office Citizenship Survey (2003). For each, it is often the third sector that provides the focus for such activity. In terms of community attachment, the household survey data reveal that, although it is lower in NDC programme areas than the national average, community attachment has grown steadily throughout the NDC programme (which commenced in 1999–2000). NDC, which 'places the community at the heart of the programme', appears to have had a positive effect here. This finding is supported by extensive analysis reported in Hickman and Manning (2005).

Table 7.1: Perceptions of attachment to the neighbourhood (%)

	NDC			National[a]
	2002	2004	2006	2006
Feel part of local community[b]	35	39	42	53
Neighbours look out for each other	59	62	61	72
Involved in voluntary work in last three years	23	24	25	23

Base: NDC 2002 (19,547), 2004 (19,633), 2006 (15,792); Comparator 2006 (3,062); National 2006 (1,989). (1) All heard of NDC 2002 (12,661), 2004 (15,749), 2006 (13,008).

Notes: [a] Ipsos MORI Omnibus 2006, [b] 'A great deal' or 'a fair amount'.

Data: NDC Household Surveys (2002, 2004, 2006), undertaken by Ipsos-MORI for the national evaluation of NDC.

The findings for support provided between neighbours indicate less change. Indeed this may be as expected, for such activities are largely a byproduct of public expenditure on community activities. Despite this, the figure (61%) is not as different from national averages (72%) as might be expected from perceptions of deprived communities becoming fractured in terms of informal social support networks. The figures do not and cannot reveal, however, the everyday structure of such support along the lines of age, ethnicity, faith and housing tenure.

The data on voluntary activity are perhaps the most striking and highlight deficiencies in policy priorities that assert a blanket equation between deprivation, non-white ethnicity, worklessness, disability, and low levels of voluntary activity. Clearly, these data are place rather than people specific, but they do reveal that levels of voluntary activity in NDC programme areas are slightly higher than the national average. There is variation across NDC areas (as there is in the Citizenship Survey across area and socio-economic groups), but nonetheless these data reveal that association through volunteering is occurring to a significant extent in many deprived neighbourhoods, in contradiction to the conclusions of some social capital and contact theorists. Although we know the third sector plays a key role in both coordinating and fostering community attachment, less is known about the differing configurations of third-sector organisations operating in deprived areas.

Associative democracy and partnership

There is a call within community cohesion discourse to local agencies for the development of partnership working, which includes, among others, the voluntary and community sector. However, central government statements on community cohesion rarely contain the detail of the purposes of such partnership working. A review by Cantle of community cohesion in Oldham reflects this delegated approach with a call for 'a new "bottom-up" approach with far more importance attributed to local communities taking responsibility for shaping and driving change in their localities' (Cantle et al, 2006, p 8). Similar themes are reflected by ministerial statements that government can only do so much. However, the 2006 Cantle review of Oldham does recognise problems in the partnership model: 'we found community leaders of the Voluntary, Community and Inter-faith sectors were restricted to a small cadre of established representatives who often felt over-stretched and unable to cope with the volume of meetings, reports and requests for consultation' (Cantle et al, 2006, p 25). However, in some recommendations Cantle et al then fail to recognise these problems, falling back on a requirement that public bodies 'tap the potential contribution of the Voluntary, Community and Inter-faith sectors' (Cantle et al, 2006, p 30; see also Furbey, Chapter Six in this volume).

The relationship between the government and the third sector over community cohesion is worthy of further examination. The relationship between the sector – or, more broadly, civil society – and the state, and with representative democracy, lies at the heart of debates about the difference between wider processes of governance, and a narrower state government. The 'rolling back of the state' (Jessop, 1994) is increasingly understood, and accepted, to mean that the state has withdrawn from many of its traditional social and economic spheres. For some, these functions should simply be surrendered to the market (Weingast, 1995), but it can equally be argued that public goods could be delivered through or in conjunction with other non-market forms of agency.

This alternative understanding is addressed by work on associative democracy (Hirst, 1994). Hirst argues that many activities can be delivered through mutual and voluntary associations whereby 'as many of the affairs of society as possible are managed by voluntary and democratically self-governing associations' (1994, p 19). Hirst also raises the broader question about the provision of welfare, and argues that the free exercise of choice through participation in an association offers the greater reward of empowerment, rather than the illusory hope of equality of outcomes (1994, p 170). This conflict appears to be reflected in the changing basis of governmental pronouncements on the third sector, where it is both given a role in the process of partnership and voice, but simultaneously is to achieve harder public service outcomes. In terms of community cohesion, the focus appears to be on the pursuit of equality of outcomes, as much as it is on the process of empowerment.

However, Anheier highlights that 'one last issue remains to be considered', which is whether voluntary associations work to promote democracy through being underpinned by good governance (cited in Deakin, 2001, p 108). That is, the associative democracy of Hirst does not consider whether the customs and practices of associations themselves are democratic. A commonly held strength of voluntary associations is that they promote values and norms based on their own internal operating styles. However, this is contingent on voluntary associations having operating styles that are held by members to be legitimate, whether through ensuring effective membership representation in decision making, or through some other form of accountability. The relationship between voluntary associations and democracy is therefore complex. It is unfair to apply standards of representative democracy to voluntary associations: they gain their legitimacy through a panoply of ways, only one of which may be through operating democratic structures. This issue is brought into sharp focus by the government's intentions to raise standards of governance in mosques and to ensure 'minimum requirements' for all imams engaged by the state (Department for Communities and Local Government, 2007b).

The findings from Cantle's review of Oldham that partnership is a resource-intensive activity, especially for resource-constrained third-sector organisations, are reflected by other studies (Armstrong and Wells, 2005). It is an irony that while concerns are raised over single group funding, the third sector faces constraints as a result of changing funding regimes. Evidence from the NDC programme evaluation, shown in Table 7.2, is illuminating here. As stated, this is a programme that 'places the community at the heart of the programme', through support for elected community representatives to sit on NDC partnerships, and in many areas community representatives hold majorities on those partnerships, and through the funding of third sector-led initiatives. Despite this, household survey evidence only shows a small shift in the extent to which residents in NDC neighbourhoods feel that they can influence decisions in their area, and this remains at a level below the national average.

Table 7.2: Perceptions of influence over decision-making (%)

	NDC			National[a]
	2002	2004	2006	2006
Feel can influence decisions in area[b]	23	24	25	34

Base: NDC 2002 (19,547), 2004 (19,633), 2006 (15,792); National 2006 (1,989) (1) All heard of NDC 2002 (12,661), 2004 (15,749), 2006 (13,008).

Notes: [a] Ipsos MORI Omnibus 2006, [b] 'A great deal' or 'a fair amount'.

Source: NDC Household Surveys (2002, 2004, 2006), undertaken by Ipsos-MORI for the national evaluation of NDC.

Calls for greater and more open partnership working and community engagement (Cantle et al, 2006) are welcome, but this alone does not provide a panacea. The symptoms of deprivation and household poverty, including low incomes, poor health and fear of crime, remain the primary concerns of residents in deprived neighbourhoods. Therefore, addressing material disadvantage remains a more important factor in improving community cohesion than the necessary, but not in itself sufficient, support for associative democracy.

Conclusion

This chapter has reviewed community cohesion discourse in the UK and sought to examine the validity of the roles it ascribes to the third sector in deprived neighbourhoods. The chapter suggests that the role of the third sector has been viewed positively in such discourse, especially around the focal points it provides for civic action, voluntarism and association. These activities have been typically supported through recourse to concepts of contact theory and social capital (especially to bridging social capital). Such conceptual readings and specific incidents around narrowly defined organisations have led policymakers strongly to favour support to organisations that are 'outward looking' and that engage with organisations working with other communities. At the same time, a strong position has been taken to rule out the funding of narrowly defined interest groups, except where communities have acute social, political and economic deficits. The chapter has also considered how these agendas then operate in deprived neighbourhoods and may have unintended detrimental consequences for cohesion.

The following challenges appear to face the third sector in forming its role in cohesion.

Cohesion and neighbourhood change

The Commission on Integration and Cohesion (2007) argues that many areas where cohesion appears to be problematic are stable with little population turnover. However, a tighter geographic analysis reveals that the picture is far more varied: deprived neighbourhoods are experiencing higher levels of population turnover as a result of their specifically transient function in local housing markets, extensive change in the housing stock through demolition and refurbishment, or the presence of significant transient populations such as students. This provides a challenge to the third sector and the extent to which it is for and of 'the community'. Broader interest and infrastructure organisations may respond positively and provide a means to engage new communities, while narrower organisations may find their membership declining.

Complexity and diversity of the third sector

Successive area-based regeneration programmes in the UK, with the New Deal for Communities being the prime example, have provided a focus for geographically contained community organisations from targeted disadvantaged areas to engage in activities around a range of agendas (from community development to employment, housing and crime reduction). However, those organisations engaged in efforts for neighbourhood renewal only represent a small part of the third sector in any locality: a medium-sized city may contain several thousand third-sector organisations. Moreover, the engagement of third-sector organisations that claim to represent faith communities or ethnic groups is itself contentious and may act against the fostering of cohesion at a small geographic scale.

This raises various issues for promoting cohesion. The third sector will, and does, have a multitude of roles to play (from engagement to service delivery) but the scope and scale of its activities related to cohesion will vary from place to place. While the capacity of local organisations to contribute to local cohesion may be built up, often over a long time, there is no guarantee that this will occur. Even well-resourced programmes such as NDC have had relatively small impacts on changing the scope and scale of the third sector. This suggests the need for responses to perceived deficits in cohesion to be specific to local capacities and needs.

Representation and accountability

Representation and accountability tend to be seen through a lens that uses representative democracy as a benchmark for assessing the degree of representation provided by other systems of governance. The role of the third sector is actually quite different and tends to focus on legitimising policy decisions made by public sector policy actors. The legitimacy of the sector itself may stem from the extent and scope of participation in a range of public-, private- and third-sector action. However, this may challenge the role of the sector as being 'independent' of the state (Kendall, 2003; see also Furbey, Chapter Six in this volume). Even in the eyes of the state, the successful engagement of the sector within the community cohesion agenda depends on the legitimacy of third-sector organisations to speak for different communities.

The implication of third-sector representation and accountability issues is one of caution: recognising the potential voice of the third sector to represent often marginalised communities, but also recognising that the sector itself, and the communities it is part of, are dynamic and changing. Risks of 'sector representatives' becoming ossified need to be avoided.

Resources

The viability of the third sector in neighbourhood renewal and community cohesion agendas stem frequently from its access to, and use of, different resources (information, political and financial). In comparison to other sectors, it is constrained in its use of traditional resources such as funding (although this has changed markedly since 1997) and political power. Its strengths appear to remain in its diversity and the ways in which it can legitimise the policy-making process as a proxy for citizen and user involvement and speak for marginalised groups. However, the closer its engagement in project and service delivery, the greater will be its financial dependency on the state.

The resource implications for community cohesion interventions are especially pertinent here. In many cases the sector may advance cohesion (or highlight cohesion deficits) through the voice it gives to marginalised groups and possibly its role as a deliverer of services to those groups. However, these services are rarely labelled as being linked to community cohesion. Rather, they remain part of wider agendas around economic regeneration, employment, community engagement, crime reduction and an array of others, which have an implicit, but crucial relationship to the levels of cohesion at both local and national spheres.

Acknowledgements

I would like to acknowledge the support from Mike Foden and Ian Wilson in analysing the NDC data and to thank Penny Withers (Department for Communities and Local Government) for helpful comments. The content of this chapter remains, however, the sole responsibility of the author.

References

Amin, A. (2002) 'Ethnicity and the multicultural city: Living with diversity', *Environment and Planning* A, vol 34, no 6, pp 959–80.

Armstrong, H. W. and Wells, P. (2005) 'Multi-level governance and civil society: The third sector in the design and delivery of EU regional policy', in I. Sagan and H. Halkier (eds) *Regionalism contested: Institutions, society and territorial governance*, London: Ashgate, pp 35–52.

Bauman, Z. (2001) *Community: Seeking safety in an insecure world*, Cambridge: Polity.

Cantle, T., Kaur, D., Athar, M., Dallison, C., Wiggans, C. and Harris, J. (2006) *Challenging local communities to change Oldham: Review of community cohesion in Oldham*, Coventry: Institute of Community Cohesion.

Commission on Integration and Cohesion (2007) *Our shared future*, London: Commission on Integration and Cohesion.

Community Cohesion Independent Review Team (2001) (Cantle Report) *Community cohesion: A report of the Independent Review Team, chaired by Ted Cantle*, London: Home Office.

Community Cohesion Panel (2004) *The end of parallel lives? The report of the Community Cohesion Panel*, London: Home Office.

Deakin, N. (2001) *In search of civil society*, Basingstoke: Palgrave Macmillan.

Department for Communities and Local Government (2007a) *Improving opportunity, strengthening society: Two years on – A progress report on the government's strategy for race equality and community cohesion*, London: Department for Communities and Local Government.

Department for Communities and Local Government (2007b) *Preventing violent extremism – Winning hearts and minds*, London: Department for Communities and Local Government.

Etzioni, A. (1995) *The spirit of community*, London: Fontana.

Gamble, A., Payne, A., Hoogvelt, A., Dietrich, M. and Kenny, M. (1996) 'Editorial: New political economy', *New Political Economy*, vol 1, no 1, pp 5–11.

Hazell, R. and Trench, A. (2004) *Has devolution made a difference? The state of the nations 2004*, Exeter: Imprint Academic.

Hickman, P. and Manning, J. (2005) 'Community involvement in neighbourhood regeneration: Who participates?' *Voluntary Action*, vol 7, no 1, pp 43–59.

Hirst, P. (1994) *Associate democracy: New forms of economic and social governance*, Oxford: Blackwell.

HM Treasury (2002) *Cross-cutting review of the role of the voluntary and community sector in the delivery of public services*, London: HM Treasury.

Home Office (2001) (Denham Report) *Building cohesive communities: A report of the Ministerial Group on Public Order and Community Cohesion*, London: Home Office.

Home Office (2003) *2003 Home Office citizenship survey: People, families and communities*, Home Office Research Study 289, London: Home Office.

Home Office (2005) *Improving opportunity, strengthening society: The government's strategy to increase race equality and community cohesion*, London: Home Office.

Jessop, B. (1994) 'Post-Fordism and the state', in A. Amin (ed) *Post-Fordism: A reader*, Oxford: Blackwell.

Jessop, B. (2002) *The future of the capitalist state*, Cambridge: Polity.

Jessop, B. (2004) 'Multi-level governance and multi-level metagovernance', in I. Bache and M. Flinders (eds) *Multi-level governance*, Oxford: Oxford University Press.

Kendall, J. (2003) *The voluntary sector: Comparative perspectives in the UK*, London: Routledge.

Keating, M. (2001) 'Rethinking the region: culture, institutions and economic development in Catalonia and Galicia', *European Journal of Urban and Regional Studies*, vol 8, no 3, pp 217–34.

Knight, B. (1993) *Voluntary action*, London: Home Office.

Laville, J.-L. (2004) *The third sector in Europe*, Cheltenham: Edward Elgar.

Lawless, P. (2005) *New Deal for Communities 2001–2005: An interim evaluation*, Research Report 17, London: ODPM.

Loughlin, J. (2001) *Subnational democracy in the European Union: Challenges and opportunities*, Oxford: Oxford University Press.

Macmillan, R. (2006) *Part of the picture: The voluntary and community sector across South Yorkshire*, Sheffield: Sheffield Hallam University.

Office of the Third Sector (2007) *The future role of the third sector in social and economic regeneration*, London: Office of the Third Sector.

Pierre, J. (2000) *Debating governance: Authority, steering and democracy*, Oxford: Oxford University Press.

Putnam, R. (1994) *Making democracy work: Civic traditions in modern Italy*, Princeton, NJ: Princeton University Press.

Putnam, R. (2007) '*E pluribus unum:* Diversity and community in the twenty first century: The 2006 Johan Skytte Prize Lecture', *Scandinavian Political Studies*, vol 30, no 2, pp 137–74.

Rhodes, R.A.W. (1996) 'The new governance: Governing without government', *Political Studies*, vol 44, no 4, pp 652–67.

Rhodes, R.A.W. (1997) *Understanding governance: Policy networks, governance, reflexivity and accountability*, Maidenhead: Open University Press.

Robinson, D. (2005) 'The search for community cohesion: Key themes and dominant concepts of the public policy agenda', *Urban Studies*, vol 42, no 8, pp 1411–27.

Salamon, L.M. and Anheier, H.K. (1998) *The nonprofit sector in the developing world: A comparative analysis*, Johns Hopkins Nonprofit Sector series, Manchester: Manchester University Press.

Shutt, J. and Kumi-Ampofo, F. (2005) *Changing funding programmes: Impact on the work of the voluntary and community sector and consequences for the Yorkshire and Humber economy*, Leeds: Yorkshire and Humber Regional Forum.

Tam, H. (1998) *Communitarianism: A new agenda for politics and citizenship*, Basingstoke: Macmillan.

Waltzer, M. (ed) (1995) *Toward a global civil society*, Oxford: Berghahn.

Weingast, B.R. (1995) 'The economic role of political institutions: market preserving federalism and economic development', *Journal of Law, Economics and Institutions*, vol 11, no 1, pp 1–31.

Woolas, P. (2006) Speech at the LGA Conference 'Community Cohesion event', London, 6 July 2006 (accessed 4 April 2008 at www.communities.gov.uk/speeches/corporate/lga-conference).

EIGHT

Welfare state institutions and secessionary neighbourhood spaces

John Flint

Introduction

The welfare state has always been associated with attempts to forge a cohesive sense of British identity and a contractual reaffirmation of the relationship between state and citizen. It is no coincidence, for example, that the housing pillar of publicly funded welfare during the 20th century was strengthened in the aftermath of the two world wars that so powerfully shaped the understanding of Britishness: the 'Homes for Heroes' campaign after 1918 and Aneurin Bevan's programme of council housing and new town developments after 1945. Bevan himself recognised the potential for the welfare state to promote cohesion and residential integration between income groups, with his vision of council estates epitomising the 'lived tapestry of the mixed community' (Cole and Goodchild, 2001, p 353).

Similarly, an expanded provision of publicly funded education was a defining characteristic of the emergence of the Western European nation state, and schools were (and are) often arenas for the historical struggle between secular and religious authorities over governance structures (Burleigh, 2005). Schools are a particularly important pillar of the welfare state and its relationship to national identity and civic obligation as they are regarded as vehicles for the inculcation of shared values and norms to future generations, evidenced for example in the citizenship component of the National Curriculum (Underkuffler, 2001).

The other pillars of the welfare state – health, employment and social insurance – also have important links to definitions of citizenship and consequences for cohesion: for example the 'postcode' lottery and growing privatisation of health services; the increasingly conditional employment and social insurance rights of the unemployed and new arrivals to the UK; and underclass theories linking welfare dependency to the socio-spatial segregation of deprived neighbourhoods from 'mainstream' British society (see Fletcher, Chapter Five, and Reeve, Chapter Nine, in this volume). This chapter focuses on schools and social housing organisations as neighbourhood institutions, and examines how particular forms of these institutions have become problematised within the community cohesion discourse. The chapter also assesses the evidence of the impacts that these institutions have on social cohesion at the neighbourhood level.

Schools, housing and secessionary spaces

Schooling and housing interact in closely analogous ways to affect the dynamics of neighbourhoods (Bramley and Karley, 2007). Housing and schooling choice and the linkages between them were strongly implicated in the neighbourhood segregation, along ethnic and religious lines identified in the various policy reports into the community tensions and street conflicts in Bradford, Oldham and Burnley that provided the catalyst for the community cohesion agenda in England and Wales (Community Cohesion Independent Review Team, 2001; Ouseley, 2001). The concept of 'parallel lives' adopted within community cohesion discourse to denote polarised cultural identities, insular social networks and a lack of interaction and engagement between ethnic or religious groups also resonates with the different policy contexts of sectarianism in Scotland and the continuing segregation of the two community traditions in Northern Ireland. The growing problematisation of Islam in the UK has led to a renewed debate about the contribution of Muslim (and other) state-funded faith schools to community cohesion and the accommodation of Islamic practices, including the wearing of the niqab, in state schools. In Scotland, similar high-profile debates continue about the social divisiveness or otherwise of a state-funded Roman Catholic school sector.

There is a growing focus within community cohesion policy and discourse in England and Wales on the impact of social housing allocation policies on levels of, and perceptions of, cohesion. More than half the respondents surveyed by the Commission on Integration and Cohesion (2007) feel that some groups in Britain get unfair priority when it comes to services, including housing and schools, with asylum seekers, refugees and immigrants most frequently mentioned, although this belief is stronger at the national than the local level. Although it has been subject to little political or media scrutiny, the presence of black and minority ethnic (BME) housing associations, providing accommodation and specialist services to particular ethnic groups, has been a longstanding feature of the social rented housing system in England; and offers further evidence on the impacts on social cohesion made by ethnically or religiously based organisations within the welfare state.

Both faith schools and BME housing associations represent the publicly resourced and state-promoted institutionalisation of diversity on ethnic and/or religious lines. There are, of course, important differences between them: BME housing associations are much less prevalent in numerical, proportional and political terms in the UK, and BME housing associations may be constituted on an ethnic as well as a religious basis. However, both types of organisation are part of a reconfigured welfare state and both constitute a physical presence within local neighbourhoods. Faith schools are often regarded as undermining social cohesion and the secular authority of government, and – particularly in Scotland and Northern Ireland – are sometimes portrayed as arenas of ambiguous loyalty to the nation state. They also raise a series of issues about how ethnic and/or religious needs should be prioritised and resourced in public spending allocations and accommodated within 'mainstream' welfare services.

Although BME housing associations have not received that much attention within community cohesion debates, the 'Islamisation' of some neighbourhoods has been portrayed as creating potential sites of insurrection (see Phillips, 2006). Although much of the community cohesion discourse focuses on 'parallel lives' creating divisions between populations, there is also an undercurrent of concern about 'parallel' modes of service provision undermining the relationship between citizen and state and the primacy and reach of traditional public authorities. The provision of differentiated services and institutions in some neighbourhoods, including religious law, courts, schools and even, in some Jewish communities a *Hatzolla* (ambulance service), and the private security and environmental services of gated communities not only generates physically distinct urban spaces, but may also be conceptualised as challenging local and national state authority (Valins, 2003; Phillips, 2006). The government response has included proposals to monitor and raise standards of governance in mosques, a growing focus on standards in independent religious schools and expressions of concern about how emergency and environmental services may access gated private residential complexes (Communities and Local Government, 2007a; Atkinson et al, 2003).

The extent to which faith schools or BME housing associations represent a secessionary movement, in both physical and political terms, by certain groups within UK society, and the consequences for social cohesion, needs to be examined within the historical and contemporary context of other secessionary processes in education and housing. First, the provision of both a universal state school system and council housing was built upon the previous and continuing presence of religious and private schools and private rented and owner-occupied housing respectively. This pattern of schooling and residential settlement was influenced by earlier waves of migration to Britain, for example of Irish and Jewish populations in the 19th century. Concerns about the creation of '*deux jeunes*' (two youths) as a result of parallel religious and state school systems have been common throughout Western Europe since the Reformation (Burleigh, 2005), while fears of 'apartheid' schools influenced the desegregation and bussing policies of the United States in the 1950s (Burgess et al, 2005).

Second, the secession and socio-spatial segregation of populations at both ends of the class and income spectrum following the economic restructuring of the 1970s and 1980s have been a prominent feature of urban commentary. The apparent discovery of a spatially concentrated and isolated 'underclass' in the UK (Murray, 1990) characterised by a 'dependency' culture reliant on state housing and benefits had as its mirror image the emergence of affluent gated communities. These are residential developments physically insulated from surrounding urban areas, and, at least in some cities of the United States, are accompanied by an attempt to withdraw from municipal governance structures, including the use of public services and the payment of local taxes (Boudreau and Keil, 2001; see also Blandy in Chapter Twelve, this volume).

Third, the poor 'performance' of schools in deprived neighbourhoods is critical in the reinforcement of disadvantage and is a barrier to social integration, partly because of the increasing use of private fee-paying schools or the ability to pay premiums on house prices to ensure residence in the catchment areas of high-performing state schools (Bramley and Karley, 2007).

Schools, faith and ethnicity

The research evidence suggests that there is significant segregation on ethnic and religious lines in the state school systems of the UK. Burgess et al (2005) found high levels of segregation among ethnic groups in England, although this varied considerably between localities, with South Asian pupils more segregated than black pupils.

They also found that children were more segregated at school than in their neighbourhood, although there was also evidence of residential segregation. In Northern Ireland, the parallel state-funded school system, mirroring ethno-religious residential segregation, results in less than one in ten pupils being from the respective minority religious tradition in most schools (Gallacher et al, 2003). These figures would appear to support the conceptualisation within the community cohesion agenda – arising from its analysis of events in Bradford, Oldham and Burnley in 2001 – of a link between schools, neighbourhoods and ethnic/religious segregation. The Cantle Report highlighted that this 'drift' towards mono-ethnic or mono-cultural educational institutions was not only occurring in faith-based schools (Community Cohesion Independent Review Team, 2001; see also Butler and Hamnett, 2007). In Scotland, although there is little evidence of residential neighbourhood segregation between Catholics and Protestants (Bruce et al, 2004), it is estimated that up to 90% of Catholic households use Catholic state schools where these are available locally (see Flint, 2009, forthcoming). It is this lack of residential segregation, combined with the absence of Church of Scotland schools within the state system, that fuels the argument that the state funding of a distinctive Catholic education sector is a primary cause of sectarian tension in Scotland.

The government in England and Wales operates a policy of encouraging the institutionalisation of religious diversity within the state sector, both through promoting the expansion of faith-based schools and through encouraging existing independent faith schools to enter the state system (Department for Education and Skills, 2001). There are Church of England, Church of Wales, Catholic, Jewish, Methodist, Islamic, Seventh Day Adventist and Hindu state-funded schools. Similarly, the Scottish and Northern Ireland governments continue to support publicly funded Roman Catholic schools within the state sector. A number of state-supported city technology colleges also have a religious ethos, most notably the Emmanuel College in Gateshead, which has been at the centre of controversies about the promotion of 'Creationism' in some schools (Randerson, 2006).

Through the 1977 Education (Northern Ireland) Act and the 1989 Education Reform (Northern Ireland) Order, the state has officially supported the development of state-funded integrated schools (see Flint, 2009, forthcoming, for a fuller account of historical and contemporary developments). Schools in England and Wales now have a duty to promote community cohesion, and the government has published guidance for schools on how they may fulfil this duty (Department for Children, Schools and Families, 2007). In Scotland, schools are identified as having a key role in interventions aimed at reducing intra-Christian sectarianism (Scottish Executive, 2006a), while in Northern Ireland the Department of Education has a duty to support the development of integrated education.

The levels of ethnic segregation within schools have an impact on racial and religious attitudes to 'other' groups (Clotfelter, 2001). A number of studies in Northern Ireland have found that pupils attending integrated schools had more friends from the 'other' ethno-religious tradition than pupils attending 'Protestant' or 'Catholic' schools (Gallacher et al, 2003; McGlynn et al, 2004; Schubotz and Robinson, 2006). Of equal importance was the fact that these studies appeared to show a significant impact of the integrated schools themselves, with pupils making new friendships within the 'other' tradition since attending these schools and that integrated schools managed to maintain a balanced intake despite growing residential segregation in the neighbourhoods in which they were located. This countering of residential segregation may be compared to findings from England and Scotland that show that many schools are more segregated on ethnic or religious lines than residential neighbourhoods (Burgess et al, 2005; Flint, 2009, forthcoming). Furthermore, the Northern Irish studies also suggest that friendships and contacts made inside school were maintained beyond the school environment, and this is supported by Bruegel (2006), whose research in England found that primary school-aged Asian children identified most of their close friendships within their classroom peers. These studies all suggest that it is the day-to-day contact between children that is required to foster robust social relations and networks between different groups, and that this daily contact may also enhance cross-group relations between adults.

This research evidence would appear to cast doubt upon the utility of a central pillar of government intervention aimed at improving neighbourhood community cohesion: twinning programmes for schools. Twinning schools was recommended in the Cantle Report as a means of bringing children from different ethnic and religious backgrounds together through a series of joint educational, cultural and sporting activities. The Department for Children, Schools and Families is supporting a programme of school twinning, while the Scottish Executive has also actively promoted twinning activities between 'non-denominational' and Roman Catholic state schools (Scottish Executive, 2006b). Several English local school-twinning schemes, such as the Unity and School Links projects in Oldham, the Shared Spaces initiative in Bradford and the twinning programme for 'mono-cultural' schools in Peterborough, have been positively reviewed (Cantle et al,

2006), and similarly positive outcomes have been claimed for projects in Scotland (Scottish Executive, 2006b).

However, Bruegel (2006) argues that the limited and sporadic nature of twinning is not sufficient to enable pupils or parents to develop more diverse social networks and Cantle et al (2006) admit that there was little evidence that the Linking project in Oldham that they cite had increased contact between children of different cultures outside school. In Scotland, the complex links between neighbourhood, schools, physical proximity and social relations have been evident in the attempts to develop new-build shared campuses, locating non-denominational and Roman Catholic state schools on the same site. One scheme in North Lanarkshire was halted due to opposition from parents and the Catholic Church, and a shared campus in Midlothian has been subject of considerable media attention focusing on alleged conflicts between pupils, parents and staff (see Flint, 2009, forthcoming).

The shared campus controversies in Scotland illustrate the complexities of state-supported institutionalised diversity in which physical and symbolic separateness are accommodated through public funding. It is evident that many secular state schools have undertaken extensive strategies of compromise and reform to meet the religious and cultural needs of their pupils and parents. However, dilemmas emerge from these developments. It is not clear that these strategies of accommodation within the regulatory and budget constraints of the secular state system are sufficient. A study for Bristol City Council found that, despite a recognition by Muslim parents that existing schools did facilitate sensitive uniform policies, appropriate meal provision and religious observance opportunities, this was not sufficient to prevent widespread support for an Islamic secondary school (Bristol City Council and MORI, 2004). Both the Bristol study and Hewer's (2001) work on Birmingham also found a desire among Muslim parents that male and female pupils should be taught separately on the same campus. Clearly, these demands cannot easily be reconciled within existing education policies and budgets. Similarly, the recent controversies over the rights of pupils and staff within state schools to wear the niqab (Bright and Peters, 2005; BBC News, 2007) illustrate how individual schools provide a microcosm of the community cohesion debate: to what extent can universal services and policies be reconfigured to adapt to the demands of certain sections of the population? There is also a risk that adapting school practices to meet the demands of one group results in the alienation, or even secession, of another. The most famous example of such a process was in Dewsbury in 1987 when a group of parents withdrew their children from a local primary school because of what they perceived as its overly Islamic ethos and attempted to establish their own educational facility (Naylor, 1989). Debates over the extent to which welfare state institutions can respond to diversity and promote cohesion are also evident in social housing, to which the chapter now turns.

Housing allocations and BME and 'faith' housing associations

Residential segregation, linked to housing market and school catchment area systems was identified as a primary causal factor in the disturbances in northern English cities and towns in 2001 (Community Cohesion Review Team, 2001). More recently, the report into the disturbances in the Lozells area of Birmingham in 2005 found that changing populations, perceived levels of refugees and asylum seekers and the fluidity of private tenancies undermined the building of community relationships and neighbourhood loyalty. The report also found concerns that 'one ethnic group is benefiting more than another from public funds' (Latchford, 2007, p 15). Cantle et al (2006) reported continuing residential segregation in Oldham, with a polarisation of inner-city private rented BME neighbourhoods and peripheral social rented white estates regarded by BME households as no-go areas (but see Phillips et al, Chapter Four in this volume for a more complex analysis of housing processes in Oldham). This section discusses two key issues through which the welfare pillar of public or social housing provision is problematised in relation to community cohesion: allocation policies and the presence of a BME and 'faith' housing association sector.

Social housing allocations

The community cohesion discourse identifies the centrality of access to affordable (publicly subsidised) housing in fostering connections within neighbourhoods and illustrates how the allocation of housing may undermine cohesion through generating social tensions between groups of the population and simultaneously eroding a perceived compact between citizen and state as manifested in the right to access welfare provision:

> Access to affordable housing can create and sustain people's affinity and sense of belonging to their neighbourhood. However if one group of people appears to be unreasonably favoured, investment in new homes and regeneration can

be a source of tensions, and be damaging to cohesion and integration. (Housing Corporation, 2007a, p 8)

Both the Housing Corporation's (2007a) and the Commission on Integration and Cohesion's (2007) identification of a perceived unfairness in social housing allocations appear to reflect the concerns of a growing proportion of the population. Findings from the 2007–08 Citizenship Survey showed that 24% of white respondents perceived racial discrimination against whites by council housing departments or housing associations, compared with 15% of respondents perceiving this discrimination in 2001. Of BME respondents, 13% perceived discrimination against their own group (Communities and Local Government, 2007b). A further concern within the contemporary community cohesion discourse is that tensions between established populations, immigrants and local state agencies over access to housing are clearly no longer confined to the northern post-industrial towns with large South Asian populations, which were the focus of cohesion policies in the immediate aftermath of the 2001 disturbances. Rather, rural areas experiencing large inflows of migrant workers from the EU accession states are identified as new arenas for social tensions (and, indeed, fleeting attention is also given to relations between established rural communities and second-home families, see Commission on Integration and Cohesion, 2007, para 1.14).

In response, the Housing Corporation (2007a) and the Commission on Integration and Cohesion (2007) argue that housing allocation and lettings decisions should be clear, fair and transparent and should coincide with attempts to tackle deprivation in areas where one racial or faith group is predominant. In a foreword to the Housing Corporation's Community Cohesion Strategy (2007a), Darra Singh emphasises the importance of how welfare services are administered by local state and quasi-state institutions: 'Trust in local institutions and ... partnerships forged between local people and institutions provide the most effective means of achieving cohesion locally' (Housing Corporation, 2007a, p 3).

However, the contemporary community cohesion agenda is also influencing far more radical proposals that would fundamentally reconfigure the rationales and priorities underpinning the allocation of social housing. Industry Minister Margaret Hodge (2007) suggested a need to rethink social housing allocation policies, which, she argued, 'prioritised the needs of an individual migrant family over the entitlement others feel they have ... we should look at policies where the legitimate sense of entitlement felt by the indigenous family overrides the legitimate need demonstrated by the new migrants'. She went on to suggest that 'need should not be the only factor' and that 'allocations should be based upon length of residence, citizenship or national insurance contributions'. Before we explore the substantive implications of this argument, it should be noted that while perceptions that whites were losing out in social housing allocation systems have been found in recent neighbourhood studies, this is not a universal finding (Watt, 2006; Hewitt and Wells, 2007). Of equal importance is the fact that empirical evidence about social housing allocations, for example to EU accession state nationals, refutes Hodge's claims (Robinson, 2007).

Hodge's arguments raise, but do not provide an answer to, a dilemma. They occur in a context in which social housing has always been the most rationed element of the welfare state, in which decisions about access or exclusion have always been more influenced by judgements (subjective as well as objective) about the character, behaviour and circumstances of claimants (Ravetz, 2001). Hodge's suggestion that 'entitlement' be the primary factor in allocation would overturn a longstanding emphasis on 'priority based on need' in the assessment of the relative circumstances of households. Her suggestions that citizenship, national insurance contributions or length of residence be determining factors would also move Britain closer to the model of citizenship and welfare in Germany (Fetzer and Soper, 2005). However, she also identifies, through her concept of entitlement, a sense that an unwritten but longstanding social compact exists between white working-class communities and the British state. It is this sense of abandonment that the British National Party (very prominent in Hodge's own constituency) exploits, often using council or social housing as a motif.

The community cohesion policy discourse regularly refers to the need to address the concerns of 'settled' communities, often code for white working-class neighbourhoods (Commission on Integration and Cohesion, 2007). However, these communities are far from 'settled'; rather they have experienced transformation in the period since the mid-1970s. Indeed, the collapse of manufacturing employment and the concentration of associated poverty and social problems characterised the residualisation of many social housing neighbourhoods. Tragically, these processes were then inverted through influential underclass theories as the deliberate social, spatial and cultural self-segregation of some deprived communities from 'mainstream' British society (Murray, 1990).

It is also important to understand that the prominence of 'community' and 'cohesion' and its interface with public/bureaucratic housing allocation policies is not confined to ethnicity. Rather, there is a growing emphasis within the social housing movement towards prioritising localised 'community-based' lettings in which fostering social mix, securing local connections and predicting the outcomes of allocations on communal dynamics reside in an uneasy tension with individualised housing needs assessments and bureaucratic state regulations (Flint, 2006). These developments occur within a realigned architecture of social housing institutions that has promoted the transfer of local state-controlled (council) housing to 'community-based' or 'arm's-length' housing associations, which have their corollary in the emergence of common interest developments and gated communities. These seek to bind their residents and regulate community relations through private legal contracts and, in some cases, utilise commercial rather than local authority environmental and security service provision (see Flint, 2006, and Blandy, Chapter Twelve in this volume). These residential processes and the increasing demand among some commentators for an end to the use of the term 'social housing' and all that this denotes (Dwelly and Cowans, 2006) reflect a much wider 'death of the social' being enacted through social and welfare policy reconfiguration in the UK and elsewhere (Rose, 1996).

BME and 'faith' housing associations

The concern over perceptions of unfairness in housing resource provision combines with a wider policy critique of multiculturalism within contemporary community cohesion discourse in a reframing of a central pillar of social housing policy since the 1960s: the promotion of a BME housing association sector and the provision of dedicated funding streams to meet BME housing needs. The Housing Corporation Community Cohesion Strategy argues: 'In line with the Commission [on Integration and Cohesion] recommendations we also intend to consider future investment to benefit a particular community group only in these circumstances where a clear business and equity case is made. This may include schemes that provide exclusive services to … BME and faith communities …' (2007a, p 9).

The BME housing association movement in England represents 'an almost internationally unique example of separate organisational development through the dedication of substantial funds from mainstream national budgets to minority ethnic self-management' (Harrison et al, 2005, p 80). The Housing Corporation's 1986 BME

Housing Needs Strategy formally promoted and facilitated the consolidation or establishment of BME-led housing associations (defined as having at least 80% of their governing members drawn from a BME background). There are around 60 BME housing associations registered with the Housing Corporation, mostly managing very small numbers of units (less than 200).

Given that BME housing associations are an example of state-funded institutionalised diversity on ethnic or religious lines, and the fact that they are a physical presence, often with a concentrated BME population in particular neighbourhoods, they may be expected to have an impact on local community cohesion. The existing research evidence suggests that these housing associations, whether based on ethnicity or religion (predominantly Muslim or Jewish), do not create divided local neighbourhoods or undermine civic development through their separatism (see Flint, 2008, forthcoming, for a full discussion). In particular, many BME housing associations now have a significant, or majority, proportion of their tenants from a different or non–BME background and therefore are not producing socio-spatial 'enclaves' of mono-cultural residential neighbourhoods. Indeed, several BME housing associations have been identified as leading good practice in fostering local community cohesion, including the AKSA BME housing association cited by Cantle et al (2006) as establishing mixed communities in Oldham, and the North London Muslim and Agusdas Israel Housing Associations developing Islamic–Jewish links (Housing Corporation, 2007b).

However, the presence of BME housing associations within local neighbourhoods, even if the consequences for social cohesion appear to be generally positive, raises a number of fundamental issues about how diversity is accommodated within social housing policy. First, equity issues arise in resourcing: for example, the perceived religious needs and practices of some tenants. This is epitomised in the attempt to provide larger family homes, with flexible room spaces and expanded kitchens to facilitate halal food preparation for Muslim tenants. Not only are these attempts sometimes based on a misunderstanding of religious practices, but the fact that almost all households would desire more living space and larger kitchens highlights the difficulties of categorising and prioritising the needs of particular groups.

Conversely, although the Housing Corporation's policy focus has shifted to meeting BME needs within mainstream social housing rather than expansion of the BME housing association sector, it is unclear whether this will always be sufficient to meet specific cultural and social needs. To give one example, in a study of refuges providing shelter for women escaping domestic violence, Wilson (2007) argues that the promotion of racial and religious equality has had little influence on the day-to-day practices of white-dominated women's organisations. She cites a lack of awareness, racial stereotyping and discriminatory practices within 'generic (essentially white)' refuges (Wilson, 2007, p 27) and argues that such 'mainstream' provision cannot provide for the cultural needs of South Asian women, necessitating the availability of Asian-only facilities. Despite equal opportunities legislation and a growing awareness of specific BME and religious needs within the social housing movement, it is unlikely that all mainstream housing providers are currently in a position to meet these needs within their resources. Given that the majority of BME tenants are in 'mainstream' tenancies in non-BME housing associations, improving the housing and neighbourhood conditions across the social rented sector is likely to have the most significant impact on enhancing cohesion at the neighbourhood level.

The continuing presence of specialist local BME or 'faith' housing organisations need not undermine this approach. Indeed, one of the successes of the BME housing association movement is that the presence of state-funded housing institutions based on ethnicity or religion has been subject to relatively little controversy and challenges to their legitimacy. This is all the more remarkable given that they are a physically manifest symbol of diversity within neighbourhoods, in which the social and cultural practices of particular ethnicities and faiths are played out visibly in urban space. This may be contrasted with a wider problematisation of the presence of Islamic or Jewish 'spaces' or 'enclaves' in local and national policy processes (Naylor and Ryan, 2002; Phillips, 2006).

Conclusion

The report into the disturbances in the Lozells area of Birmingham in 2005 recommended that: 'Decisions over priorities and allocation of resources are and should be political decisions, rather than regarded as solely being based on objective and competitive criteria whose cumulative effect can be deeply divisive' (Latchford, 2007, pp 28–9). This highlights the fact that both the welfare state and the community cohesion agenda are political projects, whose outcomes, while masked and hidden to some extent through bureaucratic state mechanisms or the promotion of 'community-based' organisations, reflect the economic, social and cultural capital of different sections of the British population.

The Secretary of State for Communities and Local Government recently wrote that: 'The benefits of globalisation are not always distributed among different communities and neighbourhoods' (Blears, 2007, p 2). She went on to state that she believed in: 'a vision of a Britain where neighbours have respect and concern for each other's welfare' (Blears, 2007, p 3). It could be argued that the development of the institutions of the welfare state, including schools and housing, during the 20th century illustrated both the political ambition to tackle inequality arising from economic forces and also the enactment of citizens' collective concern for the welfare of others. Although the secretary of state pledges a new commitment to citizenship and civic pride, these are not the same things and, as Marshall (1950) understood, the social rights of citizenship cannot easily be divorced from legal belonging or political loyalty to a cohesive polity. Rather, the longer-term viability, sustainability and legitimacy of the state and its welfare system requires an acknowledgement of the need for autonomy and diversity in its neighbourhood institutions, however complex the governing arrangements arising from this may be.

At the same time, debates about the divisiveness of the state funding of faith schools or BME housing associations need to be more directly linked to the private secession – through schooling or housing processes – of more affluent sections of the population and the impact of these secessions upon cohesion within and between neighbourhoods. The Commission on Integration and Cohesion argues that a high level of deprivation in a neighbourhood is: 'an issue that can be addressed locally, or be tackled by local institutions' (2007, para 4.17). It is fundamentally mistaken. The debates around faith schools, social housing allocation and BME housing associations occur within the neighbourhood-level economic and population flow consequences of globalisation. They also occur amid the political and civic consequences of a long-term diminution of the unwritten social contract forged after the Second World War and enacted in the primacy of the secular British nation state and its welfare system and the ethnic and religious certainties underpinning them.

Most of the debates around the impacts of faith schools, social housing allocations and BME housing associations on local neighbourhoods have focused on their consequences for social capital in localities, conceptualised as harmonious daily relations between different ethnic or religious groups. However, these debates have neglected the economic and cultural capital underpinning the extent to which social capital can enhance the life opportunities within local communities. It would appear that faith schools and BME housing associations may be important institutional vehicles for enhancing the legitimacy of the cultural capital of ethnic and religious minorities in the UK. More importantly, it is also evident that improving the overall quality of education and housing in deprived neighbourhoods and narrowing the gaps in economic capital between different populations will have the most positive impact for ethnic and religious minorities and white working-class communities in the UK. This is the role that the welfare state, and the political and taxation system underpinning it, could and should be playing in the quest for greater cohesion within and between our neighbourhoods.

Finally, the research evidence also highlights the complex balance of constraints and choices that influence educational and housing decisions within localities and the variability of the impacts of schools, allocation policies and BME housing associations in different neighbourhoods, influenced by specific local histories and contexts (Amin, 2002; Burgess et al, 2005; Phillips et al, Chapter Four in this volume). This local variation requires further study. More research is also urgently required into how schools and housing associations serving particular ethnic or religious groups actually have an impact on daily social interaction and friendship networks within, and beyond, neighbourhoods.

References

Amin, A. (2002) 'Ethnicity and the multicultural city: Living with diversity', *Environment and Planning A*, vol 34, no 6, pp 959–80.

Atkinson, R., Blandy, S., Flint, J. and Lister, D. (2003) *Gated communities in England*, New Horizons research series, London: ODPM.

BBC News (2007) 'Schoolgirl loses veil legal case', *BBC News*, 21 February 2007 (http://news.bbc.co.uk/1/hi/education/6382247.stm).

Blears, H. (2007) *Letter to Darrah Singh, Chair of the Commission on Integration and Cohesion*, London: Communities and Local Government.

Boudreau, J.A. and Keil, R. (2001) 'Seceding from responsibility? Secession movements in Los Angeles', *Urban Studies*, vol 38, no 10, pp 1701–31.

Bramley, G. and Karley, N.K. (2007) 'Homeownership, poverty and educational achievement: School effects as neighbourhood effects', *Housing Studies*, vol 22, no 5, pp 693–721.

Bright, M. and Peters, M. (2005) 'We still feel cheated and segregated', *The Observer*, 6 March 2005.

Bristol City Council and MORI (2004) *Demand for a Muslim school in Bristol*, Bristol: Bristol City Council.

Bruce, S., Glendinning, T., Paterson, I. and Rosie, M. (2004) *Sectarianism in Scotland*, Edinburgh: Edinburgh University Press.

Bruegel, I. (2006) *Social capital, diversity and education policy*, London: London South Bank University.

Burgess, S., Wilson, D. and Lupton, R. (2005) 'Parallel lives? Ethnic segregation in schools and neighbourhoods', *Urban Studies*, vol 42, no 7, pp 1027–56.

Burleigh, M. (2005) *Earthly powers: Religion and politics in Europe from the Enlightenment to the Great War*, London: Harper Perennial.

Butler, T. and Hamnett, C. (2007) 'The geography of education: Introduction', *Urban Studies*, vol 44, no 7, pp 1161–74.

Cantle, T., Kaur, D., Athar, M., Dallison, C., Wiggans, A. and Joshua, H. (2006) *Challenging local communities to change Oldham*, Coventry: Institute of Community Cohesion.

Clotfelter, C.T. (2001) 'Are whites still fleeing? Racial patterns and enrolment shifts in urban public schools, 1987–1996', *Journal of Policy Analysis and Management*, vol 20, no 2, pp 199–221.

Cole, I. and Goodchild, B. (2001) 'Social mix and the "balanced community" in British housing policy – A tale of two epochs', *Geojournal*, vol 51, no 4, pp 351–60.

Commission on Integration and Cohesion (2007) *Our shared future*, London: Commission on Integration and Cohesion.

Communities and Local Government (2007a) *Preventing violent extremism – Winning hearts and minds*, London: Communities and Local Government.

Communities and Local Government (2007b) *Statistical release: Citizenship survey: April–June 2007, England and Wales*, London: Communities and Local Government.

Community Cohesion Independent Review Team (2001) (Cantle Report) *Community cohesion: A Report of the Independent Review Team, chaired by Ted Cantle*, London: Home Office.

Department for Children, Schools and Families (2007) *Guidance on the duty to promote community cohesion*, London: Department for Children, Schools and Families.

Department for Education and Skills (2001) *Schools achieving success*, London: Department for Education and Skills.

Dwelly, T. and Cowans, J. (eds) (2006) *Rethinking social housing*, London: Smith Institute.

Fetzer, J.S. and Soper, J.C. (2005) *Muslims and the state in Britain, France and Germany*, Cambridge: Cambridge University Press.

Flint, J. (2006) 'Maintaining an arm's length? Housing, community governance and the management of "problematic" populations', *Housing Studies*, vol 21, no 2, pp 171–86.

Flint, J. (2008, forthcoming) 'Faith and housing in the UK: Promoting community cohesion or contributing to urban segregation?', *Journal of Migration and Ethnic Studies*.

Flint, J. (2009, forthcoming) 'Faith-based schools: Institutionalising parallel lives?', in A. Dinham, R. Furbey and V. Lowndes (eds) *Faith in the public realm: Controversies, policies and practices*, Bristol: The Policy Press.

Gallacher, A., Smith, A. and Montgomery, A. (2003) *Integrated education in Northern Ireland: Participation, profile and performance*, Coleraine: University of Ulster.

Harrison, M., Phillips, D., Chahal, K., Hunt, L. and Perry, J. (2005) *Housing, 'race' and community cohesion*, Coventry: Chartered Institute of Housing.

Hewer, C. (2001) 'Schools for Muslims', *Oxford Review of Education*, vol 27, no 4, pp 515–27.

Hewitt, R. and Wells, K. (2007) *On the margins: A qualitative study of white Camden households at risk of exclusion from education and employment*, London: Camden Borough Council.

Hodge, M. (2007) 'A message to my fellow immigrants', *Observer*, 20 May 2007.

Housing Corporation (2007a) *Shared places: Community cohesion strategy*, London: Housing Corporation.

Housing Corporation (2007b) *Housing Corporation assessment: North London Muslim Housing Association*, London: Housing Corporation.

Latchford, P. (2007) *Lozells disturbances summary report*, Birmingham: Black Radley.

McGlynn, C., Niens, U., Cairns, E. and Hewstone, M. (2004) 'Moving out of conflict: The contribution of integrated schools in Northern Ireland to identity, attitudes, forgiveness and reconciliation', *Journal of Peace Education*, vol 1, no 2, pp 147–63.

Marshall, T. (1950) *Citizenship and social class and other essays*, Cambridge: Cambridge University Press.

Murray, C.A. (ed) (1990) *The emerging British underclass*, London: Institute of Economic Affairs.

Naylor, F. (1989) *Dewsbury and the school above the pub*, London: Claridge Press.

Naylor, S. and Ryan, J.R. (2002) 'The mosque in the suburbs: Negotiating religion and ethnicity in South London', *Social and Cultural Geography*, vol 3, no 1, pp 39–59.

Ouseley, H. (2001) *Community pride not prejudice: Making diversity work in Bradford*, Bradford: Bradford Vision.

Phillips, D. (2006) 'Parallel lives? Challenging discourses of British Muslim self-segregation', *Environment and Planning D: Society and Space*, vol 24, no 1, pp 25–40.

Randerson, J. (2006) 'Revealed: Rise of creationism in UK schools', *The Guardian*, 27 November 2006.

Ravetz, A. (2001) *Council housing and culture: The history of a social experiment*, London: Routledge.

Robinson, D. (2007) 'European Union migrants in social housing in England', *People, Place and Policy Online*, vol 1, no 3 (www.ppp-online.org).

Rose, N. (1996) 'The death of the social? Reconfiguring the territory of government', *Economy and Society*, vol 25, no 3, pp 327–56.

Schubotz, D. and Robinson, G. (2006) 'Cross-community integration and mixing: Soes it make a difference?', ARK research update 43, (http://www.ark.ac.uk).

Scottish Executive (2006a) *Action plan on tackling sectarianism*, Edinburgh: Scottish Executive.

Scottish Executive (2006b) *Building friendships and strengthening communities: A guide to twinning between denominational and non-denominational schools*, Edinburgh: Scottish Executive.

Underkuffler, L.S. (2001) 'Public funding for religious schools: Difficulties and dangers in a pluralistic society', *Oxford Review of Education*, vol 27, no 4, pp 577–92.

Valins, O. (2003) 'Stubborn identities and the construction of socio-spatial boundaries: Ultra-orthodox Jews living in contemporary Britain', *Transactions of the Institute of British Geographers*, vol 28, no 2, pp 158–75.

Watt, P. (2006) '"Respectability, roughness and race": Neighbourhood place images and the making of working-class social distinctions in London', *International Journal of Urban and Regional Research*, vol 30, no 4, pp 776–97.

Wilson, A. (2007) 'The forced marriage debate and the British state', *Race and Class*, vol 49, no 1, pp 25–38.

NINE

New immigration and neighbourhood change

Kesia Reeve

Introduction

The UK has witnessed a significant shift in the nature of immigration in recent decades: migrants are arriving in greater numbers, and from a far more diverse range of countries, than 20 or 30 years ago. There is evidence that a new geography of immigration is emerging, resulting in the local presence of households with different motivations, aspirations and needs, raising issues for neighbourhood dynamics and trajectories. Public policy, meanwhile, has prompted renewed interest in the notion that ethnicity (and religion) is a divisive issue, suggesting that ethnic residential 'segregation' is undermining community cohesion in UK cities (Community Cohesion Independent Review Team, 2001; Ouseley, 2001). However, despite the prominence of immigration and community cohesion policy and the heated debates both issues provoke, very little connection has thus far been made between these two policy areas, particularly at the local level. In fact, immigration policy and discourse have remained largely aspatial, contrasting sharply with the rootedness of the community cohesion agenda in assumptions about the consequences of minority ethnic spatial concentration. The community cohesion agenda, meanwhile, has implicitly focused on South Asian (especially Muslim) populations and the neighbourhoods in which they live, serving to problematise these communities but neglecting the potential neighbourhood consequences of the arrival of new population groups.

Recognition of the local implications of new immigration is gradually emerging in both immigration and community cohesion discourse (see for example Audit Commission, 2007; Commission on Integration and Cohesion, 2007; Improvement and Development Agency for Local Government (IDeA), 2007); a reorientation probably prompted by the significant numbers of migrants arriving in the UK from EU accession states since 2004 and pressure from some local authorities to acknowledge the challenges this presents. However, awareness still fails to reflect the scale and pace of change. This chapter represents the beginnings of an attempt to understand the changing nature of UK immigration and the way in which new immigrant settlement is reshaping neighbourhoods and raising different challenges in different places. It explores the geography of new immigrant settlement and the localised impact of this spatial distribution, examining the ways in which new immigration is shifting the population composition and dynamics of some neighbourhoods as new groups coincide with established minority ethnic communities, or settle in locations with no previous minority ethnic presence.

This chapter draws on data gathered through a series of research projects carried out over a four-year period covering the themes of housing market change, community cohesion, minority ethnic housing experiences and new immigration. This includes information gleaned through informal contact and conversations with officers and stakeholders in the areas in which this research has been carried out.[1]

Immigration in the UK

The UK has a long history of receiving immigrant populations. Following the abolition of the slave trade, which brought Africans to the UK from the mid-16th century (Fryer, 1984), African people continued to arrive in small numbers, mainly settling in London and other port locations (Killingray, 1994). Merchant seaman from the subcontinent and Somalis recruited to the British armed forces during the First World War settled in the UK in the inter-war years, in the case of Somalis, joining compatriots recruited in the late 19th century from the British colony of Somaliland to work in English ports (Cole and Robinson, 2003; ICAR, 2007). Polish ex-servicemen migrated to the UK following the German occupation of Poland in 1939 and were joined in the immediate post-war period by other Poles, Germans, Italians, Ukrainians and Austrians recruited to address labour shortages. Other groups with a long history of settlement include Jews, whose arrival in the UK dates back to the 17th century, with subsequent waves of Jewish immigration from Russia, Lithuania and Poland in the late 19th century and again between 1933 and 1939.

It was not until the 1950s, however, that Britain witnessed mass immigration, with West Indian and South Asian households settling in the UK through the 1950s, 1960s and 1970s, alongside ongoing immigration of people from Ireland and the Old Commonwealth (Canada, Australia, New Zealand), who continued to remain greater in number during this period (Berkeley et al, 2006; Clayton, 2006). Commentators point out, however, that during this period Britain remained a country of net emigration (Hatton, 2005; Berkeley et al, 2006), and data available from 1971 onwards show that this remained the case until the 1980s (see Figure 9.1). In the early 1970s net immigration stood at approximately -50,000 per year, a figure that had shifted dramatically to 150,000 by the late 1990s (Hatton, 2005; Berkeley et al, 2006). The most recent figures show a continuation of this trend, with net immigration in 2005 standing at 185,000 (see Figure 9.2).

This shift in net immigration has been accompanied by changes in the population profile of immigrants to Britain. Economic conditions and employment opportunities in the UK, economic, social and political conditions abroad and contemporary policy and legislation all combine to influence immigration trends. Thus, legislation directed towards New Commonwealth citizens restricting their rights of abode in the UK, namely the 1962 and 1968 Commonwealth Immigrants Acts and the 1971 Immigration Act, effectively halted primary immigration from New Commonwealth countries (although family settlement

Figure 9.1: Migration, 1971–2005 (inflow and outflow)

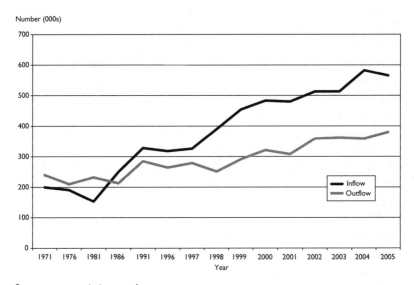

Source: www.statistics.gov.uk

Figure 9.2: Net immigration, 1971–2005

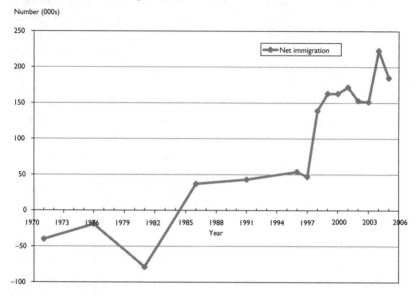

Number (000s)

Source: www.statistics.gov.uk

continued). On the same day that the 1971 Immigration Act came into force restricting the rights of some to UK settlement, Britain joined the European Community, giving freedom of movement to EC citizens and thereby extending the rights of others (Clayton, 2006). The European Community Association agreement in 1994 and the Agricultural Workers Scheme, meanwhile, provided opportunities for non-EU Europeans to live and work in the UK, prompting relatively substantial migration from Eastern Europe (Markova and Black, 2007). More recently, EU enlargement in 2004 extended the right to live and work in the UK to citizens of a further eight European countries (A8 countries), prompting an immediate rise in the numbers of people arriving from these accession states. In the year before enlargement, EU immigration represented 20% of total immigration to the UK. By 2005 this had increased to 35%, taking net immigration of EU citizens from -21,000 to 46,000 in just two years. Workers Registration Scheme (WRS)[2] data support the conclusion that much of this increase is attributable to A8 migration: between May 2004 and March 2007 a total of 630,000 applications were received from A8 nationals, estimated to represent 408,000 individuals (Border and Immigration Agency et al, 2007).

Meanwhile, changing international political conditions have also served to shift the size, profile and diversity of the new immigrant population in the UK. Outbreaks of civil war, persecution and genocide prompted the arrival of (relatively small numbers of) East African Asians, Vietnamese and Bangladeshi refugees in the 1970s, a picture significantly altered by the late 20th century. Asylum immigration has been on an upward trend since the late 1980s, from less than 5,000 in 1988 to a peak of over 80,000 by 2002 (Kyambi, 2005), with later figures showing that a total of 22,750 applications for asylum were made in 2006. In recent decades the UK has witnessed asylum immigration from an increasingly diverse range of countries including Kosovo, Afghanistan, Somalia, Iraq and the Sudan.

The geography of new immigration

Much has been written about the distinctive (regional and local) geography of minority ethnic residential settlement (eg Phillips, 1998; Bowes et al, 2000; Simpson, 2004), noting concentrations in major centres of population such as London and Birmingham as well as industrial towns and cities in the Midlands, Lancashire and Yorkshire. The concentration of minority ethnic households in urban rather than rural locations, and in inner-city rather than peripheral or suburban neighbourhoods is also well established. While the regional spatial distribution of different minority ethnic groups tends to reflect a historic geography of labour shortage, locally a range of housing-related factors come into play. For example, the reliance of many immigrant populations on the private sector has contributed to residential clustering in inner-city areas, and there is an extensive literature about the spatial consequences of discrimination in housing allocation and access that has served to steer minority ethnic households into particular neighbourhoods (Ford, 1975; Ginsburg, 1988; Jeffers and Hoggett, 1995).

There is surprisingly little known, however, about the residential settlement patterns of new immigrants and the extent to which these reinforce (or otherwise) established minority ethnic residential geographies. Certainly no national dataset exists capable of providing comprehensive and accurate information about the spatial distribution of new arrivals to the UK. The patchy evidence that does exist, combined with anecdotal insights from local stakeholders, strongly suggests, however, that a process of change is in train, expanding the spatial boundaries of minority ethnic settlement and potentially raising issues for the future trajectories of some local neighbourhoods.

Continuities in the residential geography of immigration do persist, with regions and cities with a long history of minority ethnic settlement such as London, Bradford and Birmingham still drawing new immigrants. In part, this familiar geography of settlement represents the continued migration of people from ethnic groups with an established history of settlement in the UK, usually arriving in the UK to join family. Kyambi's extensive mapping of new immigrant communities, for example, concludes that by 2001 the tendency for new immigrants to settle in locations with established communities from the same country still prevailed (Kyambi, 2005), while Stillwell and Phillips (2006) suggest that chain migration is one factor sustaining levels of minority ethnic residential concentration in established clusters. Statistics support this view. The West Midlands and the old industrial north-east and Yorkshire and Humber regions – key areas of settlement for Pakistani immigrants in the 1970s – witnessed much of the growth in the Pakistani-born population between 1991 and 2001. Similarly, much of the 49,000 net increase in the Bangladeshi-born population is found in the London boroughs of Tower Hamlets, Newham and Hackney, and in the West Midlands and Manchester – all locations with established Bangladeshi population clusters. According to the 2001 Census the port locations of Bristol, Cardiff and Liverpool, meanwhile, are home to relatively large numbers of Somali-born residents, suggesting continued immigration to cities with longstanding Somali communities (Kyambi, 2005).

Established minority ethnic residential clusters can also draw immigrants from ethnic groups with no presence in the area (Robinson et al, 2005; Robinson and Reeve, 2006). Community and religious facilities, the experience of local services in meeting the needs of a diverse population, relatively cheap housing and the perceived safety associated with ethnically mixed neighbourhoods can all serve to draw new immigrants with no community ties or networks to particular locations. This is particularly relevant in towns and cities with little history of immigrant settlement and where few such residential clusters exist. Research carried out by the author in North Lincolnshire (a rural district in the Yorkshire and Humber region centred around the small town of Scunthorpe) and in Gateshead (a city in the north-east of England), for example, found strong demand for the established minority ethnic cluster areas among newly arriving populations and those with little history of settlement there.

Continuities in established patterns of immigrant settlement therefore remain, driven by chain migration on the one hand and the benefits of traditional reception localities to new population groups on the other. But there is also evidence that a new geography is emerging, shifting the ethnic composition of the UK and potentially reshaping local neighbourhoods.

The shifting geography of new immigration: explaining 'new' patterns of residential settlement

While acknowledging that contemporary patterns of immigrant settlement cannot be reduced to a few simple determinants, a number of key influences can be readily identified. First, in response to growing concerns about the concentration of asylum seekers in London and the South-East, a policy of residential dispersal was introduced in 2001. Second, industrial restructuring and shifting labour market opportunities in the UK have served to draw large numbers of new immigrants to very particular locations. Rather than arriving in the UK to take up employment in manufacturing (as South Asian immigrants did in the 1970s) or public services (as African Caribbean immigrants did in the 1950s), it is in agriculture, food processing and the service sector where employment opportunities now exist. Third, new immigrant settlement cannot be understood in isolation from current housing market conditions. The outcome of these three processes is immigrant settlement in locations (regions, cities, neighbourhoods) with little history of accommodating diversity on the one hand, and the increasing diversification of ethnically mixed neighbourhoods on the other.

Many rural areas and small towns with very little history of accommodating diversity are witnessing rapid and substantial change, driven primarily by new migrant labour. Mainly a product of population movement from EU accession states, a process of rural immigrant settlement was already in train prior to 2004, with new arrivals from other European countries and further afield. Relatively large numbers of Portuguese workers, for example, arrived to take up employment in Lincolnshire and the east of England, while Chinese migrant workers employed in food-processing factories are recorded in West Norfolk (Taylor and Rogaly, 2004). With regard specifically to A8 migrants, the Commission for Rural Communities reports that 23% (or 120,000) of all registrations with the Workers Registration Scheme in the two and a half years following EU accession were from rural areas, and points to concentrations in Lincolnshire, the Wash, Yorkshire and Herefordshire (Commission for Rural Communities, 2007), while WRS data show that Anglia witnessed the highest numbers of workers registering with employers between May 2004 and March 2007. It is in a town in rural Lincolnshire (Boston) where the highest ratio of registrations to working age population can be found (Commission for Rural Communities, 2007).

The local geography of migrant worker settlement is less clear although it is reported that concentrations are more pronounced in rural compared with urban locations (Commission for Rural Communities, 2007). At present, insights are largely anecdotal as well as variable. In some cities (for example Bradford and Birmingham) local stakeholders report in-migration of Eastern Europeans to neighbourhoods with long-established (black and Asian) minority ethnic populations, and in others they report a more dispersed pattern of settlement. Few suggest that recent arrivals from EU accession states are gravitating towards residential clusters of people from the same ethnic group, reflecting both the absence of an established receiving population in some cases (eg Slovak or Lithuanian), and the relatively dispersed nature of established Eastern European populations in others (eg Polish).

Although not presented as such, the policy of asylum seeker dispersal introduced in 2001 was a housing-led programme, representing a way of relieving pressure on areas of high housing demand and 'redistributing' some of this demand to locations with void property. The geography of asylum seeker settlement has thus correlated with the national and local geography of housing (over)supply. The latest figures from March 2007 show that the regions and cities currently accommodating the most National Asylum Seeker Support Service (NASS)-supported asylum seekers are those with a history of immigrant settlement (for example Yorkshire and Humber, the West Midlands, Leeds and Birmingham). Continuing the tradition of immigrant settlement in some UK ports, Cardiff was home to half the asylum seeker population dispersed to Wales in March 2007, while Portsmouth was accommodating the majority of asylum seekers in the South-East. These statistics also show, however, that significant numbers of asylum seekers are living in towns and cities beyond minority ethnic population clusters. This includes Rotherham and Barnsley in Yorkshire (home to 795 and 565 NASS-supported asylum seekers respectively in March 2007), Gateshead and Middlesbrough in the North-East (345 and 625 respectively), and Peterborough in the east of England (190). But even when asylum seekers are dispersed to cities with a history of immigrant settlement, it does not always follow that they are accommodated in minority ethnic residential cluster areas: the local geography of housing supply has served to direct many asylum seekers to neighbourhoods with virtually no minority ethnic presence, including predominantly white, peripheral social housing estates. Once granted leave to remain, the reliance of many refugees on the social rented sector subsequently reinforces this local geography of settlement.

So, economic restructuring drawing migrant workers to new locations in search of employment opportunities markedly different from those in the post-war period, and the dispersal of relatively large numbers of asylum seekers, has apparently served to extend the spatial boundaries of immigrant settlement in the UK. The residential geography of immigration is also, however, influenced by housing market conditions, a fact as true in the past as it is today. The process of suburbanisation in the 1960s, for example, saw the traditional white working-class population gradually vacate the terraced housing of some inner-city neighbourhoods. This, combined with the influx of rental properties onto the market for sale following the introduction of the 1956 Rent Act, created a ready supply of affordable owner-occupied accommodation into which South Asian immigrants moved. Similarly, the upward mobility of Jewish households in the 1950s can be seen to have created 'space' in neighbourhoods such as Chapeltown in Leeds and Moss Side in Manchester where this community had clustered, making way for the in-migration of African Caribbean immigrants (see Farrar, 2001; Hudson et al, 2007 for more detailed histories of these neighbourhoods).

Similarly, a series of recent trends has opened up residential opportunities for new immigrant populations. First, the spatial deconcentration of some established minority ethnic populations (Pakistani, Indian and black Caribbean) may be creating 'gaps' in the market in neighbourhoods where relatively cheap accommodation on which new immigrants rely tends to be located. The process of minority ethnic dispersal and suburbanisation (Dorling and Thomas, 2004; Simpson, 2004) is linked by some to the emergence of a minority ethnic middle class (Stillwell and Phillips, 2006) but also follows a well-established pattern of gradual residential integration (Robinson and Reeve, 2006; Simpson et al, 2006). At present, high levels of natural population growth and continued chain migration are sustaining demand from the established community (Simpson, 2004; Stillwell and Phillips, 2006), but over time this may shift. In the course of researching community cohesion issues in Birmingham, for example, local officers in the east of the city reported that new immigrants were 'backfilling' housing vacated by the established South Asian population. Local data supported their impressions, demonstrating two parallel trends of increasing diversity of minority ethnic cluster areas on the one hand, and an emerging Pakistani population in adjacent areas on the other.

Second, eroding demand for social housing in particular locations (often, but by no means always, on large estates on city peripheries) has prompted a search for 'new markets' to fill increasing numbers of void properties. Local stakeholders interviewed by the author in cities across England have been candid about the opportunity asylum seeker dispersal and subsequent refugee settlement represented within this context. As in the 1960s, then, the shifting residential preferences and actions of white working-class households once again create a geographically concentrated housing supply, which is being filled by new immigrants.

Third, the emergence of new housing markets catering for particular population groups can serve to open up housing opportunities in the accommodation (and locations) they vacate. The development of city-centre student flats is one such example. Migrant workers and students are both served by the same market, namely the low-cost private rented sector. The recent shift in the student housing market in many cities towards purpose-built city-centre accommodation therefore releases supply in a market readily able to respond to new immigrant requirements. In Sheffield, for example, the neighbourhood witnessing significant Polish new immigrant settlement has a long history of accommodating the city's student population, many of whom are moving into the new purpose-built student flats in the nearby city centre.

Finally, housing market processes can restrict, as well as open up, residential opportunities. Rising house prices across the UK, for example, are forcing first-time buyers to consider locations they may previously have discounted. The potential for gentrification of traditional minority ethnic reception localities is therefore high, and new arrivals to the UK may find themselves priced out of neighbourhoods that have long served new immigrant populations. The virtual extinction of a low-cost owner-occupied market will also have implications for immigrant populations traditionally reliant upon this sector for accommodation (such as South Asian new immigrants), potentially serving to draw households into the social rented sector, a tenure with a geography very distinct from private sector markets.

New immigration and neighbourhood change

The previous section has crudely mapped the geography of new immigration, pointing to the ways in which the settlement patterns of new immigrants coincide with and diverge from those of previous immigration streams, both reinforcing and extending the spatial boundaries of minority ethnic settlement in the UK. This section considers some of the challenges wrought by such processes of change and the ways in which the new geography of immigration is potentially reshaping local neighbourhoods, raising questions about the future trajectories of different types of locality.

Within the context of new immigration, we are interested primarily in two processes of change (or types of place). These are, first, places witnessing a first wave of minority ethnic settlement, whether rural areas drawing migrant workers, cities with little history of accommodating diversity or white estates where asylum seekers and refugees have been housed; second, they are places experiencing the in-migration of new populations to established minority ethnic clusters and other diverse neighbourhoods. Drawing on Pratt (1991), Robinson et al (2007a) usefully apply the terms 'established contact zones' and 'new contact zones' of immigration to describe these two distinct types of place. In both new and established contact zones, the arrival of new immigrant populations can shift the character and profile of the local neighbourhood. Except in the case of chain migration to established residential clusters, ethnic diversification of the local population is inevitable, although this plays out differently in different types of place. In new contact zones immigrant settlement introduces ethnic diversity while in established contact zones diversity increases.

The pace and scale of ethnic diversification in some locations has been dramatic; we can draw on a number of examples to illustrate this fact. In 2001 the minority ethnic population of Gateshead, in the north-east of England, was far from diverse. Small numbers of Indian, Pakistani and Chinese households were living in the city but virtually no residents falling within the 'Black' or 'Other' ethnic categories employed by the census. Following the introduction of dispersal in 2001, the ethnic profile of Gateshead changed beyond recognition. It is estimated that within two years approximately 1,000 asylum seekers had arrived into a city that had previously accommodated just 5,891 minority ethnic people (Gateshead Council, 2003). Local officers working with refugees and asylum seekers and interviewed by the author in 2006 were aware of 31 new ethnic and national groups with no previous presence in the city, including people from Uganda, Angola, Iran, Iraq, the Congo, Kyrgystan and Rwanda. A similar picture of rapid change emerges if we examine two authorities reported to have experienced a significant inflow of migrant workers. Prior to EU accession the 2001 Census recorded a total of 4,174 minority ethnic people in Crewe and Nantwich. Of these, just over 1,000 were recorded as 'White Other' (ie not White British or White Irish and the category most likely to capture white Europeans). If reports that more than 3,000 A8 nationals have since arrived in the area are accurate (Border and Immigration Agency et al, 2007; Salman, 2007), then the minority ethnic population of Crewe and Nantwich has nearly doubled and the White Other population has increased fourfold. A similar picture emerges in the rural district of Kerrier where, in 2001, there were just 2,213 non White British residents, just over 1,000 of whom were 'White Other' and where there has reportedly been a recent inflow of 3,000–4,000 migrant workers (Border and Immigration Agency et al, 2007).

The arrival of new immigrant populations can alter the demographic and socio-economic profile of neighbourhoods and, as a consequence, the local profile of housing need (property type, size and design, tenure, cost) can change dramatically, reflecting the different characteristics, preferences, aspirations and circumstances of in-migrating households. Patterns of demand for other services (for example schools and healthcare) can also shift. A mismatch between available supply and housing (and other service) requirements is often the result. Thus, the stated preference for council housing among many refugee households set alongside a parallel preference for living in diverse neighbourhoods (identified in research conducted by the author in Newcastle, Gateshead, Birmingham and Sheffield, for example) is likely to raise significant supply issues. Shifts in neighbourhood demographic and economic profiles can also introduce greater stability or (more usually) transience to the local housing market. Such changes may be witnessed most keenly in new contact zones (particularly rural locations and peripheral social housing estates), which tend to have stable, ageing populations and thus provide the starkest contrast with the relatively young age profile of most immigrant groups. But regardless of age and tenure profile, high levels of mobility among some new immigrant populations can increase turnover in the neighbourhoods in which they are concentrated: asylum seekers, for example, have no choice but to vacate NASS accommodation once granted leave to remain; refugees accommodated by local authorities on predominantly white estates often make efforts to transfer to more diverse neighbourhoods (as was the case among Somali refugees interviewed by the author in Sheffield, and Southern African refugees interviewed in Gateshead); and migrant workers rarely intend to stay in the UK long (Robinson et al, 2007a).

The responsiveness of housing markets to shifting local conditions and demands adds a further dimension, with the expansion of the private rented sector a common manifestation of new immigrant settlement (as noted for example by Commission for Rural Communities [2007] and Border and Immigration Agency et al [2007], in relation to some rural locations where houses in multiple occupation (HMOs) are reported to have increased dramatically and family housing is being purchased for rent to migrant workers). We have already mentioned that Polish new immigrants in Sheffield are apparently filling a gap in the local housing market created by the movement of students into new purpose-built accommodation in the city centre. There was also evidence that the private rented sector in this particular neighbourhood was actively responding to this new migrant population, with landlords purchasing property to market to Polish residents via community internet message boards and local Polish services. Similar processes were reported to be in train in other locations where the author has conducted research, including Birmingham and several New Deal for Communities (NDC) areas where landlords were reportedly responding to the demand (or anticipated demand) from both migrant workers and asylum seekers. Across all 39 NDC areas a correlation between the in-movement of White Other households and an increase in the private rented sector may indicate a market responding to this shifting population profile and associated patterns of housing demand. Thus, in total, 18% of those who in-migrated to NDC areas between 2004 and 2006 were White Other, compared with just 3% of those who stayed within the area, and 44% of in-movers were resident in the private rented sector compared with just 7% of stayers (Centre for Regional Economic and Social Research, 2007).

The consequences of changing patterns of residential demand for the future trajectories of neighbourhoods can point in contrary directions. In buoyant, high-demand markets (which may include some minority ethnic residential cluster areas and rural locations) the increased demand arising from new immigrant settlement can be problematic, reducing housing supply for established residents. In minority ethnic residential cluster areas, where poor housing conditions are commonplace, problems of overcrowding may become more severe, while in rural areas access to affordable accommodation for newly forming households may become even more restricted. But new immigrant settlement can also serve to repopulate declining markets instantly (for example on low-demand social housing estates) and provide a source of demand in locations witnessing the gradual dispersal of the established population. In some established contact zones neighbourhood sustainability can rely on the demand provided by the minority ethnic population. Without a replacement population, the shifting aspirations and gradual dispersal of established minority ethnic households therefore raises the possibility of future housing market decline in certain inner-city neighbourhoods, a decline potentially arrested by new immigrant settlement.

To suggest that in the long term some neighbourhoods could witness complete population renewal would be, perhaps, somewhat exaggerated.

Relatively speaking, new immigrants do tend to represent a small proportion of a local population. However, this pattern of settlement may well be reinforced through subsequent chain migration and natural household growth, raising the possibility that the 'new' communities of today will become significant settled populations of the future, in both new and established contact zones. While it may seem highly unlikely that the few Somali and Liberian refugees currently living in the peripheral social housing estates in Sheffield, for example, will eventually replace the white working-class population of these neighbourhoods, or that Eastern Europeans will become the predominant population of the inner-city neighbourhoods in Bradford where the South Asian community is currently clustered, history suggests that this is not out of the question. Moss Side in Manchester and Chapeltown in Leeds, both locations of significant Jewish settlement, witnessed a process of gradual population change from the 1950s onwards, becoming residential cluster areas for the African Caribbean community. In Moss Side there is evidence that this cycle of population renewal may be continuing, with the reported in-migration and subsequent growth of a significant Somali population (Hudson et al, 2007).

Neighbourhood change and community cohesion

Neighbourhood change arising from new immigrant settlement – particularly when rapid and unexpected – inevitably raises challenges for community cohesion, not least when the precise trajectory of change in a given location is uncertain. Preserving the sustainability of neighbourhoods historically reliant on a particular, but now shifting, demand base, ensuring the needs of the local population are met and managing community relations as new groups coincide with established communities can all be undermined (as well as strengthened) by processes of change.

Local socio-economic conditions and the ethnic profile of neighbourhoods are factors consistently found to affect the potential for cohesion issues to arise, particularly in relation to tensions between communities. Although by no means inevitable, hostility from local residents, a more difficult settlement experience and lower levels of commitment to place among new arrivals can all be more likely in areas with little history of immigrant settlement, and also those areas experiencing economic and social deprivation, where newcomers are more likely to be perceived in terms of competition for scarce resources (Boswell, 2001; Amin, 2002; Wren, 2004; Robinson and Reeve, 2006). Yet it is precisely these kinds of locations that are experiencing new immigrant settlement. Asylum seekers and refugees are disproportionately concentrated in deprived areas, partly reflecting the various processes discussed earlier (a housing supply-led dispersal policy, reliance on the social rented sector, eroding demand in particular locations), which serve to steer these households into lower-demand social rented accommodation. In fact, the locations designated by the Home Office for asylum seeker dispersal correspond closely with the 88 local authority districts experiencing the highest levels of social exclusion (Chartered Institute of Housing, 2003). As noted by Flint (2006), the cohesion risks associated with new immigrant settlement therefore fall disproportionately on deprived neighbourhoods and populations. Rural areas and small towns, meanwhile, are witnessing disproportionate inflows of migrant workers, where the visibility of new arrivals and the impact of their settlement may be all the more pronounced given the virtual absence of an established immigrant population.

It is, of course, oversimplistic to suggest a direct correlation between particular types of place and particular cohesion risks (but see Robinson et al, 2007b for an attempt to develop a model linking processes of change with cohesion implications in different types of locality). The picture is far more complex than this, not least because some of those neighbourhoods that are apparently better equipped to manage increasing diversity (ie established contact zones, with a history of minority ethnic settlement) are also those suffering high levels of deprivation. Nor will different minority ethnic communities necessarily possess the 'awareness and understanding' of each other demanded by the community cohesion agenda by simple virtue of the fact that they are not white British. Thus, while the community cohesion agenda is firmly premised on a form of contact theory (arguing broadly that diversity fosters inter-ethnic tolerance, trust and solidarity), this fails to appreciate that in a context of contention over limited resources, diversity can foster conflict, rather than cohesion. Indeed Putnam's recent work suggests (in a US context at least) that diversity fosters social isolation and the development of distrust, rather than inter-group (or, for that matter, intra-group) solidarity and trust (Putnam, 2007).

Diversity and harmony do not, therefore, always go hand in hand, despite evidence that new immigrant settlement can raise greater challenges in less diverse neighbourhoods; minority ethnic communities, like white British communities, can feel hostile towards newcomers and resent the additional demands on local services, housing and employment they represent, particularly within a context of poverty and many years of struggle for local facilities, resources, recognition and political voice. The schisms that emerge in local communities can appear as inter-ethnic (whether between white British and minority ethnic households, or between different minority ethnic groups) when in fact divisions are drawn on the basis of 'established' and 'new' community identities (Beider and Goodson, 2005). Animosity, hostility and sometimes clashes between different minority ethnic groups have thus been reported in cities as multi-ethnic as Leicester and Birmingham.

In contrast, relatively few tensions have thus far been reported in the small towns and rural locations witnessing EU migrant settlement. EU migrants are certainly victims of abuse and harassment, and evidence does suggest that such experiences may be more common in rural than in urban areas (Norfolk, 2006; Commission on Integration and Cohesion, 2007). Nevertheless, the reception greeting EU migrant workers has generally been more positive than that which has greeted asylum seekers and refugees (Barclay et al, 2003; Craig et al, 2004; ICAR, 2007; Kohn, 2007). One obvious explanation for this disparity is that EU migrants are white. In a non-urban context, therefore, although EU migrant settlement alters the ethnic profile of rural locations, the whiteness of the countryside is preserved (see Agyeman and Spooner, 1997; Chakraborti and Garland, 2004; Garland and Chakraborti, 2006, for discussion about rurality and rural racism). This explanation is supported by one recent study that found that white migrants are received more positively than non-white migrants (Pillai et al, 2007). Research conducted by the author in Sheffield similarly found stark differences between the experiences of white (Polish) migrant workers and black (Somali and Liberian) refugees and asylum seekers, the latter reporting far higher and more extreme experiences of racism and harassment (Robinson et al, 2007a).

Discourses of immigration also perpetuate and reinforce differential perceptions of immigrant groups, in turn influencing their reception and treatment at a local level. Kohn, for example, notes the contrast between the prevailing perception of Polish migrant workers and previous immigration streams. He suggests that the national stereotypes applied to Polish migrant workers are largely positive (hardworking, willing) and that they are perceived as correcting problems (for example the high prices charged by British plumbers) rather than creating them. In effect, they are seen as embodying the values and attitudes of a nostalgic bygone era: they are 'keen, young, white people, taking whatever work is on offer and going to church every Sunday' (Kohn, 2007, p 9). Clayton's (2006) observations about the contradictory nature of immigration discourse make a similar point. He notes that immigrants are accused of taking jobs and depressing wages on the one hand (South Asians in the 1980s, EU migrants today), and of refusing to work and using up welfare provision on the other (asylum seekers) (Clayton, 2006).

The challenge of managing the local changes wrought by new immigration is compounded by an apparent and significant deficit of understanding. Knowledge about the size and profile of incoming populations appears, at present, to be based largely on impression and anecdote. Local officers interviewed by the author in various locations across England have rarely, for example, been able to provide robust information about shifting local populations and associated profiles of need. Although acutely aware that change is occurring, few are equipped with the knowledge to do more than guess at the direction of this change. Many are unable to identify with confidence the ethnic groups now residing in their local neighbourhood. The consequences for race equality and for neighbourhood sustainability are significant. The danger is that neighbourhood planning and management (housing, services, facilities, regeneration activity and other interventions) will be based on current understanding of local housing and service requirements and market conditions. Much is now known about the housing situations and requirements of established minority ethnic populations. It has taken time (and legislation), but knowledge has gradually accrued enabling local agencies to plan for and respond to the needs of these communities (but see Reeve and Robinson [2007] for a somewhat different picture in rural authorities). With the familiar map of ethnic spatial distribution rapidly altering, efforts to meet the needs of local populations may already be outdated in some locations. If housing and service planning forges ahead regardless, we risk reverting to a situation where the needs of minority ethnic households in particular locations are not acknowledged, understood or met.

Conclusion

This chapter has attempted to open up a particular dimension of emerging neighbourhood diversity that has been relatively neglected within community cohesion policy discourse, suggesting that new geographies of immigrant settlement are prompting significant changes and challenges at a local level. Knowledge about these 'new' resident populations and processes of change, however, is currently lacking, potentially carrying considerable consequences: if community tensions are to be averted or successfully managed, if housing and other service providers are to fulfil their race equality duties and adequately meet the needs of the local minority ethnic population, if local stakeholders are to plan for the future rather than the past and if the sustainability of local communities is to be ensured, there is an urgent need to recognise, acknowledge and understand the changed nature of immigration to the UK and the implications for local neighbourhoods.

Acknowledgements

I gratefully acknowledge the contribution made by David Robinson to this chapter. He has been centrally involved in all the research projects on which the chapter is based and many of the points contained within it originate from debate and discussion with David. Thanks also for the very useful comments and suggestions on early drafts.

Notes

[1] Where particular projects are mentioned in the text they are generally referred to as having been conducted by the author, but a number of colleagues were also centrally involved in the management and delivery of these including David Robinson, Rionach Casey, Rosalind Goudie and Ian Cole.

[2] Most A8 nationals working in the UK are required to register with the WRS although there is some evidence that many do not (Robinson et al, 2007a)

References

Agyeman, J. and Spooner, R. (1997) 'Ethnicity and the rural environment', in P. Cloke and J. Little (eds) *Contested countryside cultures: Otherness, marginalisation and rurality*, London: Routledge.

Amin, A. (2002) 'Ethnicity and the multicultural city: Living with diversity, *Environment and Planning A*, vol 34, no 6, pp 959–80.

Audit Commission (2007) *Crossing borders: Responding to the local challenges of migrant workers*, London: Audit Commission.

Barclay, A., Bowes, A., Ferguson, I., Sim, D., Valenti, M., Fard, S. and MacIntosh, S. (2003) *Asylum seekers in Scotland*, Edinburgh: Scottish Executive.

Beider, H. and Goodson, L. (2005) *Black and minority ethnic communities in the Eastern Corridor: Aspirations, neighbourhood 'choice' and tenure*, Birmingham: Birmingham City Council.

Berkeley, R., Khan, O. and Ambikaipaker, M. (2006) *What's new about new immigrants in twenty-first century Britain?*, York: Joseph Rowntree Foundation.

Border and Immigration Agency, Department for Work and Pensions and Communities and Local Government (2007) *Accession monitoring report: A8 countries, May 2004–2007*, London: Border and Immigration Agency.

Boswell, C. (2001) *Spreading the cost of asylum seekers: A critical assessment of dispersal policies in Germany and the UK*, London: Anglo-German Foundation for the Study of Industrial Society.

Bowes, A., Dar, N. and Sim, D. (2000) 'Citizenship, housing and minority ethnic groups: An approach to multiculturalism', *Housing Theory and Society*, vol 17, no 2, pp 83–95.

Centre for Regional Economic and Social Research (2007) *New deal for communities: A synthesis of new programme wide evidence: 2006–07*, Sheffield: Centre for Regional Economic and Social Research.

Chakraborti, N. and Garland, J. (eds) (2004) *Rural racism*, Devon: Willan Publishing.

Chartered Institute of Housing (2003) *Providing a safe haven: Housing asylum seekers and refugees*, Coventry: Chartered Institute of Housing.

Clayton, G. (2006) *Textbook on immigration and asylum law*, 2nd edn, Oxford: Oxford University Press.

Cole, I. and Robinson, D. (2003) *Somali housing experiences in England*, Sheffield: Centre for Regional Economic and Social Research.

Commission on Integration and Cohesion (2007) *Our shared future*, London: Commission on Integration and Cohesion.

Commission for Rural Communities (2007) *A8 migrant workers in rural areas: A briefing paper*, London: Commission for Rural Communities.

Community Cohesion Independent Review Team (2001) (Cantle Report) *Community cohesion: A report of the Independent Review Team, chaired by Ted Cantle*, London: Home Office.

Craig, G., Dawson, A., Kilkey, M. and Martin, G. (2004) *A safe place to be? The quality of life of asylum seekers in Sheffield and Wakefield*, Hull: University of Hull.

Dorling, D. and Thomas, B. (2004) *People and places: A 2001 Census atlas of the UK*, Bristol: The Policy Press.

Farrar, M. (2001) 'The zone of the other: Imposing and resisting alien identities in Chapeltown, Leeds, during the twentieth century', in S. Gunn and R.J. Morris (eds) *Making identities: Conflicts and urban space 1800–2000*, London: Ashgate.

Flint, J. (2006) 'Maintaining an arm's length? Housing, community governance and the management of "problematic" populations', *Housing Studies*, vol 21, no 2, pp 171–86.

Ford, J. (1975) 'The role of the building society manager in the urban stratification system: Autonomy versus constraint', *Urban Studies*, vol 12, no 3, pp 295–302.

Fryer, P. (1984) *Staying power: The history of black people in Britain*, London: Pluto Press.

Garland, J. and Chakraborti, N. (2006) '"Race", space and place: Examining identity and cultures of exclusion in rural England', *Ethnicities*, vol 6, no 2, pp 159–77.

Gateshead Council (2003) *Community cohesion: A summary baseline report on community cohesion in Gateshead*, Gateshead: Gateshead Council.

Ginsburg, N. (1988) 'Institutional racism and local authority housing', *Critical Social Policy*, no 24, Winter 1988/9, pp 4–19.

Hatton, T. (2005) 'Explaining trends in UK immigration', *Journal of Population Economics*, vol 18, no 4, pp 719–40.

Hudson, M., Phillips, J., Ray, K. and Barnes, H. (2007) *Social cohesion in diverse communities*, York: Joseph Rowntree Foundation.

ICAR (2007) *The Somali refugee community in the UK*, London: ICAR.

Improvement and Development Agency for Local Government (IDeA) (2007) *New European migration: Good practice guide for local authorities*, London: IdeA.

Jeffers, S. and Hoggett, P. (1995) 'Like counting deck chairs on the Titanic: A study of institutional racism and the housing allocations in Haringey and Lambeth', *Housing Studies*, vol 10, no 3, pp 325–44.

Killingray, D. (ed) (1994) *Africans in Britain*, London: Frank Cass.

Kohn, M. (2007) 'A very modern migration', *Catalyst*, March–April 2007, pp 9–11.

Kyambi, S. (2005) *Beyond black and white: Mapping new immigrant communities*, London: Institute for Public Policy Research.

Markova, E. and Black, R. (2007) *East European immigration and community cohesion*, York: Joseph Rowntree Foundation.

Norfolk, A. (2006) 'Artist's "race-hate" video divides troubled town', *The Times*, 19 August.

Ouseley, H. (2001) *Community pride not prejudice: Bradford race review*, Bradford: Bradford City Council.

Phillips, D. (1998) 'Black minority ethnic concentration, segregation and dispersal in Britain', *Urban Studies*, vol 35, no 10, pp 1681–702.

Pillai, R., Kyambi, S., Nowacka, K. and Sriskandarajah, D. (2007) *The reception and integration of new migrant communities*, London: Institute for Public Policy Research.

Pratt, M. (1991) 'Arts of the contact zone', *Profession*, no 91, pp 33–40.

Putnam, D. (2007) '*E pluribus unum*: Diversity and community in the twenty-first century, The 2006 Johan Skytte Prize Lecture', *Scandinavian Political Studies*, vol 30, no 2, pp 137–74.

Reeve, K. and Robinson, D. (2007) 'Beyond the multi-ethnic metropolis: Minority ethnic housing experiences in small town England', *Housing Studies*, vol 22, no 4, pp 547–71.

Robinson, D. and Reeve, K. (2006) *Neighbourhood experiences of new immigration: Reflections from the evidence base*, York: Joseph Rowntree Foundation.

Robinson, D., Reeve, K., Coward, S., Bennington, J. and Buckner, L. (2005) *Minority ethnic housing experiences in North Lincolnshire*, Sheffield: Centre for Regional Economic and Social Research.

Robinson, D., Reeve, K. and Casey, R. (2007a) *The housing pathways of new immigrants*, York: Joseph Rowntree Foundation.

Robinson, D., Reeve, K., Casey, R. and Goudie, R. (2007b) *Promoting equality and sustainability through housing market renewal: A strategy for bridging Newcastle Gateshead housing market renewal pathfinder*, Gateshead: Bridging Newcastle Gateshead.

Salman, S. (2007) 'Fitting response', *The Guardian*, 8 August.

Simpson, L. (2004) 'Statistics of racial segregation: Measures, evidence and policy', *Urban Studies*, vol 41, no 3, pp 661–81.

Simpson, L., Gavalas, V. and Finney, N. (2006) *Population dynamics in ethnically diverse towns: The long-term implications of immigration*, CCSR Working Paper 2006-04, Manchester: Cathie Marsh Centre for Census and Survey Research.

Stillwell, J. and Phillips, D. (2006) 'Diversity and change: Understanding the ethnic geographies of Leeds', *Journal of Ethnic and Migration Studies*, vol 32, no 7, pp 1131–52.

Taylor, B. and Rogaly, B. (2004) *Migrant working in West Yorkshire: Report to Norfolk Country Council*, Sussex: Sussex Centre for Migration Research.

Wren, K. (2004) *Building bridges: Local responses to the resettlement of asylum seekers in Glasgow*, Glasgow: Scottish Centre for Social Justice.

TEN

Too much cohesion? Young people's territoriality in Glasgow and Edinburgh

Keith Kintrea and Naofumi Suzuki

Introduction: territoriality in the 'most cohesive society in Europe'

The existence of a cohesive society is often taken for granted in Scotland, and community cohesion has not featured as a concern of government in the same way as it has in England. The term is rarely used in policy debates and there have been no reports or inquiries relating to community cohesion in Scotland. When it has been used, it has usually been introduced by those familiar with developments in England. To take the example of cohesion between religious groups and/or ethnic groups, in response to the car bomb at Glasgow Airport in summer 2007, First Minister Alex Salmond commented that the general lack of retaliatory incidents was 'a tribute to the cohesion of Scotland and the major efforts that have been made by police and others in terms of general cohesion and community support' (quoted in BBC, 2007). On the same theme at a meeting with 'Muslim leaders' he maintained: 'I think we are ahead of every other European society on this. Rather than alienation, the predominant feeling is one of identification' (quoted in Dinwoodie, 2007). As can be gleaned from these pronouncements, there is a struggle within Scotland to imagine itself – or to present itself – as a modern European nation that is socially integrated. These struggles are perhaps intensifying now under a Scottish National Party-led devolved government, as nationalism lends itself to the idea that difference starts only at the English border (McCrone, 1992).

Some might dismiss this as self-delusion, but the debate about community cohesion, as well as being more muted, is definitely different in Scotland. In England it is held in the context of a changing society, arising from differences between social, religious and ethnic groups and rapid changes in cities and neighbourhoods brought on by external migration and internal segregation. In contrast, community cohesion issues in Scotland, even if they are identified in different language, more often represent longstanding divisions in what has been for a long time a less dynamic society. A primary example of the persistence of old divisions is the previous Scottish administration's programme to tackle the embarrassment of sectarianism, in which the former First Minister presented Scotland in general as a place where 'the rich and varied traditions that make up 21st century Scotland are what makes our society so dynamic' (McConnell, 2006, p 1). A key feature of the *Action plan on sectarianism* (Scottish Executive, 2006) was an integration project targeted on pupils in council-run schools, which of course in Scotland operate along unassailably divided lines, with Catholic and 'non-denominational' schools sitting alongside each other in the same neighbourhoods but serving different groups.

This chapter focuses on territorial behaviour among young people as a persistent feature of Scottish urban areas, clearly identified as far back as the 1920s (Patrick, 1973; Davies, 1998), with origins sometimes claimed back to migrant groups in the 18th century. Territoriality can be defined as a claim over an identified geographical space, which is defended against others. It raises questions both about cohesion between places and neighbourhoods and the conflict that comes from too much cohesion. The focus on territoriality has a place in this book because it is a vivid expression of 'communities (operating) on the basis of a series of parallel lives', identified in the Cantle Report (Community Cohesion Independent Review Team, 2001, p 9) as a source of ignorance and fear between people living in different neighbourhoods. Indeed a focus on territoriality shows that segregation between people living in different areas can be the consequence of active social forces, including within groups that are otherwise identical to each other, rather than just a product of neglect of the consequences of ethnic segregation.

The aim of this chapter, then, is to explore how important territoriality is now among young people in Scotland and what are its manifestations, dimensions and implications. It draws on two studies, Suzuki and Kintrea (2007) and Suzuki (2007). The first involved interviews with youth workers and other adults familiar with territoriality in two areas of Glasgow and one area of Edinburgh. The second included interviews with a wide range of adults and focus groups of young people in one area of Glasgow.

Background

This chapter arises from the authors' 'discovery' of territoriality as an important theme of urban life as in two earlier research studies. In research on neighbourhood effects (Atkinson and Kintrea, 2001, 2004) territoriality emerged as a feature of deprived neighbourhoods. Neighbourhoods were riven by hidden boundaries; on one side were familiarity and safety, crossing the boundaries took people into areas of fear and violence. While young people seemed most affected, adults were also embroiled. The second project focused on sports projects for young people (Suzuki, 2007). In investigating their potential to sponsor processes of social inclusion, territoriality emerged as a central mechanism of exclusion, limiting the capacity of young people with respect to their leisure activities and also their effective transition to adulthood.

The literature shows that we were not the only researchers to see glimpses of territoriality while looking at other phenomena. Diverse studies, many of which have a focus on Scotland, mention in passing the importance of territoriality as a limiting factor in young people's lives, especially in disadvantaged areas. Examples include research in the contexts of local health services (Caldwell et al, 2003), mental well-being (Scottish Development Centre for Mental Health et al, 2003), substance misuse (Effective Intervention Unit, 2003), neighbourhood safety management (Atkinson and Flint, 2003), anti-poverty work (Robertson, 2000), homelessness (Fitzpatrick, 2000, 2004), drugs and crime (Bennet and Holloway, 2004), transport (Turner and Pilling, 1999) and parenting (Seaman et al, 2006). A consistent theme was the need for service provision to take territoriality into account in order to improve effectiveness.

The wider literature provides a view that territoriality is something fundamental to human social organisation, without saying much about it as a social problem. Relph (1976) and Sack (1986) put territoriality at the centre of human experience and well-being; Relph suggests that there is a 'deep human need' for attachment to 'significant places' (1976), so there is a strong link between the importance of place and the expression of territoriality over that place, and personal identity and well-being (see Dear and Wolch, 1989). Low and Altman (1992) argue that place attachment also provides access to a community through social networks; in turn, this can promote a sense of identity, particularly through learned behaviour or through a shared religion, culture or lifestyle. In other words, place attachment and territoriality appear to be mutually reinforcing, even when many people are mobile across space (Mesch and Manor, 1998).

If territoriality is fundamental, the question then arises whether it is, in principle, a positive or negative feature. Those who have studied young people's use of public spaces suggest that young people gain significant benefits at a personal level, in contrast to the view that usually labels young people on the streets as a social problem. Wallace and Coburn (2002), for example, suggest that territoriality is a sign of young people claiming some ownership of public space and that territoriality provides psychological and social benefits. Following the classic psychologist Maslow, it seems that territoriality can provide a solution to basic human needs, including security, belonging, esteem and self-actualisation (see Ardrey, 1967), especially in deprived areas where other social resources are in short supply. Indeed, many writers have explained the approaches taken to manage young people in public spaces as an inter-generational conflict over resources expressed spatially (see, inter alia, Watt and Stenson, 1998; Williamson, 1999; Cahill, 2000; Tucker and Matthews, 2001; Pain and Francis, 2004). After all:

> Teenagers have limited ability to manipulate private property. They can't own it, can't modify it, and can't rent it. They can only choose, occupy and use the property of others. This limitation is true in their communities, it's true in their schools, and it's true in their homes. (Childress, 2004, p 196)

The use of public places by young people has been further linked to the development of identity (Robinson, 2000); a sense of place was associated by Hall et al (1999) with the development of citizenship among young people, while Karsten (2005) believes life in shared public spaces across class divides is necessary for the development of full lives in a diverse society, that is, for the development of democratic values.

The literature also suggests that territoriality is not always positive, either at the neighbourhood or the individual level, with regard to its impact on the life chances of individuals. Territoriality has the potential to reinforce the inward-looking tendency often found in deprived places (Atkinson and Kintrea, 2004) and so helps to isolate residents from wider opportunities (Forrest and Kearns, 1999) and to lead to negative labelling by outsiders. The studies discussed above as providing glimpses of territoriality all regard it as placing limitations on young people's freedoms and opportunities. What is more, serious risks arise when territories are defended, (Smith and Bradshaw, 2005).

Researching territoriality

In spite of these commentaries, there have been no studies that have provided more in-depth understandings of territoriality in contemporary Scotland, perhaps because it is taken for granted as a longstanding fracture that is difficult to heal. The localities examined across our two studies were the East End and the South Side of Glasgow, and North Edinburgh. Most of the East End of Glasgow falls within the top 15% of deprived areas in Scotland, and it has been subject to many urban regeneration interventions. The built environment is a mix of council-built estates and older mixed-tenure tenement property in a set of clearly identified neighbourhoods. The East End is known for 'gangs' and it is well documented that they have a sectarian origin. The population of the East End was and is predominantly white.

The South Side of Glasgow was selected in order to research territoriality in more ethnically diverse neighbourhoods. The South Side is a less intensively deprived area than the East End, and comprises mainly older tenement housing, predominantly in private ownership, but with some presence of community-based registered social landlords. Council-built estates, where they exist, are small. Initial contacts with youth agencies confirmed that territoriality was common among young people from black and minority ethnic communities in the area, as well as white young people. The presence of 'Asian gangs' in the area has attracted considerable media attention, especially in the context of the murder of the white teenager Kriss Donald in 2004, and the conviction of his Asian attackers. Asian gangs in the South Side are said to go back to the 1960s (Azam, 2006). In 2006 Strathclyde Police set up Operation Tag to tackle the territorial violence in the area.

The third locality was North Edinburgh, comprising a set of five contiguous council-built estates fringing the Firth of Forth. Again these estates have been subject to longstanding urban initiatives pursuing the regeneration of the locality. Youth agencies in the area have tried to address territoriality through various projects. The neighbourhoods are predominantly white, with the largest minority ethnic group being Chinese.

Within each of these localities, we interviewed adults who worked with, or were directly knowledgeable about, young people and who could provide insights into territoriality in the study neighbourhoods. In the East End, some of the material also draws on Suzuki (2007), whose research included participant observation in sports projects and focus groups with young people, in addition to key actor interviews.

Understandings of territoriality

Territoriality was recognised as an important issue affecting neighbourhoods by all interviewees in both cities and all three localities. It was reported that territoriality took the form of attempts to achieve the domination of identifiable streets or areas by groups of young people, which could spill over into fights between groups, and that resulted in a pervasive feeling of lack of safety among young people, and some adult residents. A majority of those we interviewed, including local police officers, perceived territoriality as a reality of life but also as a major social problem and a significant source of disadvantage and anti-social behaviour. An alternative view – though less frequently articulated – was that the perception of territoriality was exaggerated, was unhelpfully fuelled by the media, and only affected a minority of young people.

It was common for our research participants immediately to discuss territorial groups as gangs, but some interviewees were wary of the negative connotations of the term, although gang does not imply any sophistication of organisation. The young people involved were in the age range 12 to 18, although a smaller number of younger and older individuals were also involved, occasionally children under 10 years old and, exceptionally, adults aged up to 25 years. This finding is broadly supported by Smith and Bradshaw (2005), whose research found membership of named gangs in Edinburgh peaking at the age of 16.

The main participants in gangs were boys, but there was a consensus that girls also played a part in territoriality. Some research respondents suggested that as many girls could be associated with gangs as boys, although others regarded girls' involvement as less serious as a result of their tendency to withdraw from anti-social behaviour as they reached their late teens. Girls could play a variety of roles in a gang, including spectating, carrying weapons (on the grounds that they were less likely to be searched) and sometimes fighting, albeit in a more sporadic or opportunistic manner than boys.

In both Edinburgh and Glasgow, most research participants agreed that a gang would typically have 'hard-core' and 'peripheral' members. There were also non-members, young people from the same area who were not seen as active. While individuals in the core group could be easily identified, the membership of the periphery was more obscure, and the boundary between peripheral members and non-members was blurred. What is more, many interviewees suggested territoriality affected virtually all young people in areas where gangs were active, whether they were gang members or not.

The number of hard-core members of a gang ranged from 10 up to 20 although, if those individuals on the peripheries of gangs were included, the size of a gang could be much larger. In Edinburgh it was reported that the number of young people participating in a single fight varied from 40 to 400, with this very high number of participants being explained by 'non-members' opportunistically joining in. Suzuki (2007) also found that in the East End of Glasgow, young people who did not regard themselves as gang members could still join a fight. If those loosely associated through opportunistic participation in gang fighting and 'tagging' (painting or scrawling gang names and logos in public areas) are included, in some neighbourhoods the majority of young people, or at least males, could be linked to territorial gangs.

While there were common features between the two cities, there were some important differences between Edinburgh and Glasgow. The first difference related to the scale and complexity of territories. The picture in Edinburgh was of one 'team' from each of five neighbourhoods, which were distinguished from each other by housing design and age and were mostly separated by main roads. These teams were Drylaw, Muirhouse, Royston, West Granton and West Pilton. The boundaries and the groups were well established and it was thought unlikely that a whole new team would emerge. The five teams had had a complex history of conflict with changing enmities and alliances over the years.

In both the East End and South Side of Glasgow the number of 'youth gangs' was far greater and their rivalries more complex. A youth worker from the South Side of the city suggested that it would be impossible to tell how many gangs were around in the area, as a gang could easily split at any point. Groups often had offshoots, including junior and female versions, membership was flexible and shifting and one group could be in conflict with several others at the same time:

> 'Now, if you got a young person from Lilybank, who goes to Eastbank Secondary School, [he needs] to cross a territorial barrier to go there, because gang fighting happens. There's hundreds and hundreds of gangs within the East End of Glasgow. Hundreds of them. Right? So that means they need to cross boundaries ... they need to cross boundaries all the time.' (sports project coordinator, East End of Glasgow)

A second difference between the two cities was the extent of the violence involved in territorial conflict. In Edinburgh, many interviewees considered that the incidence and seriousness of violence had died down in recent years. However, in Glasgow, the perception was generally the opposite, as we were told:

> 'Gang fighting is nothing unusual. Very common. It's near enough a ritual every night of the week.' (basketball coach, East End of Glasgow)

> 'How often did I fight when I was younger? Every night. Every week.' (football coach, East End of Glasgow)

The process of conflict across boundaries, often located at 'pinch points' such as bridges, was similar in both cities. Conflicts typically happened over a period of days or sometimes weeks, starting with rival groups congregating, then baiting and running at each other, then escalating to fights involving blunt objects and sometimes knives. After serious injuries to participants, the police became involved and the territorial activity calmed down for a while, before building up again. The main combatants were 13 to 15 years old. Older gang members did participate in the fighting on occasion, but more often played a role in arranging the fights. Younger individuals took a supporting role, carrying messages and usually staying in the background during actual incidents of fighting.

The history and geography of territorial culture

Strathclyde Police, based on 'intelligence' sources, has mapped out 110 gangs in Glasgow (see Leask, 2006). This suggests that many gang territories are small, on average just over half a square mile per territory. There is also a very uneven coverage of active gangs, suggesting even smaller territories in practice. Moreover, the distribution of gangs is skewed to areas with high deprivation levels, with no gangs known in most of the more affluent areas. This is confirmed, if not necessarily reliably, by a website claiming to list 'every gang in Glasgow' (Glasgow Gangs, 2007). Even if some of the names on this site are supplied by 'wannabes' rather than active gangs, they are still heavily clustered in deprived areas of the city.

The territoriality of today carries a strong shadow of the past. While territoriality in Edinburgh was said to go back to the 1960s and to have been based on the same territorial neighbourhood boundaries as today, Glasgow's past has a more ghostly presence. Some of today's gangs use names that are the same (or versions of) names used in more distant historical periods, well before the lifetimes of the young people and even their parents and grandparents. However, if the distant origin of territoriality was in religious, ethnic or social class differences, these seem to have been dissolved now. Interviewees were clear that contemporary territorial conflict was not linked to sectarianism, in spite of the names of some gangs being obviously associated with Catholicism and Orangeism/Protestantism. Contemporary conflict between youth groups does not appear to be based on class or social distinction, perhaps reflecting the concentration of gang activity in deprived areas. If there were past differences between areas related to perceived respectability and the deservedness of particular housing outcomes (Damer, 1989), these too seemed to have vanished. There appeared to be no sub-cultural differences between the groups of white young people and no competing or clashing preferences in terms of music, clothes or lifestyles.

Territoriality, then, seemed to be only about geographical location and attachment and allegiance to neighbourhood places. This form of territoriality was deeply embedded. Most accounts in Glasgow held that that territoriality was 'generational'; there was an acceptance by parents and other older generations that territorial behaviour among young people was normal, which was based on their own experiences when young. There was said to be a 'historical attachment' to it; young people would not always be castigated by their parents for their involvement. One police officer interviewee recalled when arriving at a house, that he was told by the mother that her son was 'away out gang fighting ... he'll be back later on', in the same way as if he been playing football or at the youth club. It was therefore regarded as part of the rites of passage for male teenagers to be involved in gang fighting.

Racial or ethnic differences were not important factors affecting territoriality in North Edinburgh. Although police officers regarded hate crimes towards minority ethnic groups as being gang-related, these were not regarded as the main causes or manifestations of conflict in the area, reflecting the fact that white people predominate and most conflicts were between whites. On the South Side of Glasgow, where there is a substantial Asian population and some residential segregation on ethnic lines, territorial difference seemed to co-exist with racial differences. It was regarded by research respondents, however, that it would be as likely for a group of Asians to fight another group of Asians as it would be for them to fight a group of whites. It was also considered to be unlikely that a white gang would team up with other white gangs specifically to fight Asians, or vice versa. The presence of any territorial gangs with both Asian and white members could not be confirmed by any interviewees, although it was believed to be unlikely.

But overall, young people seemed to care about territorial divisions much more than racial or ethnic ones. This is not to say that there are not differences between Asian and white gangs. It was suggested by research respondents that Asian youth culture, more so than white, has been influenced by the American black gang culture through music and clothing. It was also suggested that Asian gang members were more affluent, or at least displayed more explicit material aspirations, particularly related to expensive cars.

The pattern of territoriality in Glasgow may be complicated by the fact that migration and residential settlement in the city occurred among different ethnic minority groups in different historical periods. However, it appears somewhat unusual in the wider UK context, given that in other cities territoriality seems to more explicitly represent racial differences. For example, Webster (1996) describes the dynamics in which racial tension between white and Asian youths in the north of England led to territoriality, or in his term, 'localism'.

Explanations for territorial behaviour

On the whole, interviewees tended to suggest that the primary reason for territorial behaviour and gang involvement was disadvantage, in families and in places, and poor levels of achievement in education and/or employment, leading to low self-confidence and self-esteem. Young people might then pursue alternative forms of recognition and respect by taking part in gang activities. This was true of both Edinburgh and Glasgow and of white and Asian youths, and supports the findings that gang activity was heavily weighted towards disadvantaged areas. Several respondents suggested that young people living in oppressive conditions in deprived neighbourhoods also needed a 'release valve'. However, none of these circumstantial factors exactly explains why reactions to these social conditions find their expression in specifically territorial behaviour.

The second type of explanation related to the excitement that young people derived from territorial behaviour. There was a fair amount of agreement among interviewees in both cities that territoriality was a leisure activity during which 'recreational violence' could be practised; one described it as 'entertainment' and a 'big game'. Suzuki (2007) also confirms this from young people's point of view. Asked why he participated in gang fighting, one recent participant replied:

> 'Because there's nothing else to do on the streets. Cos I was
> bored senseless, and what I was doing was, I was running

about 'n' gang fightin' ... young people go and fight, because they like the adrenalin rush. And then the police come... they get chased and ... it's like, all just adrenalin. Just something to keep the night going.' (football coach, East End of Glasgow)

A third explanation suggested that, where territoriality and violence were commonplace, there was a recursive effect. Young people, threatened by gang members, might associate themselves with a gang in order to avoid being targeted. However, most respondents in fact believed the overall risk of victimisation would be much higher if a young person was a gang member.

The impacts of territoriality

The research respondents unanimously agreed that territoriality placed limits on young people's freedom to travel to areas outside their own home locality, especially during evenings and weekends. We were told repeatedly that in areas affected by gangs, young people would not go into other territories unless accompanied by adults, otherwise they would feel unsafe:

NS:	I wonder why you don't go to other places to find something else to do?
Girl 1:	Lots of different people fight us.
NS:	Could you tell me about it a bit more?
Girl 1:	Between schemes.
Boy 1:	Like, Bridgeton gangs going to Calton.
Girl 1:	And fight.
Boy 1:	Gang fighting.
Girl 1:	Gang fighting, so that we cannot really go to other places because of the gang fighting.
NS:	So gang fighting, [Name of Girl 1], do you feel it's dangerous for you to travel across [area boundaries]?
Girl 1:	Uh huh. People ask me 'Where are you from? Where's your scheme?' If I'm in another scheme or another place, people ask me 'Where's your scheme?', and people don't like me because of where I stay.
NS:	So do they actually attack you?
Girl 1:	Yes. They want to fight with you. Like, if I come up here [venue name], nothing would happen,

> but if you are in like all places like Haghill, then they will want to fight with you because you're from a different area.
>
> Girl 3: Aye.
> Girl 1: Lots of, lots of gang fighting. (transcript of focus group, East End of Glasgow)

The immediate significance of this limiting impact of territoriality was that it denied young people access to amenities and services, and even to visits to family and friends, and kept them in their own neighbourhoods where amenities were typically very limited. For youth workers to persuade young people to use major public facilities such as leisure centres and swimming pools, which are well located near major bus routes and main roads but surrounded by residential areas, it was necessary to accompany them, or to provide minibus transport, even when the facilities were within a short walking distance. For some young people the fear was so strong that even when transport was provided they were still unwilling to take up the opportunities. In both cities it was agreed that the more deeply young people had been involved in gangs, the more likely they were to withdraw into their own territory and not seek opportunities outside it. However, there are complex factors at work here. Some respondents were keen to stress that confinement to their home area not only came from the fear of attack, but also from general low self-confidence and self-esteem, which was probably the root of their territorial attachment in the first place. The extent of these impacts was not altogether clear, but it seemed in some areas that it was difficult for any young person, even non-members of gangs, to avoid some influence. Notwithstanding the discussion above, the focus groups suggested that girls tended to have more freedom to move than boys, probably reflecting their secondary status within gangs.

It was also reported by many interviewees that territoriality, especially expressed in active gang membership, carrying weapons and gang fighting tended to lead to young people becoming criminalised, as the police got involved. Police officers in particular stressed how the passive activity of carrying a knife could very quickly translate into a violent offence, with fairly random results as to who became a criminal and who a victim. However, it was said that 'intelligent' gang members would quit committing crimes when they reached the age of 16 so as to avoid being subject to the adult court system. But as far as organised criminal activities were concerned, respondents – including police officers – uniformly believed that there was no link between 'youth gangs' and adult criminal organisations. Although many suggested that there was a link between deep involvement in territorial gangs and criminality as an adult, this was not attributed to direct association with adult criminals. In both Edinburgh and Glasgow it was believed that organised criminals tended to isolate themselves from other groups so as to become less visible. An exception, however, was found in one neighbourhood in North Edinburgh, where the 'young team', men aged from 17 to 20, were increasingly becoming criminalised. But these individuals were also regarded as isolated from the rest of gangs, and to be less interested and involved in territorial fights.

This discussion also raises issues of personal safety. Information about the level of violence was provided by some of the police interviews, and we were given the opportunity to view CCTV images of fights. Personal safety also emerged as a key issue in the focus groups carried out by Suzuki (2007), for example:

NS:	OK, well, but do those people fight really seriously?
Boys 1 and 2:	Aye. Crush bottles, bricks.
Boy 1:	See, if they catch you, near enough kill you.
Boy 2:	They stab you, slash you wi' blades.
Boy 1:	Knives. Stab you.
Boy 2:	Murder.
NS:	Are they young people like youse?
Boy 2:	Aye. (transcript of focus group, East End of Glasgow)

These features of territoriality, the limitation placed on the personal freedom of most young people, the criminalisation of a smaller number of gang participants and the presence of physical risk certainly have the strong potential to result in a negative impact on the wider opportunities of young people as they make the key transitions to adulthood (Furlong et al, 2003). Criminal records induced by the involvement in gang-related activities would, for example, reduce employment opportunities. In addition, there is a risk that opportunities of jobs or further education might be unavailable where fear limits freedom to travel outside their own neighbourhoods. Certainly some respondents believed that hard-core gang members in particular were unwilling to take a job or go to college outside their home neighbourhood territory.

There was some difference between Glasgow and Edinburgh in this respect; the opinions of interviewees in North Edinburgh suggested little or no effect on young people's use of urban space, whereas many more research respondents in both study areas of Glasgow tended to think that there were genuine restrictions on young people, arising from the manifestations of territoriality. This might be related to the geographical distribution of educational or employment opportunities in the respective cities. North Edinburgh is a mainly residential locality and therefore most employment opportunities were found elsewhere, as were colleges. Therefore, young people would see fewer problems in travelling to sites of employment or further education as these were located in 'neutral ground' at some distance from their own and rival territories. Ironically, the more localised provision of jobs and college annexes in Glasgow, which have been deliberately decentralised in the city to a neighbourhood level for reasons of community outreach, might make them less accessible there because of territorial boundaries.

Altogether, what this research suggests is that there are good grounds for thinking that territoriality is an important factor in limiting young people's lives and inhibiting a successful transition to the opportunities of adult life.

Conclusion: too much cohesion?

At the time of writing this in 2008, the media is full of accounts about youth gangs, many of them black, based in urban areas and housing estates and involved in serious crime, including access to firearms. The government in England has commissioned reports looking into these problems, and funded various initiatives to stop gun crime. The territorial behaviour we have discussed here in Scotland's biggest cities appears different; territoriality is distinct from organised criminality, and violent behaviour is at a lower level and distinctly ritualistic rather than purposive, and its practitioners appear to be somewhat younger. There also appears to be limited differences between white and Asian youths' behaviour.

We sense, however, that the kind of territoriality experienced in Scotland, and Glasgow especially, is particularly disadvantageous, even if its familiarity and its relatively low levels of violence attract less attention at the UK level. In many senses this territoriality is an expression of community cohesion, and the evidence supports the theories of the importance of place to human relationships. Territoriality is a form of cohesive behaviour that has its roots far in the past and has not been shaken off by social change. Rather, it remains as a ghost image of a distant, and differently divided, past. Indeed, it is possible to surmise that what social change there has been has actually entrenched territoriality further. The East End of Glasgow and North Edinburgh, if less so

Glasgow's more variegated South Side, are dominated by very deprived housing estates, where there has been a long process of residualisation against the background of industrial decline. Regeneration efforts have done much to improve the quality of the built environment, and both cities' economies are recovering on a new services base, but these changes have done little to reduce the comparative multiple deprivation of our study neighbourhoods. Adults living in these neighbourhoods often have highly circumscribed lives, much more so than residents in poor areas in more dynamic areas of the UK (Atkinson et al, 2005), and young people, it now seems, are even more affected. Central Scotland, of course, has not been unique in its experience of industrial change, but the extent of deprived areas, in Glasgow in particular, and the importance of social housing with its close association with poverty right across the central belt of Scotland are distinctive compared with most other UK urban contexts.

One youth worker in the East End of Glasgow told us that for young people territoriality was about 'having a sense of belonging, that no one can take away from you', with the implication that place and local friendships were some of the few things that young people living in deprived neighbourhoods could call their own. Yet the impact on young people's lives, especially because the ages of those most deeply involved in territoriality coincide with the time of transition from youth to adulthood where opportunities open up possibilities or barriers close them down, is potentially very problematic, even if the disadvantages are not so spectacular as being the victim of gun crime.

There are many important questions that remain unanswered in studies of territoriality. The first question is about the scale of its adverse effects. The relationship between cohesion, territoriality, gang involvement and limited opportunities is real, but it is not fully clear how many young people are affected, and to what extent. The differences that exist between Edinburgh and Glasgow and other variants of territorial behaviour in other cities in the UK that are emerging as part of wider study on this topic (Kintrea et al, 2008) also suggest that there are specifically local cultural factors at work that need to be better understood through research into the direct experience of young people in different places. Finally, a question only touched on in this chapter is 'What is it in particular that young people get out of territoriality?'. More insight into this is essential for any successful strategy aimed at countering the negative elements of territoriality and offering alternative positive mechanisms for young people to articulate and celebrate their local identity and place attachment.

Acknowledgements

This paper is based in part on research supported by the Scottish Executive, but the views expressed are the authors' own.

References

Ardrey, R. (1967) *The territorial imperative animal: A personal inquiry into the origins of property and nations*, Glasgow: Fontana/Collins.

Atkinson, R. and Flint, J. (2003) *Locating the local in informal processes of social control: The defended neighbourhood and informal crime management*, CNR paper 10, Bristol: ESRC Centre for Neighbourhood Research.

Atkinson, R. and Kintrea, K. (2001) 'Disentangling neighbourhood effects: Evidence from deprived and non-deprived neighbourhoods', *Urban Studies*, vol 38, no 11, pp 2277–98.

Atkinson, R. and Kintrea, K. (2004) '"Opportunities and despair, it's all in there": Practitioner experiences and explanations of area effects and life chances', *Sociology*, vol 38, no 3, pp 437–55.

Atkinson, R., Buck, N. and Kintrea, K. (2005) 'British neighbourhoods and poverty: Linking place and social exclusion', in N. Buck, I. Gordon, A. Harding and I. Turok (eds) *Changing cities*, Basingstoke: Palgrave Macmillan.

Azam, I. (2006) 'Asian gang life in glasgow' (www.asianimage.co.uk/display.var.1020787.0.asian_gang_life_in_glasgow.php?act=login).

BBC (2007) 'Salmond praises airport heroes', *BBC News Scotland*, 3 July (http://news.bbc.co.uk/1/hi/scotland/glasgow_and_west/6266906.stm).

Bennet, T.H. and Holloway, K.R. (2004) 'Gang membership, drugs and crime in the UK', *British Journal of Criminology*, vol 44, no 3, pp 305–23.

Cahill, C. (2000) 'Street literacy: Urban teenagers' strategies for negotiating their neighbourhood', *Journal of Youth Studies*, vol 3, no 3, pp 251–77.

Caldwell, C., McCann, G., Flower, C. and Howie, J. (2003) *Have you been PA'd?: Using participatory appraisal to shape local services*, Glasgow: Oxfam.

Childress, H. (2004) 'Teenagers, territory and the appropriation of space', *Childhood*, vol 11, no 2, pp 195–205.

Community Cohesion Independent Review Team (2001) (Cantle Report) *Community cohesion: A report of the Independent Review Team, chaired by Ted Cantle*, London: Home Office.

Damer, S. (1989) *From Moorepark to Wine Alley: The rise and fall of a Glasgow housing scheme*, Edinburgh: Edinburgh University Press.

Davies, A. (1998) 'Street gangs, crime and policing in Glasgow during the 1930s: The Case of the Beehive Boys', *Social History*, vol 23, no 3, pp 251–67.

Dear, M. and Wolch, J. (1989) 'How territory shapes social life', in M. Dear and J. Wolch (eds) *The power of geography*, London: Unwin Hyman.

Dinwoodie, R. (2007) 'Salmond: Scotland leads the way in social cohesion', *The Herald*, 1 August (www.theherald.co.uk/search/display.var.1586553.0.0.salmond_scotland_leads_way_in_social_cohesion.php).

Effective Intervention Unit (2003) *Services for young people with problematic drug misuse: A guide to principles and practice*, Edinburgh: Scottish Executive.

Fitzpatrick, S. (2000) *Young homeless people*, Basingstoke: Macmillan.

Fitzpatrick, S. (2004) 'Poverty of place: Keynote address given at the University of York', JRF Centenary Conference: Poverty and Place: Policies for Tomorrow, York: Joseph Rowntree Foundation (www.jrf.org.uk/conferences/centenary/pdf/povertyofplace.pdf).

Forrest, R. and Kearns, A. (1999) *Joined up places: Social cohesion and neighbourhood regeneration*, York: Joseph Rowntree Foundation.

Furlong, A., Cartmel, F., Biggart, A., Sweeting, H. and West, P. (2003) *Youth transitions: Patterns of vulnerability and processes of social inclusion*, Edinburgh: Central Research Unit, Scottish Executive.

Glasgow Gangs (2007) (http://glasgowgangs.freewebspace.com/custom2.html).

Hall, T., Coffey, A. and Williamson, H. (1999) 'Self, space and place: Youth identities and citizenship', *British Journal of Sociology of Education*, vol 20, no 4, pp 501–13.

Karsten, L. (2005) 'It all used to be better? Different generations on continuity and change in urban children's daily use of space', *Children's Geographies*, vol 3, no 3, pp 275–90.

Kintrea, K., Bannister, J., Pickerinig, J., Reid, M. and Suzuki, N. (2008, forthcoming) *Young people and territoriality in British cities*, York: Joseph Rowntree Foundation.

Leask, D. (2006) 'Gang map of Glasgow 2006', *Evening Times*, 7 February.

Low, S. and Altman, I. (1992) 'Place attachment: A conceptual inquiry', in I. Altman, and S. Low (eds) *Place attachment*, London: Plenum Press.

McConnell, J. (2006) 'Foreword', in Scottish Executive, *Action plan on sectarianism*, Edinburgh: Scottish Executive.

McCrone, D. (1992) *Understanding Scotland: The sociology of a stateless nation*, London: Routledge.

Mesch, G. and Manor, O. (1998) 'Social ties, environmental perceptions and local attachment', *Environment and Behaviour*, vol 30, no 4, pp 504–19.

Pain, R. and Francis, R. (2004) 'Living with crime: Spaces of risk for young homeless people', *Children's Geographies*, vol 2, no 1, pp 95–110.

Patrick, J. (1973) *A Glasgow gang observed*, London: Eyre Methuen.

Relph, E. (1976) *Place and placelessness*, London: Pion.

Robertson, J. (2000) 'Boys, girls, and gangs', Oxford: Oxfam.

Robinson, C. (2000) 'Creating space, creating self: Street frequenting youth in the city and suburbs', *Journal of Youth Studies*, vol 3, no 4, pp 429–43.

Sack, R. D. (1986) *Human territoriality: Its theory and history*, Cambridge: Cambridge University Press.

Scottish Development Centre for Mental Health, Scottish Council Foundation and OPM (2003) *Building community well-being: An exploration of themes and issues*, Edinburgh: Scottish Executive.

Scottish Executive (2006) *Action plan on sectarianism*, Edinburgh: Scottish Executive.

Seaman, P., Turner, K., Hill, M., Stafford, A. and Walker, M. (2006) *Parenting and children's resilience in disadvantaged communities*, York: Joseph Rowntree Foundation.

Smith, D. and Bradshaw, P. (2005) *Gang membership and teenage offending*, Edinburgh: Centre for Law and Society, University of Edinburgh.

Suzuki, N. (2007) 'Sport and social inclusion', PhD thesis, Glasgow: University of Glasgow.

Suzuki, N. and Kintrea, K. (2007) *Young people and territoriality in Scotland: An exploratory study*, Glasgow: Department of Urban Studies.

Tucker, F. and Matthews, H. (2001) 'They don't like girls hanging around there: Conflicts over recreational space in rural Northamptonshire', *Area*, vol 33, no 2, pp 161–8.

Turner, J. and Pilling, A. (1999) 'Integrating young people into integrated transport: A community based approach to increase travel awareness', paper presented at the Planning and Transport, Research and Computation Young People and Transport Conference, Manchester, 24 November 1999.

Wallace, D. and Coburn, A. (2002) '"Space – the final frontier": An exploration of territoriality and young people', *Scottish Youth Issues Journal*, no 5, Winter 2002, pp 73–92.

Watt, P. and Stenson, K. (1998) 'The street: It's a bit dodgy around there: Safety, danger, ethnicity and young peoples' use of public space', in T. Skelton and G. Valentine (eds) *Cool places: Geographies of youth cultures*, London: Routledge.

Webster, C. (1996) 'Local heroes: Violent racism, localism and spacism among Asian and white young people', *Youth and Policy*, vol 53, pp 15–27.

Williamson, H. (1999) 'Self, space and place: Youth identities and citizenship', *British Journal of the Sociology of Education*, vol 20, no 4, pp 501–14.

ELEVEN

Geodemographics and the construction of differentiated neighbourhoods

Roger Burrows

Introduction

This chapter is concerned with the relationship between social geography and digital representations of it. It argues that it is increasingly the case that vernacular, proximate, immanent perceptions of neighbourhood identity are losing their influence to a range of urban informatics technologies able to ascribe powerfully the supposed essential character of localities from afar (Burrows and Gane, 2006; Parker et al, 2007). Further, it argues that there are good theoretical reasons to suggest that these digital attributions of neighbourhood character are forming ever-more recursive associations with whatever passes for 'ground truth' (Pickles, 1995), to the extent that we may need to start thinking far more profoundly about the contemporary constitution of place as a complex process of co-construction between software and material social relations (Parker et al, 2007). The notion that we have entered an era of the automatic production of space (Thrift and French, 2002) is not just a theoretical issue; it is also one that will have profound implications for policy, practice and everyday life. The fact that new forms of technology are being utilised to construct ever-more diverse and segmented notions of neighbourhood, and that these constructions may in turn influence dynamics of cohesion within and between neighbourhoods, linked to residential location choices and the imagery of neighbourhood characteristics, has to date been absent from policy discourses on community cohesion in the UK.

The social codification of neighbourhoods

Although the social codification of neighbourhoods has a long history, with a lineage that stretches back at least as far as Charles Booth's *Descriptive map of London poverty* in the late 1880s (Harris et al, 2005, pp 30–7), it was only with the introduction of a now very mundane technology for the social production of spatial location, the common postcode (or, in the US, zip code), that the construction of modern geodemographic systems – our main focus in this chapter – became a possibility. Of course, postcodes were not introduced with this purpose in mind. They were originally devised solely for the purposes of sorting and directing mail. The history of postcodes will not be the most compelling of topics for many people, but several of the historical decisions taken about their functioning and formatting in different countries have turned out to be crucial antecedents in explaining cross-national variations in neighbourhood informatisation processes.

The UK was quite late in introducing its postcode system. The fully fledged version was only fully implemented in 1974, nine years after the US and a full 33 years after the first system had been introduced in Germany in 1941. In the UK the postcode is divided into four distinct parts. The first one or two letters is the postcode area and it identifies the main Royal Mail sorting office that processes the mail. There are currently 124 such areas. The second part is the postcode district and this tells the sorting office to which delivery office the mail should go; there are currently 3,064 such districts. The third part is the sector and this tells the delivery office to which local area or neighbourhood the mail should go. There are currently 11,598 such sectors. The final part is the unit code, which identifies a group of, on average, about 15 addresses. There are over 1.78 million unit codes, covering over 27.5 million individual delivery points.

This means, of course, that knowledge of a postcode allows anyone to locate that spatial location with a fair degree of accuracy. If social space was structured in a random manner, such spatial knowledge would be of little interest. However, social space is very highly structured. From the classic account of the city by the Chicago School in the 1920s (Park and Burgess, 1925) through to more contemporary conceptualisations (Davis, 1999), it has long been recognised that cities possess a particular socio-spatial structure – an 'urban ecology' – often given emblematic expression in one of the most famous diagrams in the social sciences, a combination of half-moon and dartboard depicting the five concentric urban zones of 1920s Chicago, representing the sorting of social and housing classes into distinct zones produced by 'ecological' determinants such as incomes, land values, race, class and so on. Indeed, describing the changing nature of the social patterning of space and then attempting to explain the underlying determinants of this patterning is the *raison d'être* of much of urban studies and, as such, is at the very heart of the concerns of the current volume.

The manner in which the social patterning of space is described varies, of course. We are all familiar with the vernacular social geographies of the towns and cities that we know – the 'posh' bits, the 'poor' neighbourhoods, the 'safe' areas, the 'rough' places and so on – that overlay in complex ways the more formal administrative geographies of places: parishes, housing estates, boroughs, place names and so on. More formal accounts of variable social geographies take the form of academic or policy-driven 'community studies' – usually involving a mix of qualitative and descriptive statistical data that attempt to summarise the salient features of particular neighbourhoods and, often, the relationship between different neighbourhoods – while different composite statistical measures are also used to construct neighbourhoods and to reveal the differences between them. Prime among these have been various state-sponsored iterations designed to measure place-based differences in deprivation. The most recent are the Indices of Multiple Deprivation (IMD) (Noble et al, 2004), which use a huge amount of spatially referenced statistical data in order to divide England into 32,482 areas of roughly equal population size. Each area is given an IMD score constructed using a large number of data items covering seven different domains of deprivation: income, employment, health and disability, education, skills and training, barriers to housing and services, living environment and crime. A rank of 1 is assigned to areas with the highest levels of multiple deprivation and a rank of 32,482 to the area with the lowest levels – essentially it is a league table of place-based misery.

What all of these vernacular, academic and policy-related descriptions of social space reveal in their different ways is that it is inherently 'segmented' or 'clustered' or, better still, 'fractal' in its form. The social basis of this segmentation, clustering or fractal patterning is complex; both in the sense that it manifests itself in multifaceted ways as particular configurations of social variables such as class, ethnicity, age, religion, sexuality and so on, but also in the sense that the mechanisms that are generative of this patterning are ontologically emergent (Johnson, 2001). Now, this is not the place to enter into a prolonged discussion of the application of complexity theory to community and neighbourhood formation; that has already been brilliantly summarised by Byrne (1998; 2001). However, it is appropriate to note that there is a very strong mathematical basis for accepting that a range of local bottom-up behaviours by individuals and households can lead to emergent 'segregated' socio-structural spatial forms that were not necessarily intended to be the outcomes by the actors engaging in the original behaviours. The classic statement of this is the paper by Schelling (1971) – one of the few authors published in a sociology journal to have won a Nobel Prize – who demonstrates that even small individual preferences for living close to others 'similar' to oneself can lead to hugely disproportionate residential 'segregation' effects. This inherent underlying 'flocking behaviour' in neighbourhood formation is, of course, just one element in a whole set of socio-economic, cultural, political and, increasingly, technological, forces that contribute to residential zoning processes and practices that generate patterns of social differentiation between localities (Ellison and Burrows, 2007).

Geodemographics

From the mid-1970s onwards the availability of postcoded data of various sorts made possible a new way of describing such complex forms of neighbourhood differentiation – what came to be known as geodemographics. The history of this development has been detailed elsewhere (Harris et al, 2005; Burrows and Gane, 2006) and space here precludes a further detailed discussion. Suffice it to say that it came to be recognised by some in the academy – specifically Jonathan Robbin in the US and Richard Webber in the UK – that the clustered nature of the social ontology of towns and cities could be increasingly well described by applying emerging techniques of statistical cluster analysis to the myriad forms of spatially referenced – postcoded – social data that were emerging. So, crudely, the clustered differentiated 'reality' of 'ground truth' could be modelled using algorithms that, it was hoped, could produce homologous statistical constructs. The family of 'cluster analysis' methods all involve cases being 'sorted out' into clusters based on a chosen set of relevant attributes, such that the cases within a cluster are more 'alike' or 'similar' than those outside a cluster (see Aldenderfer and Blashfield, 1984; and Parker et al, 2007, for a fuller account). This apparently simple idea quickly becomes complex, however, as various conceptualisations of the notions of 'similarity', 'dissimilarity', 'distance' and 'proximity' all vie with each other in order to determine which cases are included in a cluster and which are not.

The skill of both Robbin and Webber was not only to apply these techniques to data in which the case was the postcode but also to possess the cultural insight and literary flair that enabled them to produce qualitative narratives effortlessly able to translate dull statistical output to compelling ideal typical characterisations of neighbourhoods and the people that animated them (Weiss, 2000; Phillips and Curry, 2002). Although geodemographics was born in the academy, in the world of sociology, urban economics and social statistics, in the cases of both Robbin and Webber the development and exploitation of the technique quickly moved into the world of commerce and marketing. It was in the commercial sphere that the importance of being able to understand the socio-economic and cultural attributes of someone – especially their consumption tastes and preferences – as a simple function of where they happened to live was recognised as being of huge importance. As noted elsewhere (Burrows and Gane, 2006, p 794), the huge investment in these systems by the commercial sector has occurred autonomously from developments in academic urban studies with the result that, until recently (Burrows and Gane, 2006; Parker et al, 2007; Webber and Butler, 2007; Webber, 2007), the social sciences were 'almost wholly ignorant of the empirical knowledge that has been built up by marketers on the relationship between purchasing patterns and the patterns of neighbourhood segregation which characterize modern societies' (Webber, 2004, p 220).

With the advent of widespread processes of digitisation and the routine production of huge amounts of postcoded transactional data the informational base for the production of ever-more subtle forms of geodemographic neighbourhood differentiation is likely to continue apace (Savage and Burrows, 2007), and it is likely that we will see more systems entering the marketplace. At the moment, in the UK it is possible to identify a number of different classifications (Harris et al, 2005) including, *inter alia*: Acorn, Cameo, Censation, Likewise, Locale, Mosaic, P2, People & Places, PRIZM and SONAR. The most widely used system is currently the Mosaic classification owned by the global data corporation Experian, and designed by Richard Webber (Burrows and Gane, 2006). As we will discuss, the Mosaic system classifies each of the 1.78 million postcodes in the UK to one of 11 different Mosaic Groups (big clusters) and 61 different Mosaic Types (smaller clusters nested within the 11 big ones). However, the Mosaic system is a schema that now also has a global reach. There are parallel Mosaic schemas for Australia, China (at least for Beijing, Guangzhou and Shanghai), Denmark, Finland, France, Germany, Greece, Hong Kong, Japan, the Netherlands, New Zealand, Norway, the Republic of Ireland, Spain, Sweden and the US. At the time of writing, schemas are in development in Austria, Canada, the Czech Republic, Italy and Switzerland. There is also a Global Mosaic system that maps all of these national Mosaic systems to a set of supposedly common global socio-spatial classes.

According to one influential social policy commentator, such classifications have been transformed into 'the basic fuel on which economic activity runs … Companies offering geodemographic profiling data are the 21st-century equivalents of the great energy companies of the 20th' (Perry 6, 2005, p 17). Now this is almost certainly overstating things, but there is no doubt that geodemographic classifications play an important role not just in contemporary capitalist (and increasingly public sector) marketing strategies but also in the contemporary constitution of neighbourhoods and neighbourhood differentiation. In the rest of this chapter we examine in some detail the UK Mosaic classification by way of a concrete illustration of how such systems function.

The Mosaic system

Not only is the Mosaic system the most widely used in the UK, it is also the most sociologically nuanced and familiar. Indeed, the current author has access to the software as part of a research project that aims to evaluate the efficacy of the system compared with other (academic and government) classifications when carrying out sociological research on the 'spatialisation of class' thesis (Savage et al, 2005; Parker et al, 2007). The technical details of how Mosaic has been built can be found in Harris et al (2005, pp 147–83) but essentially it is a form of weighted cluster analysis applied to some 400 different postcoded variables. Over half of these variables are sourced from the 2001 Census and just under half come from other sources such as the electoral roll, lifestyle survey data, consumer credit records, the shareholders' register, house price and council tax data, Office for National Statistics (ONS) local area statistics and so on. Once the initial clusters have been derived from these variables, their 'accuracy' is validated 'on the ground' by way of extensive qualitative fieldwork and observation. Each cluster is then subject to a detailed characterisation, some examples of which are discussed later.

Table 11.1 is complex, displaying as it does a large amount of information. In the first column the 11 different UK Mosaic Groups are shown and in the second the 61 UK Mosaic Types are shown nested within the these Groups. The claim is that these 61 ideal typical clusters can mutually exclusively and exhaustively 'map' all of the residential postcodes in the country; that the neighbourhood differentiation we can all observe around us can, in fact, be reduced to 61 different types of place. In a more sociological argot we might think of these 61 clusters as being ideal typical attempts to socio-spatially codify differences in *habitus* (Burrows and Gane, 2006; Parker et al, 2007; Webber, 2007) – the embodied, often non-discursive, tastes, preferences and practices that form the social basis for many types of distinction in a culture (Bourdieu,1984).

The third column shows how each of the 61 Mosaic Types might be ranked in terms of the level of deprivation that each – on average – experiences. Using the IMD (discussed earlier) each Type has been ranked from 1 (the most deprived Type) through to 61 (the least deprived Type). So, the Mosaic Types that are the most deprived are: 'Sharing a Staircase'; 'South Asian Industry'; and 'Low Horizons', while the least deprived are: 'Corporate Chieftains'; 'Golden Empty Nesters'; and 'Semi-Rural Seclusion'.

The fourth column shows the estimated number of individuals living in England in 2005 (50,271,465) and the Mosaic Type within which each currently resides. The fifth column shows this number expressed as a percentage. So the most 'common' Mosaic Type is 'Industrial Grit', which is nested within the 'Ties of Community' Group. It is estimated that some 2,012,400 individuals (4% of the English population) live in postcode areas so classified. The least 'common' Mosaic Type in England is 'Sharing a Staircase' (with just 8,309 individuals or 0.02% so classified) but closer inspection reveals that this Mosaic Type is mostly found in Scotland and is designed to capture areas where households with young children living predominantly in urban tenements reside. If we leave this anomaly to one side the next least populous Type is the rather more pleasant sounding 'Summer Playgrounds' – postcodes dominated by incoming visitors and locals in areas of great natural beauty – where 76,576 (0.15%) of the population reside.

The examples of Sheffield and York

The rest of Table 11.1 displays data about two cities – Sheffield and York – in the north of England. Although these are arbitrary selections based upon the institutional locations of the book editors and the chapter author, they are two very different types of place located just 30 miles distant from each other, and as such allow us to make some useful illustrative comparisons using the Mosaic schema. Sheffield is a regenerating post-industrial urban centre with a population of over 500,000, while York is a far smaller historic walled city with a population of just over 180,000, with a small industrial base but a large service sector and tourism industry. Anyone with even the vaguest

Table 11.1: UK Mosaic Groups and Types: England, Sheffield and York compared

Mosaic Group	Mosaic Type	IMD Rank 1–61	England	England %	Sheffield	Sheffield %	Sheffield: England	York	York %	York: England
Symbols of Success	A01 Global Connections	46	361,149	0.72	0	0.00	0	4	0.00	0
	A02 Cultural Leadership	54	525,851	1.05	5,069	0.99	94	552	0.30	29
	A03 Corporate Chieftains	61	739,136	1.47	4,330	0.84	57	40	0.02	1
	A04 Golden Empty Nesters	60	691,685	1.38	7,464	1.45	106	1,816	0.98	71
	A05 Provincial Privilege	55	825,176	1.64	14,755	2.87	175	6,449	3.49	212
	A06 High Technologists	58	1,150,346	2.29	3,943	0.77	34	4,470	2.42	106
	A07 Semi-Rural Seclusion	59	1,203,803	2.39	3,713	0.72	30	3,269	1.77	74
Happy Families	B08 Just Moving In	27	174,336	0.35	1,742	0.34	98	1,402	0.76	219
	B09 Fledgling Nurseries	40	655,591	1.30	1,950	0.38	29	3,200	1.73	133
	B10 Upscale New Owners	49	828,093	1.65	4,416	0.86	52	3,448	1.86	113
	B11 Families Making Good	45	1,244,662	2.48	11,390	2.22	89	5,235	2.83	114
	B12 Middle Rung Families	33	1,662,730	3.31	14,383	2.80	85	6,021	3.26	98
	B13 Burdened Optimists	30	1,035,132	2.06	6,577	1.28	62	3,553	1.92	93
	B14 In Military Quarters	56	142,860	0.28	0	0.00	0	775	0.42	147
Suburban Comfort	C15 Close to Retirement	51	1,649,420	3.28	8,822	1.72	52	6,984	3.78	115
	C16 Conservative Values	38	1,413,975	2.81	14,213	2.76	98	10,008	5.41	192
	C17 Small Time Business	42	1,599,211	3.18	8,343	1.62	51	5,269	2.85	90
	C18 Sprawling Subtopia	39	1,741,784	3.46	13,736	2.67	77	9,743	5.27	152
	C19 Original Suburbs	53	1,427,166	2.84	13,884	2.70	95	3,921	2.12	75
	C20 Asian Enterprise	21	786,593	1.56	891	0.17	11	0	0.00	0

Table 11.1: continued

Mosaic Group	Mosaic Type	IMD Rank 1–61	England	England %	Sheffield	Sheffield %	Sheffield: England	York	York %	York: England
Ties of Community	D21 Respectable Rows	37	1,293,559	2.57	15,061	2.93	114	5,254	2.84	110
	D22 Affluent Blue Collar	25	1,643,562	3.27	24,396	4.74	145	6,245	3.38	103
	D23 Industrial Grit	19	2,012,400	4.00	29,714	5.78	144	3,494	1.89	47
	D24 Coronation Street	11	1,388,462	2.76	15,284	2.97	108	2,251	1.22	44
	D25 Town Centre Refuge	18	485,762	0.97	642	0.12	13	1,171	0.63	66
	D26 South Asian Industry	2	774,023	1.54	13,456	2.62	170	0	0.00	0
	D27 Settled Minorities	13	986,460	1.96	1,545	0.30	15	0	0.00	0
Urban Intelligence	E28 Counter Cultural Mix	14	707,691	1.41	473	0.09	7	0	0.00	0
	E29 City Adventurers	24	581,269	1.16	304	0.06	5	1,226	0.66	57
	E30 New Urban Colonists	43	717,456	1.43	1,201	0.23	16	105	0.06	4
	E31 Caring Professionals	31	576,922	1.15	24,013	4.67	407	17,735	9.59	836
	E32 Dinky Developments	34	408,189	0.81	603	0.12	14	2,121	1.15	141
	E33 Town Gown Transition	22	384,787	0.77	28,883	5.62	734	6,283	3.40	444
	E34 University Challenge	16	303,784	0.60	12,401	2.41	399	4,116	2.23	368
Welfare Borderline	F35 Bedsit Beneficiaries	9	155,861	0.31	2,566	0.50	161	1,430	0.77	249
	F36 Metro Multiculture	7	993,557	1.98	1,185	0.23	12	0	0.00	0
	F37 Upper Floor Families	6	711,281	1.41	10,864	2.11	149	2,777	1.50	106
	F38 Tower Block Living	4	117,781	0.23	2,532	0.49	210	0	0.00	0
	F39 Dignified Dependency	5	342,937	0.68	13,917	2.71	397	2,412	1.30	191
	F40 Sharing a Staircase	1	8,309	0.02	0	0.00	0	0	0.00	0

Table 11.1: continued

Mosaic Group	Mosaic Type	IMD Rank 1-61	England	England %	Sheffield	Sheffield %	Sheffield: England	York	York %	York: England
Municipal Dependency	G41 Families on Benefits	8	712,358	1.42	6,110	1.19	84	3,772	2.04	144
	G42 Low Horizons	3	1,297,450	2.58	38,816	7.55	293	2,797	1.51	59
	G43 Ex-industrial Legacy	10	1,111,295	2.21	45,432	8.84	400	2,158	1.17	53
Blue Collar Enterprise	H44 Rustbelt Resilience	12	1,204,159	2.40	17,198	3.34	140	2,098	1.13	47
	H45 Older Right to Buy	20	925,885	1.84	19,213	3.74	203	2,746	1.48	81
	H46 White Van Culture	29	1,748,358	3.48	3,771	0.73	21	4,869	2.63	76
	H47 New Town Materialism	17	1,406,929	2.80	5,639	1.10	39	7,874	4.26	152
Twilight Subsistence	I48 Old People in Flats	15	217,172	0.43	6,929	1.35	312	132	0.07	17
	I49 Low Income Elderly	26	565,513	1.12	7,861	1.53	136	2,661	1.44	128
	I50 Cared for Pensioners	23	448,827	0.89	5,949	1.16	130	1,441	0.78	87
Grey Perspectives	J51 Sepia Memories	44	250,275	0.50	1,000	0.19	39	1,587	0.86	172
	J52 Childfree Serenity	50	547,377	1.09	3,538	0.69	63	2,685	1.45	133
	J53 High Spending Elders	52	698,684	1.39	2,697	0.52	38	2,883	1.56	112
	J54 Bungalow Retirement	36	549,914	1.09	1,139	0.22	20	4,604	2.49	228
	J55 Small Town Seniors	32	1,214,339	2.42	7,354	1.43	59	5,484	2.97	123
	J56 Tourist Attendants	28	111,807	0.22	0	0.00	0	0	0.00	0
Rural Isolation	K57 Summer Playgrounds	35	76,576	0.15	0	0.00	0	0	0.00	0
	K58 Greenbelt Guardians	57	1,096,593	2.18	1,080	0.21	10	2,241	1.21	56
	K59 Parochial Villagers	41	716,591	1.43	194	0.04	3	552	0.30	21
	K60 Pastoral Symphony	51	586,400	1.17	1,387	0.27	23	642	0.35	30
	K61 Upland Hill Farmers	47	142,627	0.28	0	0.00	0	84	0.05	16
	U99 Unclassified	-	189,585	0.38	200	0.04	10	839	0.45	120
	Population estimate 2005	-	50,271,465	100	514,168	100	100	184,928	100	100

ethnographic sensibility wandering about these two cities would very soon get a profound sense of aggregate differences between the two. Obviously the urban fabric and infrastructures and the physical locations are very different, but so too are the characters who populate the urban *mise-en-scène*. The remaining columns in Table 11.1 give us some more quantitative purchase on the profound differences in the social mix of the two populations. The figures for Sheffield show the number of individuals in the city who reside in the 61 different Mosaic Types, the figures expressed as a percentage of the total population of the city; the eighth column shows a comparison of the proportions living in any Mosaic Type in Sheffield compared to those living in same Type in England as a whole. If this figure is 100 it would mean that the same proportion live in this Mosaic Type in both Sheffield and England. A figure over 100 shows that this Mosaic is type is *over*-represented in Sheffield compared to England and a figure below 100 that the Type is *under*-represented. The next three columns show parallel data for York. This list of Mosaic Groups and Types is, in itself, a powerful way of describing places. However, the analytic utility of such classifications is considerably extended when one is able to 'map' each cluster to be able to visualise the complex juxtapositions of different types of neighbourhood. Needless to say there is nearly always a higher-level clustering or patterning to the different geodemographic categories that reveals the complex human ecology of wider areas. It is very rare, for example, for an agglomeration of 'Symbols of Success' Types to abut an agglomeration of 'Municipal Dependency' Types.

Both cities are bereft of 'Global Connections', but compared with York Sheffield has a far higher proportion of 'Corporate Chieftains' although, having observed that, it only has just over half of the national average. Sheffield also has proportionately more residents located in postcodes classified as 'Cultural Leadership' and 'Golden Empty Nesters'. York, on the other hand, has proportionately more living in 'Provincial Privilege', 'Semi-Rural Seclusion' and, especially, 'High Technologists'. But given the analytic and policy focus of this volume it is perhaps more important to examine different characterisations of the poverty of place than it is distinctions between different types of affluence.

If we extract from Table 11.1 the 10 Mosaic Types that are identified by the IMD as being the most deprived and present them in rank order we can more easily see how the distribution differs between the two cities. This is shown in Table 11.2.

Table 11.2: The 10 most deprived UK Mosaic Types in England, Sheffield and York

Mosaic Type	IMD Rank 1–61	England	England %	Sheffield	Sheffield %	Sheffield: England	York	York %	York: England
F40 Sharing a Staircase	1	8,309	0.02	0	0.00	0	0	0.00	0
D26 South Asian Industry	2	77,4023	1.54	13,456	2.62	170	0	0.00	0
G42 Low Horizons	3	1,297,450	2.58	38,816	7.55	293	2,797	1.51	59
F38 Tower Block Living	4	117,781	0.23	2,532	0.49	210	0	0.00	0
F39 Dignified Dependency	5	342,937	0.68	13,917	2.71	397	2,412	1.30	191
F37 Upper Floor Families	6	711,281	1.41	10,864	2.11	149	2,777	1.50	106
F36 Metro Multiculture	7	993,557	1.98	1,185	0.23	12	0	0.00	0
G41 Families on Benefits	8	712,358	1.42	6,110	1.19	84	3,772	2.04	144
F35 Bedsit Beneficiaries	9	155,861	0.31	2,566	0.50	161	1,430	0.77	249
G43 Ex-industrial Legacy	10	1,111,295	2.21	45,432	8.84	400	2,158	1.17	53
% of Population in these 10 Mosaic types			12.38		26.24	212		8.28	67

The first thing to note is the relative distribution of the population living in these, the 10 most deprived types of postcode. In England as a whole 12.38% of the population live in such places, whereas in Sheffield the proportion is over twice this – at 26.24% – and in York it is only two thirds of the national total – at 8.28%. The second thing to note is the very different nature of the poverty in the two cities. In Sheffield the Mosaic Type 'Ex-industrial Legacy' not only makes up almost 9% of the entire population it is also four times more prevalent in Sheffield than it is in England as a whole. In York no particular Mosaic Types stand out. The largest group are those classified as 'Families on Benefits', and the most disproportionately represented compared with England as a whole are those classified as 'Bedsit Beneficiaries', who are over two and a half times more likely to be found in York than they are in England as whole.

Mosaic Types

Space precludes an examination of all of these Mosaic Types, but in order to get a better sense of the narratives and characterisations that underpin the 'headline' labels associated with these clusters we can examine a couple in detail. What is perhaps of most interest is the manner in which the combination of variables that have been fused together to form each cluster is characterised via the production of a detailed narrative aimed at producing a sense of the 'sort of people' who reside within the postcodes so classified. This involves a process of what Curry (2002) terms 'discursive displacement', in which a discourse based on what he calls the 'topographic' – the statistical clusters – is translated to one about the 'chorographic' – an ideal typical descriptive map of a place – and then, in the end, to one about actual 'physical' places, a particular street, for example.

The mechanics by which this process occurs is clearly an iterative one. The clusters are mapped, a sample of 'real' places within the cluster are visited, images are taken, streets are trod, statistics are re-examined, people are spoken to, focus groups are organised, narratives and characterisations are recalibrated, visualisations of the localities are constructed – pictures of houses, their occupants, the brands they consume, the cars they drive, the newspapers they read, the technologies they have a predilection towards, the shops they favour and so on. A complex and expensive process of geodemographic *co*-construction occurs in this hitherto relatively hidden world of commercial sociology (Parker et al, 2007). The outcome of this process is a detailed qualitative and quantitative codification of each particular *habitus*. In the case of the UK Mosaic Types this takes the form of 12 dense pages of text, photos, graphs and charts that summarise the 'ideal typical' character of each cluster under headings such as: sociology and environment, culture and consumer psychology, who we are, how we make a living, where we live, our home lives, *weltanschauung*, time use and measures of deprivation. We might consider by way of illustration the 'Ex-industrial Legacy' Mosaic Type that is so disproportionately prevalent in Sheffield, and the 'Families on Benefits' Type that is the modal Type of deprived neighbourhoods in York.

The 'Ex-industrial Legacy' Mosaic Type is summarised as being a poor but relatively stable, predominantly elderly population living in low-rise council-owned properties typically 40 or more years old. Many people are described as being towards the end of their working lives, or already in retirement. These neighbourhoods are described as having been traditionally reliant on employment in mining, shipbuilding and other heavy industries. These neighbourhoods are usually large council estates, where few people have exercised their right to buy and where people live quite simple existences little affected by the more dramatic changes that have occurred elsewhere. There are areas where pubs, clubs and cooperatives continue to play an important role in the community and where traditional gender roles persist. The names 'Fred' and 'Lilly' are the most disproportionately represented in these postcodes. These are neighbourhoods where much of the new consumerism has had little impact. However, higher than average proportions of household income are spent on items such as: alcohol, tobacco, sitting-room furniture, videos, televisions, audio systems, entertainment outside the home and foreign package holidays. Football clubs are supported with passion. The people in such postcodes are summarised in the software as 'being remnants of the old proletariat ... left struggling in the new economy ... [but] not as disenfranchised as some other, more alienated types'.

The 'Families on Benefits' Mosaic Type is described as being predominantly young families on very low incomes living in extensive areas of low-rise public housing on the outskirts of provincial cities where few people have exercised their right to buy. Education qualification levels are described as low and many people in such postcodes start a family at an early age. A large proportion of children are described as living in single-parent households and, of those that do not, disproportionate numbers live with half-brothers and half-sisters in often rapidly changing household formations. The names 'Damien' and 'Donna' are the most disproportionately represented in these postcodes. These neighbourhoods are described as poor markets for almost all consumer products. Levels of indebtedness are very high. People in these neighbourhoods are described as purchasing large quantities of frozen food, and the quality of diets is generally poor. People in such neighbourhoods also smoke a great deal. Not surprisingly, health is generally poor. People in such neighbourhoods are said to watch a great deal of TV, especially soaps and quiz shows. The people in such postcodes are summarised in the software as no longer possessing 'the stability provided by regular employment and reasonable levels of income [which] ... together with other disruptive influences ... [have led to] ... a serious weakening of the conventions and obligations of working class life'. Further, the 'absence of stable employment and the self-identity that this can provide, has not been replaced by a sense of purpose beyond that which derives from the security of the mundane or the pleasures of the trivial'. This, it is suggested has generated a 'marked and very fatalistic pessimism ... [which] ... can become a self destructive nihilism'.

The language used in these descriptions is sometimes shocking to the sensibilities of social science and policy audiences used to the anodyne terminology of academic research and policy reports on poverty. However, as reported elsewhere (Burrows and Gane, 2006; Parker et al, 2007), it is not just in the most impoverished places that such sensibilities might be ruffled; the archetypical descriptions of the postcodes populated by the majority of social and policy analysts – 'Cultural Leadership', 'Counter Cultural Mix', 'New Urban Colonists', 'Caring Professionals', 'Town Gown Transition' and the rest – also pull no punches. But in the end, it is not the particular form of language that is used to describe these clusters of similar places that is really significant. For, although the rhetorical devices used to describe each cluster vary between different propriety geodemographic schemas, there does appear to be a strong concordance between them as to the socio-economic and cultural basis for neighbourhood differentiation.

Elsewhere (Parker et al, 2007) we have reported on the nature of this geodemographic concordance in four very different case study streets, with perhaps the clearest illustration being from our audit of the classificatory regime that pertained in a street not very far away from Hoxton Square in the East End of London – an area often characterised as the epitome of certain sort of 'cool'. Ethnographically this was a densely populated, multi-ethnic, noisy and dynamic environment. The buildings were a complex mixture of low-rise 1960s council estates, trendy modern apartments and flats and small new-build houses. At the corner at one end was an off-licence and at the other was a plethora of small shops, bars and take-aways. Those properties in owner-occupation were relatively expensive – flats often being over £300,000 and houses closer to £400,000. The street cut across five different postcodes (reflecting the density of the population here). At the more 'trendy' end of the street the IMD classifies it as in the 3,992nd (11th percentile) most deprived place in England, while at the other (predominantly low-rise council estate) as in the 1,824th (5th percentile) most deprived. This division was mirrored in more detail in the various geodemographic classifications to which the street was subject. Acorn classifies three contiguous postcodes as instances of 'Urban Prosperity' of a particular form – 'Educated Urbanites' – and even more specifically as 'Prosperous young professionals, flats'. Their neighbours, at the poorer end of the street, were, however, classified very differently, as instances of the 'Hard Pressed' of a particular form – 'Inner City Adversity' – or more specifically as 'Multi-ethnic purpose-built estates'. Mosaic offers a slightly more nuanced characterisation still. The first three postcodes are all considered to be instances of 'Urban Intelligence', the first two postcodes are considered to be 'City Adventurers', while the third – a sort of zone of transition perhaps – is considered an instance of 'Counter Cultural Mix', while the last two postcodes are classified as part of the 'Welfare Borderline' Group and the 'Metro Multiculture' Type. The other five geodemographic classifications to which we were able to gain access characterised the postcodes in very similar ways, albeit using different labels. So, although the descriptions of the clusters vary slightly, the lines of geodemographic division are all drawn in roughly similar places.

Conclusion

The important theoretical and policy issue is where these various classifications of neighbourhoods reside and how they function. The migration of these classifications into software systems of various sorts forms one important element of creation of an emerging 'technological unconscious' so brilliantly dissected by Thrift (2004); a nascent software substrate to the social structure able to function in a myriad of ways to 'sort out' people and places (Burrows and Ellison, 2004; Graham, 2005) in a manner that is only now becoming apparent, and whose social cohesion consequences are yet to be investigated.

For some commentators this potential for the automatic production of space (Thrift and French, 2002) is just one element of a far broader and complex set of emergent technological assemblages that are suggestive of a fully fledged sentient city (Crang and Graham, 2007). For those with perhaps more grounded concerns it is not difficult to see how these geodemographic classifications can function to co-construct differentiated neighbourhoods because of their insertion in the myriad of commercial and governmental algorithms that influence: where private and public services are located; the distribution and allocation of resources related to crime, education, health and so on; insurance premiums; credit ratings (see, for example, www.checkmyfile.com); and, increasingly, the judgements and decisions of those members of the public willing and able to make informed decisions about the neighbourhoods in which they buy or rent their homes (Burrows et al, 2005). However, the function of geodemographic classifications in contributing to the segmentation and diversity of neighbourhoods and the changing dynamics of segregation or clustering occurring within them has, to date, been largely ignored in academic and policy debates about social cohesion in the UK. Fundamentally, what needs to be realised by the policy community concerned with issues of social cohesion is that there is an emerging software substrate to the existing social structure that is pulling in the direction of ever-more nuanced material patterns of differentiation and segmentation in society.

References

Aldenderfer, M. and Blashfield, R. (1984) *Cluster analysis*, London: Sage.

Bourdieu, P. (1984) *Distinction: A social critique of the judgement of taste*, London: Routledge.

Burrows, R. and Ellison, N. (2004) 'Sorting places out? Towards a social politics of neighbourhood informatisation', *Information, Communication and Society*, vol 7, no 3, pp 321–36.

Burrows, R. and Gane, N. (2006) 'Geodemographics, software and class', *Sociology*, vol 40, no 5, pp 793–812.

Burrows, R., Ellison, N. and Woods, B. (2005) *Neighbourhoods on the net: Internet-based neighbourhood information systems and their consequences*, Bristol: The Policy Press.

Byrne, D. (1998) *Complexity theory and the social sciences: An introduction*, London: Routledge.

Byrne, D. (2001) *Understanding the urban*, Hampshire: Palgrave.

Crang, M. and Graham, S. (2007) 'Sentient cities: Ambient intelligence and the politics of urban space', *Information, Communication and Society*, vol 10, no 6, pp 789–817.

Curry, M. (2002) 'Discursive displacement and the seminal ambiguity of space and place', in L. Lievrouw and S. Livingston (eds) *Handbook on new media*, London: Sage.

Davis, M. (1999) *Ecology of fear*, London: Picador.

Ellison, N. and Burrows, R. (2007) 'New spaces of (dis)engagement? Social politics, urban technologies and the rezoning of the city', *Housing Studies*, vol 22, no 4, pp 295–312.

Graham, S. (2005) 'Software-sorted geographies', *Progress in Human Geography*, vol 29, no 5, pp 562–80.

Harris, R., Sleight, P. and Webber, R. (2005) *Geodemographics, GIS and neighbourhood targeting*, Chichester: Wiley.

Johnson, S. (2001) *Emergence: The connected lives of ants, brains, cities and software*, London: Allen Lane.

Noble, M., Wright, G., Dibben, C., Smith, G.A.N., McLennan, D., Anttila, C., Barnes, H., Mokhtar, C., Noble, S., Avenell, D., Gardner, J., Covizzi, I. and Lloyd, M. (2004) *Indices of deprivation 2004. Report to the Office of the Deputy Prime Minister*, London: Neighbourhood Renewal Unit.

Park, R. and Burgess, E. (1925) *The city*, Chicago: University of Chicago Press.

Parker, S., Uprichard, E. and Burrows, R. (2007) 'Class places and place classes: Geodemographic classifications and the automatic production of space', *Information, Communication and Society*, vol 10, no 6, pp 902–21.

Perry 6 (2005) 'The personal information economy: Trends and prospects for consumers', in S. Lace (ed) *The glass consumer: Life in a surveillance society*, Bristol: The Policy Press.

Phillips, D. and Curry, M. (2002) 'Privacy and the phenetic urge: Geodemographics and the changing spatiality of local practice', in D. Lyon (ed) *Surveillance as social sorting: privacy, risk and digital discrimination*, London: Routledge.

Pickles, J. (1995) *Ground truth: The social implications of geographic information systems*, New York: Guilford Press.

Savage, M. and Burrows, R. (2007) 'The coming crisis of empirical sociology', *Sociology*, vol 41, no 5, pp 885–99.

Savage, M. Bagnall, G. and Longhurst, B. (2005) *Globalization and belonging*, London: Sage.

Schelling, T.C. (1971) 'Dynamic models of segregation', *Journal of Mathematical Sociology*, vol 1, pp 143–86.

Thrift, N. (2004) 'Remembering the technological unconscious by foregrounding knowledge of position', *Environment and Planning D: Society and Space*, vol 22, no 1, pp 175–90.

Thrift, N. and French, S. (2002) 'The automatic production of space', *Transactions of the Institute of British Geographers*, vol 27, no 3, pp 309–35.

Webber, R. (2004) 'Designing geodemographic classifications to meet contemporary business needs', *Interactive Marketing*, vol 5, no 3, pp 219–37.

Webber, R. (2007) 'The metropolitan habitus: Its manifestations, locations, and consumption profiles', *Environment and Planning A*, vol 39, no 1, pp 182–207.

Webber, R. and Butler, T. (2007) 'Classifying pupils by where they live: How well does this predict variations in their GCSE results?', *Urban Studies*, vol 44, no 7, pp 1229–54.

Weiss, M. (2000) *The clustered world*, Boston: Little, Brown and Co.

TWELVE

Secession or cohesion? Exploring the impact of gated communities

Sarah Blandy

Introduction

This chapter explores the implications for social cohesion arising from the recent increase in the number of gated communities in England, focusing on their impact both for residents and for those outside the gates.[1] Starting with perceptions and definitions of gated communities, the chapter goes on to outline the academic and policy debates about these residential developments. It then examines their implications for social cohesion among individual residents within gated communities, and for cohesion in areas within which gated communities are situated, drawing on findings from recent empirical studies. The chapter concludes by discussing the implications of gated communities for cohesion at the national scale.

The term 'gated community' has been imported from the US, where developers and sellers of this type of housing emphasise its community aspects, conjuring up an image of a socially cohesive group of residents living in a geographical neighbourhood with well-defined boundaries to enhance secure feelings of community identity and belonging. In both the US and in England these developments have two equally important characteristics – physical and legal – but, as we shall see, 'community' is not an essential feature.[2] In physical terms, a gated community is a walled or fenced housing development to which public access is restricted and often guarded using CCTV and/or security personnel. These developments inevitably reduce the public realm, defined as 'the space between and surrounding buildings and open spaces that are accessible to the public' (Planning Advisory Service, 2007). It is therefore not surprising that concerns about gated communities consistently emerged from interviews with local planning officers in England (Atkinson et al, 2003). The concept of permeability is a central principle of planning and urban design; urban sustainability and hence social cohesion depend on the free movement of people around urban space. Nor does a built form obviously designed to exclude, described by one planner as '"sod-off" architecture' (Atkinson et al, 2003), sit comfortably with the ideal of inclusiveness in planning and design: 'You should not underestimate the symbolism of the physical … [t]he physical fabric is testimony to separateness' (local authority planning officer, quoted in Manzi and Smith-Bowers, 2005, p 352).

All gated communities have a legal framework designed to ensure that residents are involved in managing and taking responsibility for the privatised space, internal roads and any facilities within its physical boundaries. In the most prevalent legal form for English gated communities, residents purchase long leases of 200 years or more, and sign up to covenants in those leases. The residents' management company (of which all leaseholders automatically become members at the time of purchase) is responsible for enforcing these covenants. As well as requiring residents to contribute their share of the cost of running the development, covenants might for example forbid residents to keep dogs, or require them to clean their windows each month. Breach of any covenant can be enforced ultimately by forfeiture of the lease, which could lead to the resident's eviction through the courts. The key question to be addressed is whether this collective legal framework leads to greater community cohesion than in similar neighbourhoods that have no formal legal ties between neighbours.

Policy context and academic discussion

Gated communities have provoked much academic debate. Their supporters argue that the combination of physical boundaries and a clear legal framework that binds the residents together should engender greater feelings of ownership in, and responsibility for, the area and increased social cohesion between residents. However, critics of gated communities would stress their impact in reducing interactions outside the immediate area, causing insularity and fear of others among residents as well as resentment by those excluded. These debates are grounded in conflicting ideas of the city as either diverse and exciting, or alternately as a site of crime, fear and anonymous isolation. The arguments are underpinned by deep-seated beliefs about democratic rights and the value of open public space. Reflecting these opposing views, gated communities are frequently cited as examples of the decline in community, and conversely, albeit less often, as a potential solution for complex urban problems.

When David Blunkett was Home Secretary, he suggested that establishing gated communities in deprived areas would 'make available to the many what is currently available to the few' (2004). He emphasised the collective nature of resident self-management, which he considered would lead to a sense of identification with the neighbourhood and of belonging to a community. In Blunkett's view, the legal framework establishing management by residents would further help to engage 'people in making decisions, and to reinforce the message that they are part of the solution' (2004). However, one of the key government strategic housing policy objectives is to create 'sustainable, inclusive, mixed communities in all areas, both urban and rural' (Department for Communities and Local Government (DCLG), 2006, para 9) and gated communities are arguably the opposite of inclusive and mixed residential areas. Those able to afford to buy into a gated community can be seen as choosing to withdraw into an exclusionary and homogeneous residential space.

Although the government's mixed community agenda has not been received uncritically (see for example, Cole and Goodchild, 2001; Galster, 2007), recent research on this topic accepts that mix at different scales may prove successful in enhancing social cohesion in different ways. At a very local scale, 'without pepper-potting of different tenures, or mix at least within the same street, it is hard to gain much interaction between residents of different tenures' (Tunstall and Fenton, 2006, p 26). Research indicates that where developers of gated communities cannot avoid planning obligations to include affordable housing on the same site, such housing tends to be internally segregated within the development and visibly different from the more upmarket homes for sale – hardly a recipe for social cohesion (Atkinson et al, 2003). However, on a slightly wider scale, different groupings of residents who live separately but nonetheless use the same shops or primary schools could also support a beneficial diversity.

The socio-economic changes that have taken place over the past few decades, and the perceived need for greater security, have led to increased use of what Reich describes as the 'sorting mechanism' (2000, p 197), by means of which citizens are moving 'into more and more finely distinguished "lifestyle enclaves", segregated by race, class, education, life stage, and so on' (Putnam, 2000, p 209), epitomised by gated communities. Described by Atkinson (2006) as 'mob mentality', is this tendency anything more than a reflection of the psychoanalytic theory that it is 'natural' to want to live with 'people like us'? (For further discussion, see Wilton, 1998). We know, for example, that many gentrifiers seek to establish middle-class enclaves in response to the perceived difficulties of urban diversity (Butler with Robson, 2003). Gating such enclaves could be seen as merely adding a physical demarcation. However, at the neighbourhood scale, the socio–spatial segregation represented by gated communities increases the possibility of a hermetically sealed existence. If you live behind walls, there is little chance of an encounter with anyone who is not a fellow resident, and when you leave through the electronic gates it is likely you will do so in a car that takes you on your 'time–space trajectory' to another safe space, thus eliminating any contact with the immediately surrounding neighbourhood (Atkinson and Flint, 2004). What is more, these choices of the affluent are obvious to all because of the built form of the gated community.

What is known about gated communities in England?

Despite the interest generated by gated communities, there is a dearth of robust research data from England. Two national studies provide snapshots: a telephone survey about attitudes to gated communities carried out on behalf of the Royal Institute of Chartered Surveyors in 2002 (Live Strategy, 2002; for further details see Blandy et al, 2003) and a postal survey of all English planning authorities (Atkinson et al, 2003). The remainder of the research evidence comprises a series of small-scale case studies of individual gated communities (Castell, 1997; Atkinson et al, 2003; Blandy and Lister, 2005; Manzi and Smith-Bowers, 2005; Thomas, 2006) and some pieces of investigative journalism (Thorp, 2003; Vallely, 2007).

Some broad conclusions emerged from the national survey of English planning authorities conducted by Atkinson et al (2003). In 2002 there were 1,000 gated communities, distributed throughout the country but concentrated in the South-East. These gated communities were usually small developments (only four local authorities had one or more gated communities with over 300 dwellings) and they were mainly located in suburbia or in the centre of towns and cities. Planners estimated that the vast majority of gated communities were built by private developers, a very small proportion by social landlords, and the remainder (around 10%) developed through a public–private partnership (Atkinson et al, 2003).

In terms of general attitudes towards gated communities, a national random survey of 1,001 individuals throughout the UK found that one third of respondents would like to live in a gated community (Live Strategy, 2002). 'Greater security' (72%) was the dominant motivation, with only 6% of respondents being attracted by 'living with people of similar background'. Half of those respondents not attracted to living in a gated development stated that they 'would rather be part of a community', thus making a distinction between a gated community and other forms of neighbourhood (Live Strategy, 2002).

Gated communities in England present a very diverse picture but do fall into three main types: infill, heritage conversion and village developments (Blandy, 2006a). The third type can be virtually discounted, as there is little land available in the UK for the huge, self-contained, gated municipalities now prevalent in the US. However, the first two types are widespread in England and, from anecdotal evidence, growing in number. Heritage conversions make use of already walled sites no longer needed for their original purpose, such as disused factories, institutions including schools and hospitals, and minor stately homes. To create a gated community, the developer installs electronic gates, converts the original building and adds new-build homes within the walls, with the option of further facilities such as a gym or swimming pool. Infill developments are gated communities developed through the opportunities presented by small urban and suburban spaces created, for example, by the demolition of one large building. The developer then walls or fences off the road frontage and builds a small courtyard development of four or six townhouses as a gated community. Many heritage conversion gated communities, and most of the infill development type, are therefore inserted into existing residential neighbourhoods.

Community cohesion, the built form, and legal relations within gated communities

It has been asserted that 'residentially based networks ... perform an important function in the routines of everyday life [which] are arguably the basic building-blocks of social cohesion – through them we learn tolerance, co-operation and acquire a sense of social order and belonging' (Forrest and Kearns, 2001, p 2130). In considering the extent to which gated communities facilitate such cohesive dynamics within a neighbourhood, the size of the development and the type of surrounding neighbourhood into which it is inserted are extremely important factors. The few studies that have researched social relationships between residents in English gated communities have, however, identified some common themes. A range of factors have an impact on cohesion within the gated community: the degree of security provided, the extent of social interaction between residents and whether they are 'people like us', and the importance afforded to individual privacy in a collective residential setting. These issues are interlinked in a complex manner: the value of living with similar residents is enhanced if the surrounding area is seen as hostile, while feelings of security are based on exclusion of outsiders; in many gated communities, 'community means sameness, while "sameness" means the absence of the Other' (Bauman, 2001, p 115).

In one gated community inserted into and hermetically sealed off from its surrounding deprived area of East London, respondents felt that residents were generally 'like minded', although there was a diverse age range (Thomas, 2006, p 22). Certainly, women residents with young children valued the social contact with others at a similar stage in their lives, and these views were also echoed by older residents here and in other gated developments. Interviews with gated community residents in deprived areas and in mixed urban areas have revealed a pervasive discourse of liberation from fear, resulting from the physical enclosure of such developments. Residents felt that 'peace of mind adds to the quality of life' (Vallely, 2007, p 37). One tenant commented that the retro-gating of his local authority estate had made it feel safer, which had led to 'a sense of pride that, you know, the estate looks better, it is our space because it's quite defined by that gate'. This had heightened the sense of community and increased the use of communal space. However, the collective and enclosed nature of gated communities can conflict with the need for privacy expressed by residents of more middle-class gated communities: 'if we found we were getting on top of other people we would move' (resident quoted in Blandy and Lister, 2005). A number of residents in a study of an East London gated community also emphasised their need for privacy and attempted to keep themselves to themselves (Thomas, 2006, p 20), while a couple were reportedly moving from a gated community in a sought-after suburb of Manchester because they wanted more privacy (Vallely, 2007, p 37).

Although a sense of security apparently made residents 'more relaxed, [so they] will say "hello" and stop and talk to you and wish you a nice day' (Vallely, 2007, p 37), some residents felt critical of the 'superficial nature' of this social contact (Thomas, 2006, p 20) and one commented ironically: 'you never know, eventually after being here a year or so we may build up to a three-sentence chat!' (Thomas, 2006, p 18). A study of the same gated community in East London carried out 10 years earlier found many respondents complaining about their neighbours, while the lack of a stable community was clear in that over one third of respondents planned to move within the next two years (Castell, 1997).

It is therefore difficult to generalise about cohesion within gated communities. Some studies report residents speaking appreciatively about social events and neighbourliness, including communal Christmas dinners and musical concerts in a community hall. In contrast, residents in other developments complained of 'a number of cliques' based on ethnicity, status, or politics, or asserted that 'there is no community spirit here' (Atkinson et al, 2003). One detailed study of social relations within a gated community found that community involvement and neighbourliness was limited, manifested by 'people just say[ing] hello as you are going past ... I don't want to live in everybody's pockets' (resident quoted in Blandy and Lister, 2005). Analysis of purchasers' motivations showed that property values, followed by security, were the most important factors when deciding to buy into this gated community, while only just over half the respondents cited 'moving into a community' as important (Blandy and Lister, 2005).

These findings may echo criticisms of non-gated suburban life as providing 'poor facilities for meeting, conversation, collective debate and common action' (Mumford, 1961, pp 512–13, cited in McKenzie, 1994, p 229). However, weak social ties (Granovetter, 1973) were overwhelmingly considered to be important by suburban residents in creating a 'feeling of home', 'security' and 'practical as well as social support' (Henning and Lieberg, 1996, p 22), so should not be dismissed too quickly. Whatever the nature of the social ties between residents, the supposedly collective nature of gated communities can provide fertile ground for resentments to build up between residents. For example, the director of one residents' association commented that 'there are some residents who seem to think there are bin fairies who put the dustbins out' and was moving to a non-gated house in the same area largely because neighbours were not pulling their weight (Vallely, 2007, p 37).

Contentions over issues such as noise, children playing football in the wrong place and car parking cause disputes in many gated communities just as in other non-gated neighbourhoods. However, residents in gated communities are bound into a formal legal structure, usually a company limited by guarantee, and must all comply with the same rules expressed as a term of their lease. The issue is whether this legal framework aids the resolution of disputes. Even in non-gated areas, law and regulatory codes tend to be used as an external reference for shared standards of behaviour in more affluent areas (Merry, 1993), so it could be argued that these legal rules provide an effective alternative to the informal social controls once typical of poorer neighbourhoods. However, research has found that most residents in a middle-class gated community were ignorant of the covenants in their lease; yet, interestingly, they felt that restrictions on their own behaviour were a small price to pay for ensuring that all other residents kept to the terms of the lease (Blandy and Lister, 2005). It is possible that in time the legal framework of gated communities will become more familiar; in North America, where common interest developments have a far longer history, one study found that 86% of residents said that they were familiar with the legal rules (Kirby et al, 2006).

Enforcement of the covenants is the responsibility of the residents' management company. In practice, this responsibility usually falls to a few residents elected as officers of the company, or to a professional managing agent employed by the company. Blandy and Lister (2005) found that most residents were unaware that they were members of the residents' management company and were not motivated to participate in the committee. In the absence of a specific problem that would transform gated community residents into a coherent group to deal with it, a passive majority usually allows an active minority to take over. In new developments, the developer can play a key role; one candidly explained that 'we cultivate the right people to lead' the residents' management company (Blandy and Lister, 2005). Interviews with gated community residents have found that many were dissatisfied with how their development was managed. They either wanted stricter enforcement of the covenants, or felt that a 'power-hungry' group of residents was running the development with 'a rod of iron', leading to 'resentment and distrust' (Atkinson et al, 2003). However, the legal structure of a gated community does have the advantage of providing a third party to deal with neighbour disputes, unlike most owner-occupied neighbourhoods. In place of the typical suburban 'avoidance culture' (Baumgartner, 1988), gated community residents can continue to 'say "Hello" every morning while somebody faceless and nameless in authority actually clamps down on the bad behaviour' (developer, interviewed for Blandy and Lister, 2005).

It therefore seems that the legal framework of the gated community does not automatically lead to greater internal community cohesion, and the research provides little encouragement for the advocates of self-managed neighbourhoods setting their own rules. As discussed later, evidence also suggests that gated communities may produce negative consequences for cohesion between residents and wider residential neighbourhoods. On an individual level, residents of gated communities must also contend with the effects of routine but time-consuming security practices, with the walls and gates as a physical reminder of risks beyond their sanctuary. Bauman suggests it is likely that residents will 'find to their dismay that the safer they feel inside the enclosure, the less familiar and more threatening appears the wilderness outside, and more and more courage is needed to venture past the armed guards and beyond the reach of the electronic surveillance network' (2001, p 117). This speculation is confirmed by Low's (2003) anthropological study of American gated communities, which found that children who have grown up in such surroundings exhibit disproportionate fear of others. Low suggests that gated community residents exhibit 'social splitting' that 'is reinforced by cultural stereotypes and media distortions, allowing people to psychologically separate themselves from people who they perceive as threatening their tranquility and neighbourhood stability. The walls and gates of the community reflect this splitting physically as well as metaphorically' (Low, 2003, p 139).

No similar study has been carried out in the UK, but there is growing evidence from anecdotal and journalistic sources that many gated community residents are in effect retreating into a completely sealed world. One resident, living in a high crime area, commented that 'We're a mini-enclave and keep the big bad world out. It's like being in the womb' (Vallely, 2007, p 37). Another resident happily explained how life was experienced through virtual reality: 'If I didn't have a television I wouldn't know what's happening outside' (Thomas, 2006, p 17). These views are encapsulated in the words of a resident who had become thoroughly accustomed to living in a gated community, to the extent that he felt this withdrawal and hermetic security was necessary: 'You can enjoy everything that the capital has to offer, but at the end of the day when you walk through that gate, it's like stepping into a different world. I would only live in a gated community in London now' (Vallely, 2007, p 33). As Kearns and Forrest point out, '[o]ne place's cohesion may be society's deconstruction' (2000, p 1001).

The impact of gated communities inserted into host neighbourhoods

Some commentators argue that the negative impact of 'inserted' gated communities is solely due to their built form and can therefore be addressed architecturally:

> Discreet security, which makes use of the surrounding Victorian walls or historic gates, is perfectly sensible. What you don't want to see is developments surrounded by spikes or glass. The risks come when you have a large number of developments looking like a fortified enclave – that's

when it starts dividing communities. (Louis Armstrong, chief executive officer of the Royal Institute of Chartered Surveyors, quoted in Thorp, 2003, p 24)

Most planning authorities are concerned that the 'overtly fortress like appearance of gates can raise the fear of crime and prevent ... natural surveillance' (Birmingham City Council Planning Department, 2001, p 27). However, the point was made by one respondent to the national survey of local authorities, that gated communities are a powerful physical indicator that the area as a whole is acquiring both higher status and property values, so should be welcomed by residents of the host neighbourhood (Atkinson et al, 2003).

In terms of a gated community's impact on cohesion at the wider neighbourhood level, the characteristics of the host area are critically important. It is worth noting that these characteristics, including the degree of existing community cohesion in the area, can even determine whether a gated community is built in the first place. Gooblar (2002) compared the response and influence of two groups of residents to gated community planning issues in two London boroughs. In Southwark, an impoverished area, there was no community response to the planning proposal by a developer for the heritage conversion of a former Victorian school, and the local authority approved the proposal. By contrast, a proposal in affluent Kensington and Chelsea to gate off an existing public road, a cul-de-sac that had originally (when first built in the early 19th century) been gated, met with considerable opposition. Influential local residents were concerned about the message of social exclusivity, and the proposal was turned down, both by the local authority and by the planning inspectorate on appeal.

The remainder of this chapter explores the impact of gated communities in areas placed at different points on the 'socio-spatial continuum that runs from highly demarcated "exclusive" areas inhabited by the wealthy, through a range of mixed localities marked by the physical contiguity of better-off and low-income social groups, to "excluded" areas that are also demarcated' (Ellison and Burrows, 2007, p 300).

Super-affluent gated developments in suburban and rural locations

There are very few completely self-sufficient and isolated gated communities in England. Therefore even in super-affluent surroundings a gated development has an impact. This effect was noted by respondents in case studies undertaken by Atkinson et al (2003). One resident of a gated community in a semi-rural location on the outskirts of an affluent village within commuting distance of London explained that residents of the area did 'regard the development as exclusive'. A police officer commented about the same gated community that 'It is very much a separate community, whose residents use their own schools and shops. ... There is very little interaction with other local residents' (Atkinson et al, 2003). Far from being integrated into the surrounding area, the extremely wealthy, mainly expatriate gated community residents were said also to own properties 'in several of the major economic cities of the world', and so had no real connection with their English 'home', being merely transient residents there.

Gated developments fitting comfortably into suburbia

As an increasing number of individual suburban houses are 'forted up' with electronic gates, high walls and surveillance equipment (Atkinson and Blandy, 2007), it seems unlikely that a small infill gated development would look out of place, or attract much interest from neighbours. Although suburbia is conventionally seen as lacking in neighbourhood activities and social interaction, in one case study suburban area there was a lively community association in which the gated development residents fully participated (Atkinson et al, 2003). It could tentatively be concluded that gated community residents fit very comfortably into such surroundings, taking their lead from the existing suburban population that mirrors their own socio-economic demographic profile.

Gated developments inserted into mixed urban areas

Research shows that some middle-class residents of socially mixed areas feel very much at home there, and positively value their neighbourhood's diversity (see Butler with Robson, 2003). The impact of inserting a gated community into such an area can be detrimental to social cohesion. Opposition to one such new gated community was expressed in letters to the local newsletter:

> By shutting themselves in, and thereby excluding us local 'undesirables', they have failed to realize that life in [name of area] is also about people; about sharing and caring; about the rich variety of culture in our local community, the inclusion of those who have different values and beliefs.

> Inclusion will not make life more insecure, exactly the
> reverse.

This was given further expression by graffiti stating 'This way to the middle class ghetto' (Blandy and Lister, 2005).

From this admittedly very limited evidence, it seems that the combination of a new fortified development and an established mixed neighbourhood may potentially cause the greatest difficulties of integration at the wider neighbourhood scale.

Gated developments inserted into a deprived area

In this scenario, the issues surrounding social cohesion between residents within and outside the gated community are thrown into stark relief. On the one hand, it has been argued that such developments reduce social segregation 'in areas that otherwise would have accommodated ... multi-deprived households exclusively' (Manzi and Smith-Bowers, 2005, p 357). Castell (1997) points out that inserting gated communities draws in middle-income professionals to such areas without displacing local residents, and argues that this results in more money being brought into areas in need of regeneration. On the other hand there is considerable evidence that residents of gated communities inserted into a deprived area go to great lengths to avoid contact with local residents. A developer acknowledged the benefit of integrating owner-occupiers into such areas, but continued: 'the trouble is, the home-buying public don't have a social conscience, they're worried about their car being stolen, so they will say: "yes, I will buy on the edge of a council estate, or an area of deprivation, but I will want a six foot high wall". And that's a huge dilemma' (Blandy, 2006b, p 250).

This dilemma is usually 'solved' by developing ultra-secure and self-contained gated communities in such areas. The website of a converted factory in the East End of London, now a large gated community, boasts: 'You'll find everything here from your morning paper and your evening DVD, to freshly baked bread and vegetables straight from nearby Spitalfields' (Bow Quarter Residents' Management Ltd, 2008). In other words, residents do not have to risk leaving the gated community to derive benefits from the surrounding neighbourhood, even when that includes Spitalfields, which is well known as a vibrant and creatively diverse area. When Castell (1997) interviewed the residents of this gated community, 10% said that a major drawback of living there was its location in a 'rough neighbourhood'. This study found that 'outside' residents and shopkeepers were mainly indifferent to the gated community in their midst; the two populations hardly came into contact with each other as over half of the gated community residents never ventured into the surrounding area at all and no residents of the gated development sent their children to the local schools.

In her study of a gated community in East London, Thomas reported many respondents mentioning the 'cultural and racial differences between insiders and outsiders' (Thomas, 2006, p 22). The same lack of community cohesion at the neighbourhood level can be seen in the development researched by Manzi and Smith-Bowers (2005), where 200 owner-occupied dwellings were created from the gated wing of a 19th-century asylum, surrounded by about 600 units of social housing, shared ownership and privately rented accommodation, which were built within the original walls but not gated. Research found that the gated community residents tended not to walk around the estate, and did not use the local shops. Although they felt safe behind the gates, most residents installed additional security measures in their properties (Manzi and Smith-Bowers, 2005).

In some instances gentrification of deprived areas is spearheaded by urban pioneers (Butler with Robson, 2003), but in the case of gated communities developers are providing and marketing fortified enclaves, which local residents may feel are 'rubbing our noses in it' (Atkinson et al, 2003). The differences in wealth and tenure between the populations inside and outside the gates has a deleterious effect on social cohesion, with the host neighbourhood deriving little benefit from the more affluent gated community residents who seal themselves off and do not use local facilities. Recent national planning guidance acknowledges that:

> Gated communities may increase the sustainability and social mix of an area where problems of crime and image could otherwise lead to the development's failure. The Government believes, however, that it is normally preferable for new developments to be integrated into the wider community and that the gating of developments should only be considered as a last resort. (Office of the Deputy Prime Minister (ODPM)/Home Office, 2004, p 30)

The retro-gating of social housing estates

Security features such as target-hardening, CCTV, concierge schemes and neighbourhood wardens are widespread in the social rented sector. These factors, in combination with the current policy enthusiasm for neighbourhood agreements and tenant management (ODPM/Home Office, 2005), could potentially fulfil both the physical and legal aspects to create a genuine gated community. Cromer Street, an estate owned and managed by the London Borough of Camden, is known for its successful retro-gating. In the late 1990s, to protect residents from serious criminal activity, Camden enclosed the space between housing blocks and installed entrance security systems on the estate. Although Cromer Street is not self-managed by the tenants and therefore cannot be properly described as a gated community, some significant legal changes accompanied the physical redevelopment. A new tenancy agreement was introduced, making it a breach of tenancy to allow anyone else to use the key, and this has been rigorously enforced (ODPM/Home Office, 2004, annex 1, pp 54–5). Cromer Street is seen as a success, with crime displaced elsewhere and the estate gaining in popularity. The London Borough of Camden has subsequently retro-gated more of its estates, at the request of tenants.

It is likely that we will see more such developments in the social rented sector, as tenants are more attracted to gated communities than owners and more affluent respondents (Live Strategy, 2002). Certainly, in the US, there is now a prevalence of low-income, racial minority, renters in gated communities (Sanchez et al, 2005). However, given that neighbourhood dissatisfaction and fear of crime disproportionately affect people on low incomes living in rented housing, retro-gating such estates raises questions about who exactly is being kept out, or locked in. The tenant of another Camden estate expressed uneasy concerns when discussing an earlier, unpopular, attempt at gating, which had felt 'like a prison then, because there was a big wall involved … like you're being sectioned off, like we were being contained, like social outcasts' (interview with author, 2007). However, the more recent (and better-designed) gates and railings installed on this same estate are now very popular with tenants, nor was there any evidence that these new gates were resented by other residents in the area. Perhaps, like the gated communities inserted into suburban areas sharing similar socio-economic characteristics, retro-gated social housing estates merge into their surroundings and have little or no negative impact on social cohesion at the neighbourhood level.

As for the concern that gated communities might exacerbate segregation on ethnic lines, there is simply no English evidence on this issue. In a 'mystery shopping' exercise, gated community sales agents were asked whether fictional black or mixed race purchasers would find it hard to fit in at their development, and their responses did not suggest any kind of prejudice (Atkinson et al, 2003). Interestingly, the most recent study of gated communities in the US, where they have been established much longer and are far more widespread, draws on census data analysis by Sanchez et al (2005) and confirms that gated housing enclaves 'may even be a refuge for minorities who are strongly outnumbered in the city in question' (Kirby et al, 2006, p 23). The East London gated community discussed earlier has a high number of gay couples, indicating that perhaps those who understandably feel vulnerable to harassment on open streets may be more attracted to the security of a gated community.

Conclusion

It would be unwise to extrapolate too far from the limited available data discussed in this chapter, particularly as there has been no research specifically directed at the issue of community cohesion in relation to gated communities. However, it would be safe to say that many gated communities represent a voluntary secession from the wider community. In England this is a social rather than political form of secession, unlike in the US, where constitutional law allows gated communities to become incorporated municipalities. Nonetheless it has important consequences at the local area level. The physical structure of gated communities decreases urban and suburban permeability and consequently chance encounters in streets and everyday public spaces. These unplanned social interactions arguably enhance community cohesion and encourage a view of diversity as enjoyable, or certainly as tolerable, rather than frightening. Many gated community residents, in contrast, become acculturated to their seclusion and increasingly dependent on it, potentially leading within the development to a 'destructive, negative cohesion ... [based on] a nervous determination to exclude people seen as outsiders' (Urban Design Alliance, 2003). This social segregation also negates or reduces the possibility of 'cohesive local responses to issues of putative common interest' (Ellison and Burrows, 2007, p 306). At the same time, the physical enclosure and legal framework that could encourage collective responsibility and a sense of identity do not actually appear to enhance community cohesion between the residents of gated developments.

As most gated communities are 'inserts' into existing neighbourhoods, their impact on social cohesion at the wider level depends on the characteristics of the host neighbourhood. An affluent 'insert' into a similar suburban area probably causes the least disruption, along with the retro-gating of deprived estates, while the worst impact on social cohesion ensues from inserting a more affluent gated community into a deprived neighbourhood. Similar concerns may arise if the host neighbourhood is mixed, but prides itself on being an open and vibrantly diverse area, so that the imposition of a segregated, walled development causes resentment.

Gated communities raise important questions that can only be addressed at the national scale. These fenced-off enclaves represent an extra layer of withdrawal, beyond the social segregation that appears increasingly to divide citizens from one another at the local scale. If retro-gating is allowed in owner-occupied areas as well as on social housing estates, and developers are given free rein by the planning system to build new gated communities, this socio-spatial segregation could spread literally wall to wall. It is at this scale that we would do well to learn lessons from the US. Over the past 20 years in Los Angeles, for example, innumerable small 'interdictory spaces' have appeared, causing little or no comment or public dissent, and are now taken for granted: 'considered in the aggregate, such infill interdictions extend spatial exclusion into the fine-grain interstices of [the] everyday landscape' (Flusty, 2001, p 659). Once this happens, 'the dream of the city as an open, civilised, and civilising habitat for the existence of free citizens' (Osborne and Rose, 1999, p 754) will have been lost, along with the ideals of community cohesion.

Notes
[1] The recent growth of gated communities in England echoes a previous era of extensive gating in the 18th and 19th centuries (see Blandy, 2006).

[2] Of course, debates about 'community' have generated a literature (see for example, Hoggett, 1997; Bauman, 2001; Delanty, 2003), which cannot be engaged with here for reasons of lack of space.

References
Atkinson, R. (2006) 'Mob mentality: The threat to community sustainability from the search for safety', in P. Malpass and L. Cairncross (eds) *Building on the past: Visions of housing futures*, Bristol: The Policy Press.

Atkinson, R. and Blandy, S. (2007) 'Panic rooms: The rise of defensive home ownership', *Housing Studies*, vol 22 , no 4, pp 443–58.

Atkinson, R. and Flint, J. (2004) 'Fortress UK? Gated communities, the spatial revolt of the elites and time–space trajectories of segregation', *Housing Studies*, vol 19, no 6, pp 875–92.

Atkinson, R., Blandy, S., Flint, J. and Lister, D. (2003) *Gated communities in England*, New Horizons research series, London: ODPM.

Bauman, Z. (2001) *Community: Seeking safety in an insecure world*, Cambridge: Polity.

Baumgartner, M.P. (1988) *The moral order of a suburb*, Oxford: Oxford University Press.

Birmingham City Council Planning Department (2001) *Places for living, Supplementary planning guidance*, Birmingham: Birmingham City Council.

Blandy, S. (2006a) 'Gated communities in England: Historical perspectives and current developments', *GeoJournal*, vol 66, nos 1–2, pp 15–26.

Blandy, S. (2006b) 'Gated communities: A response to, or remedy for anti-social behaviour?', in J. Flint (ed) *Housing, urban governance and anti-social behaviour*, Bristol: The Policy Press

Blandy, S. and Lister, D. (2005) 'Gated communities: (Ne)gating community development?', *Housing Studies*, vol 20, no 2, pp 287–302.

Blandy, S. and Parsons, D. (2003) 'Gated communities in England: Rules and rhetoric of urban planning', *Geographica Helvetica*, vol 58, no 4, pp 314–24.

Blandy, S., Lister, D., Atkinson, R. and Flint, J. (2003) *Gated communities: A systematic review of the research evidence*, CNR paper 12, Bristol: Centre for Neighbourhood Research.

Blunkett, D. (2004) 'Decentralising government: Choice, communities and the role of local authorities', speech to New Local Network annual conference, 22 January (http://press.homeoffice.gov.uk/Speeches/speeches-archive/sp-hs-new-local-govt-network-?view=Binary).

Bow Quarter Residents' Management Ltd (2008) 'Shopping' (www.thebowquarter.co.uk).

Butler, T. with Robson, G. (2003) *London calling: The middle classes and the remaking of inner London*, Oxford: Berg.

Castell, B. (1997) 'An investigation into inward-looking residential developments in London', unpublished M.Phil. thesis, London: University College, University of London.

Cole, I. and Goodchild, B. (2000) 'Social mix and the "balanced community" in British housing policy – A tale of two epochs', *GeoJournal*, vol 51, no 4, pp 351–60.

Delanty, G. (2003) *Community*, London: Routledge.

Department for Communities and Local Government (DCLG) (2006) *Planning policy statement 3*, London: Communities and Local Government.

Ellison, N. and Burrows, R. (2007) 'New spaces of (dis)engagement? Social politics, urban technologies and the rezoning of the city', *Housing Studies*, vol 22, no 3, pp 295–312.

Flusty, S. (2001) 'The banality of interdiction: Surveillance, control and the displacement of diversity', *International Journal of Urban and Regional Research*, vol 25, no 3, pp 658–64.

Forrest, R. and Kearns, A. (2001) 'Social cohesion, social capital and the neighbourhood', *Urban Studies*, vol 38, no 12, pp 2125–43.

Galster, G. (2007) 'Should policy makers strive for neighbourhood social mix? An analysis of the Western European evidence base', *Housing Studies*, vol 22, no 4, pp 523–46.

Gooblar, A. (2002) 'Outside the walls: Urban gated communities and their regulation within the British planning system', *European Planning Studies*, vol 10, no 3, pp 321–34.

Granovetter, M.S. (1973) 'The strength of weak ties', *American Journal of Sociology*, vol 78, no 6, pp 1360–80.

Henning, C. and Lieberg, M. (1996) 'Strong ties or weak ties? Neighbourhood networks in a new perspective', *Scandinavian Housing and Planning Research*, vol 13, no 1, pp 3–26.

Hoggett, P. (ed) (1997) *Contested communities: Experiences, struggles, policies*, Bristol: The Policy Press.

Kearns, A. and Forrest, R. (2000) 'Social cohesion and multilevel urban governance', *Urban Studies*, vol 37, nos 5–6, pp 995–1017.

Kirby, A., Harlan, S.L., Larsen, L., Hackett, E.J., Bolin, B., Nelson, A., Rex, T. and Wolf, S. (2006) 'Examining the significance of housing enclaves in the metropolitan United States of America', *Housing, Theory and Society*, vol 23, no 1, pp 19–33.

Live Strategy (2002) 'Telephone survey into attitudes towards gated communities in England', for the Royal Institute of Chartered Surveyors, unpublished data, on file with author.

Low, S. (2003) *Behind the gates: Life, security and the pursuit of happiness in fortress America*, London: Routledge.

McKenzie, E. (1994) *Privatopia: Homeowner associations and the rise of residential private government*, New Haven, CT, and London: Yale University Press.

Manzi, T. and Smith-Bowers, W. (2005) 'Gated communities as club goods: Segregation or social cohesion?', *Housing Studies*, vol 20, no 2, pp 347–61.

Merry, S. (1993) 'Mending walls and building fences: Constructing the private neighbourhood', *Journal of Legal Pluralism*, vol 33, pp 71–90.

Mumford, L. (1961) *The city in history: Its origins, its transformations, and its prospects*, New York: Harcourt, Brace, Jovanovich.

Office of the Deputy Prime Minister (ODPM)/Home Office (2004) *Safer places: The planning system and crime prevention*, London: HMSO.

Office of the Deputy Prime Minister (ODPM)/Home Office (2005) *Citizen engagement and public services: Why neighbourhoods matter*, London: ODPM.

Osborne, T. and Rose, N. (1999) 'Governing cities: Notes on the spatialisation of virtue', *Environment and Planning D: Society and Space*, vol 17, no 6, pp 737–60.

Planning Advisory Service (2007) 'Glossary: Public realm' (www.pas. gov.uk/pas/core/page.do?pageId=12486).

Putnam, R.D. (2000) *Bowling alone: The collapse and revival of American community*, New York: Simon & Schuster.

Reich, R.B. (2000) *The future of success: Working and living in the new economy*, New York: Vintage.

Sanchez, T.W., Lang, R.E. and Dhavale, D. (2005) 'Security versus status?: a first look at the Census's gated community data', *Journal of Planning Education and Research*, vol 24, no 3, pp 281-91.

Thomas, L. (2006) 'Disconnection: The perceptions of gated community residents in the UK', unpublished MSc Environmental Psychology dissertation, University of Surrey, on file with author.

Thorp, S. (2003) 'Enemy at the gates?', *Housing*, March 2003, pp 24–6.

Tunstall, R. and Fenton, A. (2006) *In the mix: A review of research on mixed income, mixed tenure and mixed communities*, London: The Housing Corporation.

Urban Design Alliance (2003) *Design for cohesive communities*, Memorandum in Evidence to the Select Committee on ODPM, SOC 09 Session 2002/03, London: The Stationery Office.

Vallely, P. (2007) 'Gated Britain', *The Independent Magazine*, 3 February.

Wilton, R.D. (1998) 'The constitution of difference: Space and psyche in landscapes of exclusion', *GeoForum*, vol 29, no 2, pp 173–85.

Conclusions

John Flint and David Robinson

Community cohesion: a political project of governance

This chapter identifies the key themes that have emerged in the book and sets out some future research agendas for the analysis of cohesion and new dimensions of diversity and difference.

This collection has explored the political project of governance being pursued through the active reinvigoration of the community realm, the stated objective of which is the promotion of greater 'cohesion' within British society. The most vivid articulation of this policy agenda was the government response to the disturbances in northern England in 2001. Both the functional and political elements of governance were evident in the resulting community cohesion agenda, which subsequently expanded to encompass far broader themes, including national identity, citizenship, civic allegiance, migration and governmental authority. In part it has been reactive, seeking explanations and solutions to specific localised problems or events and reflecting a wider quest for evidence-based policy making – thus, the use of investigative national commissions on community cohesion (Community Cohesion Independent Review Team, 2001; Commission on Integration and Cohesion, 2007) supported by a series of local reports and recommendations and indeed the establishment of the Institute of Community Cohesion in 2005. There has also been a broadening of the range of agencies assigned key roles, with, for example, schools and housing associations being given new roles and duties to promote community cohesion (Department for Children, Schools and Families, 2007; Housing Corporation, 2007).

However, many of the chapters in this book also identify the political nature of the new politics of community, which sets limits on which elements of social division fall within the remit of the cohesion paradigm and which areas and populations are to be subject to government action. This cohesion agenda therefore represents the contemporary manifestation of a civilising offensive through which governments seek to inculcate particular values and to reshape the morals and behaviour of the population (Elias, 2000; Burnett, 2007).

This agenda has focused on cultural explanations based on assumptions about the motivations and allegiances of particular groups within British society. In doing so, it neglects the wider structural processes that constrain the choices of individuals. In addition, as Burnett points out in this volume, the agenda is wedded to particular interpretations of cohesion and citizenship and represents a retreat from a multiculturalism that is deemed to have failed. It is also located within a broader national discourse of perpetual modernisation aimed at building an orderly society capable of responding to the challenges of globalisation (see Pow, 2007).

The weakness of evidence and lack of history

This book has attempted to provide new empirical research evidence about the dynamics of diversity and difference, operating at the neighbourhood level, in contemporary Britain. In doing so, it reveals the complexity of local circumstances and the myriad of factors underpinning social cohesion or division. It also illustrates the paucity of evidence upon which the community cohesion agenda has been constructed and challenges some of the main conceptual paradigms through which this agenda is articulated in policy discourse.

Many of the contributions in the volume highlight our lack of knowledge about how the dynamics of diversity are playing out in different localities and how these dynamics are changing (rapidly) over time. Cole and Ferrari, for example, point to the need for more nuanced analysis of local housing sub-markets and the interaction between them in explaining the demographic trajectories of neighbourhoods. Reeve describes the scale and pace of new immigration and the inability of policy processes to capture these new developments and their impacts on cohesion at the neighbourhood level. Kintrea and Suzuki argue that we do not as yet have a full understanding of the motivations underpinning territorial behaviour among young people, while Burrows concludes that policymakers and academics are only beginning to investigate what impacts new technologies may have on neighbourhood sorting mechanisms and their effects upon cohesion.

However, the evidence in this book also directly challenges some of the assumptions of the new politics of community explicit within the community cohesion agenda. Most importantly, several chapters dispute the prominence of cultural or behavioural explanations for the segregation of communities. The notion of self-segregation and 'parallel lives' was the most powerful motif to emerge from the investigations into the 2001 urban disorder, and the symbol of polarised enclaves (of working-class South Asian and white populations) continues to dominate the conceptualisation of the community cohesion 'problem' in Britain. However, Phillips, Simpson and Ahmed present findings that there is little deliberate preference for segregation among South Asian and white communities in Oldham and Rochdale; rather there is a desire for integrated and mixed neighbourhoods, in which different communities can gain the benefits that arise from congregation (social networks, facilities and so on). However, as Robinson reveals, this desire for integration is often impeded by factors including the housing market, racial harassment and anti-social behaviour. Cole and Ferrari, and Reeve also examine how housing markets and employment opportunities shape the residential decisions of ethnic groups and new immigrants.

Moving beyond the specific focus of the community cohesion agenda to consider the application of the new politics in other policy realms, Fletcher critiques cultural explanations of social disconnection through unemployment by describing a strong work ethos among residents of the estate he studied, which replicates the desire for employment, income and status existent in 'mainstream' society. He shows how economic restructuring and the collapse of manufacturing occupations were the principal causes of some of the social problems evident in his study neighbourhood. Wells uses data from the 39 New Deal for Communities neighbourhoods in England to illustrate the diversity within these localities and to review some of the assumptions made about change and neighbourhood dynamics in deprived communities. Flint argues that the available evidence does not support linear relationships between the presence of faith schools or black and minority housing associations and levels of cohesion within local neighbourhoods.

This book has also shown the importance of a historical perspective, which is usually lacking in the problematising discourses of community. The chapters by Fletcher and by Kintrea and Suzuki explore the complex histories of localities. In doing so, they reveal how these histories continue to have an impact on cohesion at the neighbourhood level and also identify how social conflict and concerns about cohesion are nothing new, providing evidence of territorial disputes and urban disorder dating back to the early 20th century. Similarly, Reeve discusses how historical patterns of residential settlement are shaping the neighbourhood impact of new migration to the UK.

In addition to challenging the robustness of the evidence base underpinning the new politics of community, this book also critiques several of the academic theories that have influenced the agenda to date. Fletcher challenges the underclass theories developed in the 1980s and 1990s that suggested that the socio-spatial disconnection of some deprived communities was largely a product of deviant cultural or behavioural norms (Murray, 1990). Fletcher's findings are particularly important because the same premises of underclass theory are increasingly being applied to Muslim communities in the UK (Phillips, 2006; Burnett, 2007). Robinson, meanwhile, reveals that the principles of political communitarianism that provide this new politics with its philosophical underpinnings have been selectively sampled, raising questions about the integrity of this ideological superstructure. In particular, he points to the way in which the concerns of communitarian thinkers regarding the erosion of valued forms of communal life and social responsibility at the hand of unregulated free market capitalism have been conveniently put to one side and ignored.

This book also provides support for those critical of the contact theory underpinning the Cantle Report (Community Cohesion Independent Review Team, 2001; see Amin, 2002). Contact theory suggests that it is physical residential proximity and daily encounters and interactions between individuals from different backgrounds that promote a sense of social solidarity. This theory has not only been influential in the community cohesion agenda, but has also shaped the government's quest to develop 'mixed communities', with neighbourhoods characterised by diversity on income, tenure, age and ethnic dimensions (Cole and Goodchild, 2001). Although Flint presents some evidence that contact between school pupils may be beneficial for wider social engagement between ethnic or religious groups, the chapters by Phillips et al, Reeve, and Kintrea and Suzuki illustrate how proximity can also lead to tensions, misperceptions and conflict.

Social capital theory is often used in debates about the need to reinvigorate community in a bid to address social problems, and particularly the concepts of 'bonding' and 'bridging' social capital. Furbey suggests the need for a much more complex analysis of how social capital plays out between individuals and collectives. He argues that the functional and consensual interpretation of community and social capital denies the ubiquity of struggles and conflicts within policy processes, and this argument is also made by Burnett and Flint. As Blandy points out, the evidence from her studies of gated communities also casts doubt on the communitarianism underpinning the community cohesion agenda. The divisions and conflicts within these gated developments mirror social tensions described at the neighbourhood level in several other contributions to this book. These findings, coupled with the importance of individual agency identified earlier, casts doubts on the simplistic equation of community, neighbourhood and social solidarity that characterises the community cohesion agenda. As Blandy, Wells and Flint argue, there is a need to explore how 'community' mechanisms of neighbourhood governance may be reconciled with state attempts to foster societal cohesion.

Neighbourhoods and the importance of the local and the individual

To date debates about the crisis in cohesion have largely been at the national level, or focused on the localities affected by the urban disorder in 2001. However, this book has presented evidence that the Commission on Integration and Cohesion (2007) is right to emphasise that place matters. The neighbourhood is the arena in which the dynamics of community and cohesion play out. Cole and Ferrari, Phillips et al, and Fletcher describe how local neighbourhood contexts are often very different and require localised practices and interventions. A number of the chapters, including those by Cole and Ferrari, Reeve and Blandy, attempt to offer a more complex and insightful classification of specific contexts within local neighbourhoods and how these might affect cohesion. Burrows also highlights that the classification of neighbourhoods can now be exceptionally detailed. There is a need to place neighbourhoods within their wider city or regional contexts, and as Cole and Ferrari, Reeve and Blandy point out, to examine the connectivity of neighbourhoods within economic and housing processes. Crucially, this brings all neighbourhoods and citizens within the frame of analysis of a contemporary crisis in cohesion. Given the importance of structural explanations of segregation or conflict identified earlier, it is not sufficient to target only those neighbourhoods where problems are manifested.

The book also challenges the lack of emphasis within the community cohesion agenda upon the agency of individuals, and the complexity of their relationship to their neighbourhood, ethnicity, faith or other elements of identity. Furbey illustrates the diversity of individual religious practice and engagement, locally and nationally, and the myriad of outcomes that this may generate for social cohesion. Similarly, Phillips et al, Kintrea and Suzuki, and Blandy reveal how individuals respond in very different ways to their personal and neighbourhood circumstances and their interaction with other groups. Such complexity undermines some of the generalised assumptions presented within the community cohesion discourse about collective attitudes and behaviour, for example, South Asian, Muslim, young, white working-class and so on.

Towards a future research agenda

It has been impossible in one collection to capture all of the dynamics of diversity and difference currently playing out in neighbourhoods in Britain. One of the key messages arising from this book is the need for further research to deepen our understanding of what cohesion actually means and what factors support or inhibit its development in particular contexts. What is clear is that the cohesion agenda is based on a very limited and disputed evidence base, and the vacuum that this creates is filled with assumptions, anecdotes and particular political interpretations about the extent and nature of a crisis of cohesion in contemporary British society. We would suggest that a future research agenda should include:

- studies of the relationship between cohesion, age, gender, sexuality, health and disability;
- the generation of a far broader evidence base on how the dynamics of diversity and difference play out in different neighbourhood, city and regional contexts and within the national environments of the constituent political entities of the UK, particularly during a process of devolution. This would enable a better understanding of the broad similarities between areas and the specifics of their differences;
- more complex analysis of the role of individual agency in determining social interaction and residential settlement patterns;
- focused attention on the consequences of changes wrought by the unregulated market forces of global capitalism for the nature and form of communities, as well as impacts on community life;
- analysis of the community consequences of related patterns of socio-spatial differentiation driven by contemporary patterns of wealth accumulation;
- international comparisons with other states with regard to the dynamics of difference and diversity and the policy responses put in place to promote cohesion;
- further work that examines the connectivity and disconnections between, rather than within, neighbourhoods and how the trajectories of neighbourhoods are linked;
- studies of emerging forms of diversity and difference, including new immigration, information technology and new forms of residential development;

- placing the contemporary community cohesion agenda within a longer-term historical framework;
- studies that link different academic disciplinary approaches.

This research is urgently required. The cohesion agenda raises fundamental questions about national identity, 'Britishness' and the relationship between state and citizen. More importantly, it demands a better understanding of how societies actually function in the 21st century. The danger inherent in the current political agenda is that it is increasingly limited to a focus upon governmental management of the manifestations of community tensions rather than addressing the underlying causes of these tensions. Thus, in her response to the Commission on Integration and Cohesion, the Secretary of State for Communities and Local Government acknowledged that 'the benefits of globalisation are not always distributed equally among different communities and neighbourhoods', and that she wished to see 'a vision of a society of equal opportunities' (Blears, 2007, pp 2–3). However, the emphasis on building cohesion is then presented as 'tackling prejudice and tensions' and 'increasing perceptions of fairness' (Blears, 2007, pp 2–3). How equal opportunities and fairness, rather than perceptions of them, are to be achieved is not made clear. In his foreword to the Commission that he chaired, Darrah Singh states that: 'Integration and cohesion is no longer a special programme or project. It is also not about race, faith or other forms of group status or identity. It is simply about how we all get on and secure benefits that are mutually desirable for our communities and ourselves' (Commission on Integration and Cohesion, 2007, p 5).

However, the cohesion agenda is a project and programme of governance, and cohesion is precisely about race, faith and other forms of group status (including income and class) and the unequal struggle among groups to secure benefits that may not be mutually desirable for others.

References

Amin, A. (2002) 'Ethnicity and the multicultural city: Living with diversity', *Environment and Planning A*, vol 34, no 6, pp 959–80.

Blears, H. (2007) *Letter to Darrah Singh, chair of the Commission on Integration and Cohesion*, London: Communities and Local Government.

Burnett, J. (2007) 'Britain's "civilising project": Community cohesion and core values', *Policy and Politics*, vol 35, no 2, pp 353–7.

Cole, I. and Goodchild, B. (2001) 'Social mix and the "balanced community" in British housing policy – A tale of two epochs', *GeoJournal*, vol 51, no 4, pp 351–60.

Commission on Integration and Cohesion (2007) *Our shared future*, London: Commission on Integration and Cohesion.

Community Cohesion Independent Review Team (2001) (Cantle Report) *Community cohesion: A report of the Independent Review Team, chaired by Ted Cantle*, London: Home Office.

Department for Children, Schools and Families (2007) *Guidance on the duty to promote community cohesion*, London: Department for Children, Schools and Families.

Elias, N. (2000) *The civilizing process*, rev edn, trans Edmund Jephcott, Oxford: Blackwell.

Housing Corporation (2007) *Shared places: Community cohesion strategy*, London: Housing Corporation.

Murray, C.A. (ed) (1990) *The emerging British underclass*, London: Institute of Economic Affairs.

Phillips, D. (2006) 'Parallel lives? Challenging discourses of British Muslim self-segregation', *Environment and Planning D: Society and Space*, vol 24, no 1, pp 25–40.

Pow, C.-P. (2007) 'Securing the "civilised" enclaves: Gated communities and the moral geographies of exclusion in (post-)socialist Shanghai', *Urban Studies*, vol 44, no 8, pp 1539–58.

Index

W

Y

Z